FURTHER PRAISE FOR NAIL 'EM

"Dezenhall's cutting-edge approach reflects a business climate where attacks are much more than communications problems—attacks represent conflicts that can only be resolved with a true understanding of the agendas at work."
—Don Olsen, Senior Vice President, Huntsman Corp.

". . . revealing insight on who gets attacked, who survives, and why."
—Dr. Richard B. Wirthlin,
pollster for Pres. Ronald Reagan and
Chairman of Wirthlin Worldwide

"Eric Dezenhall has dissected the phenomenon [of attacks] with the skill of a neurosurgeon and the wit of an essayist. For anyone who wonders why the mud in our media is so thick, *Nail 'Em!* is must reading."
—Roger D. Masters, author and Professor Emeritus
of Government, Dartmouth College

"From my vantage point deep in the cultural trenches where the battles of personal and corporate destruction are waged, I can say that no one has offered a more provocative critique of what we have become."

—Frank Luntz, President, Luntz Research

"This book offers invaluable insight and advice for anyone confronted with a vicious public attack of the type that now pervades our sensation-seeking culture."

—Peter Barton Hutt, Covington & Burling, Attorneys at Law

". . . a long-overdue handbook."

—Dr. Sally Satel, Yale University School of Medicine

"Dezenhall's writing style is lively, his flashes of wit are frequent, and he argues a case that will evoke much support in all kinds of haunts, and not just among those at the business roundtable."

—Colman McCarthy, syndicated columnist

nail 'em!

nail 'em!

Confronting High-Profile Attacks
on Celebrities
& Businesses

ERIC   DEZENHALL

PB **Prometheus Books**

59 John Glenn Drive
Amherst, New York 14228-2197

Published 2003 by Prometheus Books

07 06 05 04 03   5 4 3 2 1

Library of Congress Cataloging-in-Publication Data

Dezenhall, Eric.
    Nail 'em : confronting high-profile attacks on celebrities & businesses / by Eric Dezenhall.
        p.   cm.
    Includes bibliographical references and index.
    ISBN 1–59102–047–6 (pbk. : alk. paper)
    1. Public relations. 2. Crisis management. I. Title. II. Title: Confronting high-profile attacks on celebrities & businesses.
HD59.D49   2003
659.2—dc21   2003003710
                                                                          CIP

Printed in the United States of America on acid-free paper

Contents

5

Acknowledgments

This book would not have been possible without the help of my family, Donna, Stuart, and Eliza, who permitted my frequent—but much-needed—disappearances into my study to write. My partner, Nick Nichols, was an essential touchstone, encouraging me not to dilute my core messages despite marketplace pressure to reach gentler conclusions about the Culture of Attack. My friend Audrey Wolf taught me the "facts of life" about the unpredictable (and often cruel) world of book publishing. Her admonition to "focus" was a core element in this book's development. My friend and editorial critic Diana Morgan proved that there are few people more frightening than a petite woman with a red pen. Diana's counsel provided this book with the structure it desperately needed. My friends and colleagues at Nichols-Dezenhall helped me with critical ad hoc support. Special thanks to Maya Shackley, Terri Evans, Jim McCarthy, Ann Matchinsky, and Mari Ines Arroyo. My clients, despite their anonymity in this book, provided me with the experiences necessary to write it. I am also grateful to Steven Mitchell at Prometheus Books whose belief in this project allowed it to be, and my thanks to Kathy Deyell at Prometheus for her editorial dedication to this project. My thanks also to Andrew Lewis of Nichols-Dezenhall who played a critical editorial role in synthesizing additional information for the paperback–post 9/11 chapters of *Nail 'Em!*

Eric Dezenhall
Washington, D.C.

7

To Sondra Byer Dezenhall (1939–1987),
the last great crisis manager

He said, "In a certain city there was a judge who neither feared God nor had respect for people. In that city there was a widow who kept coming to him and saying, "Grant me justice against my opponent." For a while he refused; but later he said to himself, "Though I have no fear of God and no respect for anyone, yet because this widow keeps bothering me, I will grant her justice, so that she may not wear me out by continually coming."

The Parable of the Widow and the Unjust Judge
Luke 18:1–5

Introduction

"We're gonna nail 'em!"

This threat against my clients—usually corporations and well-known people—defines my career. It means destroy them. Hunt them down. Humiliate them. *"Nail 'em!"* has become the credo of activists, litigants, reporters, business competitors, and ordinary citizens. A reporter friend of mine once pointed to the home of a prominent Washington powerbroker and told me straight out, "We're gonna nail him in an upcoming news story." An activist group once promised that my client's entire industry "will not exist in ten years" if it did not cede to their demands of a product reformulation.

My expertise goes by such names as crisis management, risk communications, and damage control. My job is to stop the attacks. I am fighting all day long so it's hard to concentrate on the gnawing "larger" questions my friends and clients sometimes ask me about our hostile climate, questions such as:

How did "Nail 'em!" become such a popular battle cry?

Who gets attacked?

Who survives? And why?

When night falls, I think about these questions because I am haunted by what my clients go through—and what I go through with them. During the past fifteen years, I've spent endless evening hours taking notes, trying to explain the dynamics of what I call the "Culture of Attack."

The result is this book, the uncensored "facts of life" on how and why public attacks really work. I write for people who are concerned about high-profile attacks, but who aren't necessarily involved with defusing them. My intent is to help readers look at these attacks with a greater appreciation of what they have in common. This book is written from the inside out; that is, from the vantage point of someone who defuses attacks for a living and sees the world from a foxhole.

I focus on "bad" attacks; those that do more harm than good. In a bad attack, malice, falsehoods, distortions, and hidden agendas smother the search for justice and crusades for the public good. I differentiate bad attacks from legitimate ones, those that really press for justice or public good, such as Bob Woodward and Carl Bernstein's relentless pursuit of Richard Nixon during Watergate. Many attacks are hybrids; that is, they contain a mixed recipe of nobility and malice.

Sometimes, one person's attack may be another's holy war and there is no acid test that registers one or the other like a pregnancy kit. My work here rests on the premise that malice—with a thin layer of nobility icing on top—has become the dominant flavor of attacks in general.

While a few attackers have told me that they want to "nail" my clients, they are rarely so crude. Their agendas are equally positioned as crusades of moral weight, insuring the public's "right-to-know" or protecting consumers against fraud or health risks. Attackers confuse brutal scrutiny with healthy, democratic give-and-take. I reject the often proposed view that my clients' attackers are all helpless victims with a "right" to destroy them. Behind the facade of concern for public welfare I often find a malcontent with a selfish agenda or *schadenfreude*—a term that means enjoying the misfortune of others.

The most damaging attacks occur when there "something in it" for everyone, from the core attackers to the public that traffics in the news. Attacks require elements that I call the "Six Vs": a victim, a villain, a vindicator, a void, a vehicle, and a value:

1. The **victim** is someone who claims to have suffered injustice. For maximum impact, it must be an injustice that audiences identify with; an ordinary citizen wronged by a powerful person, or a population harmed by an unsafe product. Victims are the motivated parties who launch attacks, often after being prompted by someone adept at manipulating the media and the courts.

2. The **villain** is the demon who allegedly inflicted the evil on the victim and becomes the target of the attack. This role is inevitably played by the haves: life's "overdogs," celebrities, and business interests. The villains tend to be my clients.

3. The **vindicator** is the redeemer sent down to right the wrong. This part is played by activists, whistleblowers, and investigative reporters who promise to restore order. The vindicator is a catalyst in attacks.

4. The **void** is an unfilled need that the public demands be met: a complex issue that needs simplification; a conflict that must be resolved; an urge that must be acted out; or air time that needs to be filled. The void is passive: The public does not consciously demand action, but is curious and will tune in if the void can be filled in a resonant way.

5. The **vehicle** is the medium in which the attack is delivered. Vehicles include the media, the Internet, lawsuits, and person-to-person gossip.

6. The **value** is the social principle under which the attack is justified—free speech, public safety, right-to-know.

Volumes have already been written on moral crusades and dueling agendas. I set out to write about high-profile acts of aggression against celebrities and businesses that are fueled by base motives, hidden agendas, and warped priorities.

Most of the attacks against my clients fall into the more-harm-than-good category. Attacks have gotten meaner, more relentless, and less verifiable. We catch scent of an attack in the morning paper and hear the ensuing hue and cry in the evening news. We see the prey, Cardinal Joseph Bernardin, publicly vilified by a former altar boy. The altar boy's cry is picked up and repeated until we all know exactly how and where Cardinal Bernardin supposedly molested him. Motorola's stock plunges after a grieving widower claims wrongly on *Larry King Live* that cellular phones cause brain tumors. Panic erupts when syringes are found in cans of Diet Pepsi.

As we graze the millennium, a prankster with a modem has the power of a respected reporter—fashion designer Tommy Hilfiger was falsely accused on the Internet of making bigoted remarks. He never did, which the public learned when Hilfiger informed the media that he had never even been on the television program where the remarks had allegedly been made.

In turn-of-the-century colonial Salem, Massachusetts, witch hunts culminated by extinguishing a life. In turn-of-the-century modern America, witch hunts end by extinguishing characters, debates, reputations, and consumer products.

One bad news germ can become a "fact." I spend my days refuting the claims of laypersons who don't hesitate to label a product a carcinogen on the grounds that they *think* it's one. Chutzpah rules the information frontier. To be vindicated, Cardinal Bernardin's lawyers had to decimate the altar boy and his spurious story. For Motorola to be cleared, toxicologists had to spar with a widower about the safety of cell phones. We watched a store camera show a pleasant-looking woman slip a syringe into a Pepsi can.

This is what modern crisis management is all about—fighting altar boys, mourners, and little old ladies. It's what I do, and sometimes it looks bad.

The Culture of Attack is the result of discontentment, new media that reward absolute conclusions, and declining standards of decorum in which once-repugnant forms of behavior are now accepted. Attackers are angry because they mistake opportunities with guarantees and confuse disappointment with betrayal. They are guerrilla soldiers engaged in a battle for the American Dream, which many see as a perk they're owed just for being alive. When they don't get it, they attack. Few people become attackers, but Americans have become increasingly willing—and able—to traffic in attacks.

Americans are the richest people on Earth, yet prosperity hasn't neutralized all forms of misery. A few act out their misery by exchanging the pursuit of happiness for the destruction of the celebrity and the faceless big-business. These "haves" possess the power and success that symbolizes what is wrong with the attackers' lives. Attackers strike at villains, real and imagined, using questionable—but catchy—allegations and grievances. They level charges of wrongdoing and supposed hazards shamelessly and with impunity. The accusations fly through the media and Internet at incredible speeds, leaving the accused with no chance to respond.

If discontentment is the engine that drives the Culture of Attack and proliferating media are the vehicles that transport it, a lack of shame and proportion are the faulty brakes that keep our hostile society hurtling forward. The death of restraint has made people meaner and more hysterical. Every human rights violation becomes another Holocaust; every military flare-up is another Vietnam; every breach of ethics is another Watergate; and every corporate foul-up becomes another Bhopal.

Ours is not the first society to traffic in attacks. What makes our culture different is that contemporary Americans *think* it is different. Modern society takes pride in its enlightenment, in "knowing better" than its cruder forbears. C. S. Lewis wrote in *The Screwtape Letters* of attacks on the mighty: "The delightful novelty of the present situation is that you can sanction it—make it respectable and laudable even—by the incantory use of the word *democratic.*" America's self-congratulation over its love of democracy makes it hard to distinguish between a vigorous debate and a lynching.

Even the heartiest battlers can't fight in this climate. Take Admiral Jeremy "Mike" Boorda, who was our nation's highest-ranking naval officer until he shot himself to death in 1996. The suicide, by most accounts, was Boorda's reaction to questions by *Newsweek* magazine and the National Security News Service, which reported on military affairs, about allegations he was not entitled to wear the navy's valor medals. Most military experts now believe that Boorda was qualified to wear them, a conclusion that came too late to save the admiral.

When the news of the suicide broke, I told a colleague standing near the television that the only thing that amazed me was that incidents like this didn't happen more often. She understood. We see attacks on people, products, and institutions every day.

Boorda killed himself because he was afraid of the Culture of Attack. He had seen attacks on others—their constant badgering by the press, the global assumption of their guilt, their transformation into an emblem of evil—just as my colleague and I had.

Admiral Boorda took his critics at face value when one of them labeled his medal wearing "the worst thing that a military man can do." Was dubious medal wearing really the "worst thing that a military man can do"? Genocide strikes me as being worse. The attack on Boorda was a classic "bad" attack because his "punishment" far exceeded his alleged violation.

Admiral Boorda came from a time when Americans—including attackers—felt shame and cared about the proportions of their remarks. Today's survivors don't worry about pride because they understand that attacks are a part of something much bigger: Attacks are an accepted form of cultural expression. Everyday life seems to have become a zero sum game: Attackers win when Boorda, Bernardin, or General Motors lose.

The culture is fond of attributing crisis survival to "spin"—alchemy and public relations tricks that can fool all the people all the time. I reject this thesis. "Spin" is dead because the public knows what it is. The whole idea behind spin is to convey sincerity. Today, the media openly cover spin itself, so we're on guard and tune out.

America attributes good crisis management to spin in order to avoid responsibility for its own flawed standards. It's easier to conclude that Bill Clinton survives scandal after scandal due to the handiwork of "spin doctors" than it is to admit that people like the guy, "sleaze factor" and all. I horrified a television audience with my answer to a question about Clinton's high approval ratings in the wake of constant scandal:

"What do Clinton's high approval ratings mean?" a reporter asked.

"They mean we approve," I said.

The audience was upset because they wanted no personal role in Clinton's waltz from the flames of a sordid controversy.

The very contention that the public plays a role in the Culture of Attack is incendiary. My clients, whose careers depend on public support, have become indignant at the suggestion that their audiences could turn on them. They like to think that an evil cabal is going after them independent of the community. I have even been asked to delete or "tone down" references to attacks being "market-driven" in client case reports. So frantic are these requests that I know I have hit a raw nerve. My options, then, are to avoid the nerve or to probe if deftly. In this volume I have tried to do the latter.

The rules of defending against public attacks have forever changed. Damage control used to be about soft, fuzzy concepts like image. Now, it's about survival, and this has made the battle bloodier. Flacks and lawyers quibble over words in press releases while their attackers fabricate allegations with impunity. Traditional public relations assumes that the attackers need to be better informed. In order for a message to be communicated, however, it has to be received. Attackers are not receiving, they are attacking. Public relations is like spraying perfume on a mugger: He'll smell nice, but he'll mug you anyway.

Attacks are deeper than communications problems; they are conflicts that only stop when the aggressors themselves are put at risk. This is what I do—introduce a down-side to aggression.

My approach terrifies some of my new clients (I call them "targets") who believe that by fighting attacks, they are conceding that somebody doesn't like them. Well, somebody doesn't. Many targets play by rules from a long-ago era when there were things decent people neither did nor got away with. It's easier to deny our hostile climate than it is to wrestle with it. When somebody has a knife to your throat, your best weapon isn't a gerund.

My clients' attackers appear to be the helpless victims of corporate greed, mismanagement and even malice. Perhaps, but I hear this day in and day out, and I believe it less and less. To repulse the attack I assemble a team of professionals who are expert in unconventional warfare: attorneys, private investigators, pollsters, law enforcement representatives, media specialists, and lobbyists. If this all sounds like a revolution or a counter-revolution, that's because it is. But it's a strange revolution. It's not a war on the haves by the have-nots, it's a war on the haves by the want-mores. In any other era, the want-mores would be considered lucky. Not today. The want-mores don't want to live in their nice houses. They want *your* house. In a public battle, the attackers call this "equality."

During the last decade, I have seen the number of attacks grow exponentially. Many are the result of a new ethic in which blaming someone else—a person or an institution—for your problems is okay. Attackers believe that once the villain is punished and the evil purged, society's values will be preserved. The drama of the attack incorporates biblical themes of vengeance ("an eye for an eye") and revolution ("The first will be last, and the last will be first"). Legendary journalist I. F. Stone echoed this sentiment when he said, "It is the job of the journalist to comfort the afflicted and afflict the comfortable."

The views contained here have helped my clients survive brutal public fights. Unlike insightful but esoteric "social critics," I have a business incentive to get things right. If I were wrong a lot, I'd be out of business.

Nor am I writing to defend everyone who has ever been under siege: Some companies really do pollute, some government officials really do lie, and some celebrities really do get away with outrageous things. It's infuriating to sit face-to-face with a guilty party who blames an imaginary cabal or liberal media for his woes, and I have turned down clients with character disorders. The Constitution may guarantee a bad actor the right to a fair trial, but it does not guarantee him an untarnished image. No one is hurt more grievously by our culture's passion for "nailing" than the genuine victims of injustice for whom the American watchdog ethic was created. On the other hand, I believe that the current state of public scrutiny is harmful and that we should be very concerned.

That people, products, and institutions could be wrongly accused is not a popular concept for educated Americans. We have a vague sense of a less enlightened past when there were witch hunts in Salem and of a dark time in the 1950s when a paranoid senator saw Communists under his kitchen sink. A few may even be aware of political cartoons from past centuries that harshly depicted candidates as baboons. This behavior was vicious, but to many these are irrelevant schoolbook lessons. The danger is that America's confidence in its enlightenment and its ignorance of past witch hunts has made the country vulnerable to savage, albeit more sophisticated, attacks. Today's generations are, after all, the ones that are supposed to know better. Colonial cartoonists made no such claim.

I will discuss many attacks in varying degrees of detail. Some of them are case studies based upon my own experiences. They are all based on true cases, but I have created composites and changed the identities of the players to protect innocent parties. In order to avoid making the book too ponderous and difficult to read, I have chosen to relegate my sources to the bibliography rather than to use footnotes or to always state the sources in the text itself. Each controversy discussed can be supported with solid evidence, and many may even be characterized as "common knowledge" because of the widespread publicity they received.

What lies ahead is a blunt assessment of attacks as a core feature of our times and recent efforts to fight this trend. A lot of people are fed up with the Culture of Attack, including presidents, journalists, and my clients. They recognize attacks for what they are: threats to their—and our—way of life.

1. *Why It Has Become a Culture of Attack: Entitlement and Rage*

Unfulfilled entitlement causes rage.

YOU, ME, AND KATHIE LEE

No matter how I look at the Culture of Attack, it keeps coming back to Kathie Lee Gifford, the hostess of *Live with Regis and Kathie Lee.* I could search for deeper roots to the American mind, but Kathie Lee's beaming face would still be there. There were those who thought she needed to be cut down. This is how and why the attack on her happened.

On April 30 and May 1, 1997, Kathie Lee's husband, former football star and ABC broadcaster Frank Gifford, met a TWA flight attendant named Suzen Johnson at the Regency Hotel in New York City. The rendezvous was a sting on Frank orchestrated by the *Globe,* a tabloid newspaper, which paid Johnson in the neighborhood of $75,000, according to the *Washington Post.*

The "facts," according to the *Globe* account of the rendezvous, were that "lusty Frank pulled the already loosened cork from the chilled bottle of Grgich Hills Chardonnay with his teeth." Other facts-only reporting included that, "as the minutes slipped by, Frank inched ever closer, picked up a strawberry from a tray of fruit and cheese on the cocktail table in front of them and fed it to Suzen. The twosome sipped their wine, chatted—and gazed longingly into each other's eyes."

The *Globe* attacked the Giffords—entrapping Frank in a story it had concocted—because a core team of editors thought the story would sell a lot of papers. They were right. *Globe* circulation in 1997, a year that included the Giffords as well as the murder of JonBenet Ramsey, was up 13.5 percent from the year before.

Attack Summary: Kathie Lee Gifford—April–May 1997

Victim(s):   Readers of the *Globe*
Villain: Kathie Lee Gifford
Vindicator(s): The *Globe,* Suzen Johnson
Void: Doubt and resentment about Kathie Lee's perfect life
Vehicle: The *Globe*
Value: Exposing the hypocrisy of a public figure

POOR KATHIE LEE

The Giffords initially called the *Globe*'s allegations a "total fabrication." The *Globe* responded in their May 27, 1997, edition by publishing video frames from the sexual encounter, "to prove to the 43-year-old *Live* hostess that her cheating husband is the one not telling the truth."

The Giffords issued a statement. "This has been as painful for us as it would be for any other couple," they said. "However, we will get through this together. We ask that our privacy be respected at this difficult time."

I thought this was a very reasonable statement, precisely what the couple should have issued. The Giffords showed they were human. People like that. It's what the *Globe*'s readers had wanted to see all along. Kathie Lee had spent years carefully constructing her public image, one in which hers was the perfect American family—and when you live by the media, chances are you die by the media.

Kathie Lee—not Frank—was the real target of the *Globe* attack. One had only to look at the predominant image presented in the press. When the Suzen story broke, the tabloid pasted a big photo on its cover not of Frank, but of Kathie Lee. It splashed the headline, "POOR KATHIE LEE," across the front page like a WANTED poster from the old west.

The media's daggers were out for Kathie Lee long before the Suzen Johnson affair. At odds with her kid-cuddling image was the serious charge of using Honduran child labor to make her Wal-Mart clothing line. On his radio show Howard Stern was fond of pointing out that the father of the born-again Christian is Jewish. Kathie Lee was as fake as her religion, he implied. "She looks like the biggest idiot," *People* magazine quoted Stern as saying when the Johnson incident went public.

Kathie Lee knew her image created problems. "Yes, I am fully aware that there are people out there who look at me and want to throw up," she said. While hosting *Talk Soup,* actor Greg Kinnear played a lullaby from Kathie Lee's album and proceeded to hang himself. There was such hostility in the media toward Kathie Lee, said actor Ron Liebman on Comedy Central's *The Daily Show,* "because she asks for it."

What tweaked the *Globe* and consumers alike was Kathie Lee's marketing of her personal life. She referred to her "Lambchop" husband as a "human love machine" and complimented the curve of his rear on *Live with Regis & Kathie Lee.* Their beautiful children, Cody and Cassidy, were features on the morning talk show from the time they were a few weeks old. She was fortune's pet and the *Globe* wagered that its readers felt about her the way school kids feel when the teacher's pet shows up in new shoes. They silently cheer as the playground bully smudges them with dirty sneakers.

The *Globe* editors (vindicators) printed the story that its readers wanted and had the diverse ingredients to bring the attack together, including readers (victims) who likely resented Kathie Lee (villain); a vulnerable mark in Frank who was in a position to hurt Kathie Lee; a motivated and unscrupulous flight attendant in Suzen (co-vindicator) with the assets to prove the too-good-to-be-true Gifford marriage (void) was flawed; a massive circulation to get the story out (vehicle); and a convenient principle in which the attack could be justified (value): exposing the hypocrisy of a deceitful public figure.

When the more mainstream media began reporting on the affair, readers of upscale media could feel socially responsible about covering it, too. "When one of these stories arrives in the frame of a chin-scratcher about media ethics," wrote William Powers in the *New Republic,* gutter journalism becomes "perfectly respectable."

Kathie Lee had flaunted her good fortune and the *Globe* came to believe that she had asked for her public comeuppance. The "she asked for it" argument, however, is a slippery slope with terrible consequences. All Kathie Lee really did was parade her happiness. Perhaps she "asked" not to be liked. Perhaps she "asked" for people to turn the channel. But by what standard did she become a villain who invited an attack on her marriage? By the standards of the Culture of Attack, where any visibly successful person is vulnerable to the sport of taking them down.

CONFUSING COMMUNICATIONS PROBLEMS WITH CONFLICTS

It's my job to make attacks like the one on Kathie Lee go away. Reasoning politely with the attackers doesn't work. When I'm meeting with a corporate head, his PR people often call the bad press "a communications problem." I tell them we've got a situation that may entail playing hardball. The crux of the difference between public relations and crisis management is that PR people want to educate and persuade attackers. I want to *stop* them, which is a much bigger task.

The first thing I do is find out everything about the claim and the attacker. Then I come up with a strategy. If the allegation is genuine, I may suggest giving the attacker the money or attention he wants. If it's not, I may suggest exposing him to the press or in the courts. Either way, it's not communications, it's armed conflict.

Sometimes, no matter what tactic I suggest, the attacker wins. A few years ago, I worked with an executive under siege. I'll call her Diana. A former employee and rival for Diana's position—call her Natalie—was threatening to release to a major magazine embarrassing personal information about Diana. To make her attack more respectable, Natalie was also claiming that Diana had deprived her of pay she was due. For a certain amount of money, Natalie would keep the embarrassing information to herself.

Diana was in a high-profile position in a high-profile business. She feared a lurid exposé in a publication that often runs stories about people like her. Given Diana's lifestyle, Natalie's allegations, though exaggerated, were plausible.

Diana was mad and wanted to fight. I wanted to fight, too, because even with a nondisclosure statement, I didn't trust Natalie to keep quiet.

I asked to borrow Diana's word processor, then I shut the door and got to work. An hour later I printed out and handed her three pages of copy.

"I just wrote the story they'll want to write," I said.

Diana read the story and turned white.

"This is all bullshit," she said.

"So what," I said. "This is the story they'll write if Natalie talks."

I explained she would be asked by a high-profile reporter to respond to allegations of drug use and of exchanging sex for job advancement. Even if they were untrue, readers would believe the allegations, because in a Culture of Attack they *want* to believe them.

I was torn between my nature, which is to fight, and my professional obligation to Diana, which was to make the problem go away. Crisis management is like black jack. Sometimes you play a hand conservatively and "stick," not because you're happy with what you've got, but because the odds say it's the smarter move.

So Diana settled with Natalie. No media ever ran a story, but the aftertaste of extortion still lingers. There are few shut outs in the attack business.

THE GLOBE'S READERS AS VICTIMS

Given what I've learned on the job, I know why the *Globe* attacked Kathie Lee. The exceedingly happy television hostess appeared to have stolen what should have been distributed more evenly. Kathie Lee had everything: fame, money, looks. She enjoyed a monstrous helping of good luck, beauty, healthy kids, and an all-American winner for a spouse.

The *Globe* understood its readers: they wanted blood and the *Globe* was going to give it to them. They gave the *Globe* its proxy to entice her flawless husband, Frank, into a hotel with a buxom stewardess. The *Globe* wanted to validate an existing suspicion for its tabloid audience— that Kathie Lee's fairytale existence was a charade, that she was a mugger who stole their birthrights and made them victims.

Kathie Lee flagged the imperfections of the lives of the *Globe*'s readers. Very few couples, even those who are happily married, speak about their spouses the way she did. Very few *think* about their spouses that way. Instead Americans watch *Melrose Place, Pacific Palisades,* and support no-fault divorce. In a TV drama, when somebody's perfect, it's entertaining. But in real life when somebody's perfect, it's threatening. Kathie Lee evoked subliminal fears in the *Globe*'s readers that somebody else got a better deal in life than they did. "In short," wrote the *New Republic*'s Powers, "the people demanded the head of Kathie Lee Gifford, and the *Globe* delivered."

When attackers believe a person has victimized them, they don't step back to calmly ask what's going on, or how it can be fixed. They rage for revenge. It makes sense, for instance, for a community to want to hurt an executive whose factory has dumped dangerous acid in a lake where kids swim. I used to get these kinds of cases all the time. My clients were the corporations but I had to agree with the arguments of many of their attackers.

In the late 1980s, the attacks stopped making sense. My cases became more like the attack on Kathie Lee, because the demand for punishment was disproportionate to the "crime"—the aggrieved had vague medical reactions, underperforming cars, unmet career goals. The nature of the "crimes" grew increasingly trivial. The attackers became more spiteful.

Whenever there is so much distorted rage, I look beneath the surface of the attacker's charge. In Gifford's case, I don't believe the *Globe*'s dislike of her was personal. She was a symbol of a larger hurt and of a far deeper anger, and she became a projection screen for this pain. My business partner, Nick Nichols, calls this "filling our villain void."

Attacking Kathie Lee filled a void because she was a potent symbol of injustice for having the power or lifestyle that others want. This phenomenon was aggravated in the late 1980s, when a series of cultural factors that had been moving toward each other finally collided.

THE ENTITLEMENT VOID

The foundation of my work is getting into the minds of the attackers—disappointed consumers and disgruntled employees—whether it's from behind a focus group mirror or in actual confrontations. What I usually find is people who have been sold a bill of goods about the kind of life they have a right to expect. The impossibility of these expectations creates a void that needs filling. I see this not only in the attackers I am hired to fight, but in corporate clients who don't want to be bothered with adversity. It's true of my friends and I, who seem to be surprised that putting in a hard day's work is, well, hard. "Countless millions of Americans feel, in one way or another, that they have been deprived (or might be deprived) of something they deserved or have been promised," writes Robert Samuelson in *The Good Life and Its Discontents*. The economist and journalist argues that Americans have become "prisoners of entitlement." While only a few of these "prisoners" become actual attackers, there are enough angry members of society to supply reliable markets for attacks.

Americans' sense of entitlement was forged by the massive business and government boom that followed the Great Depression of the 1930s and World War II. An extraordinary partnership between business and government brought temporary security, mortgages, and insured bank deposits. The Allied victory in World War II and the United States' subsequent role in rebuilding Europe boosted our national self-esteem and economic confidence. After President Roosevelt launched massive relief programs during the Great Depression, including Social Security, Americans assumed that government would take care of them. In the 1950s, prosperity became a cultural backdrop, as opposed to something to be cherished as our good fortune. In the 1960s, our economic horizons continued expanding.

After Vietnam, the country lost this sense of endless possibility. The oil crisis promoted a slump and consumers had less money. And yet there were more consumer products and services than ever before. Americans could watch TV, travel by jet, and air-condition our houses, but many couldn't find a job they liked. Antibiotics kept the republic healthy, long-distance communication kept them in touch, the Pill and other contraception kept them dating, but there was so much more many wanted from life. "Our enthusiasm for entitlement has rested on a massive misunderstanding," Samuelson writes. "It is the myth of the unbounded power of prosperity."

Although there is no limit to human imagination, there are ceilings to achievement. Many feel like they've hit that ceiling, but Kathie Lee broke through. On a certain level, it's true. The rich *have* gotten richer, and everybody else is just walking in place. The incomes of the top 1 percent of Americans "more than doubled in real terms between 1979 and 1989," Robert H. Frank and Philip J. Cook, write in their 1995 work titled *The Winner-Take-All Society.* At the same time "the median income was roughly stable and . . . the bottom 20 percent of earners saw their incomes actually fall by 10 percent." Winner-take-all markets occur when a lot people compete for a few huge payoffs. A few win big. Many, though, are losers, and are angry about it.

According to some theorists, times are economically good. According to others they are bad. Samuelson believes that times are good, but our expectations are unrealistic because prosperity indeed has limitations. As a result, consumers buy more than they can afford. The amount of debt the average American family is managing, for instance, is a higher percentage of his income than it has been in decades. Credit card debt has surged 78 percent since 1995. Personal bankruptcies are at their highest level in recorded history (1.1 million filings in 1996), according to *U.S. News & World Report.* Yet the average American, bad credit risk be damned, is tempted by twenty credit card offers each year.

Times, you might say, are bad despite how good things are. Like wages, benefits have steadily eroded. Between 1979 and 1993, the number of workers getting health benefits from employers dropped from 79 to 64 percent. The Commerce Department reported in early 1997 that savings have fallen as a portion of disposable income from 8.4 percent in 1984 to 4.8 percent in 1989 and continue at this level.

FANTASY AS A CULTURAL TEMPLATE

I don't like attackers, but my job has taught me that they're not all evil. They can be the people next door who complain about chemicals in food or about fat in popcorn and muffins. Once I strip away the rage, I find a desperate person looking for credit, recognition, or celebrity. I find an exile from an exciting world that has passed him by.

The world he wants to join never really existed. Americans feel exiled, but from a place located inside the TV screen. Attackers feel entitled to the same sense of community they see there. It's the community shared by the super-functional Huxtables, where the mom and dad have great jobs, the kids are good looking, and everyone is funny. It's the cast of *Friends,* who despite cosmetic struggles, end up with a cozy hearth in the world. Or the gathering of cancer-stricken characters on *Melrose Place* and *Party of Five* who look gorgeous and come out of their ordeals giving each other high fives. If all of us managed our affairs better, couldn't we be this lucky? To be sure, fantastic programs existed earlier, but were anchored in an ethic teaching that good things are earned, not bestowed.

As much as attackers crave a place in this electronic bombardment of perfect happiness, they don't resent TV characters, because they aren't real. Some, however, feel entitled to be them. They are emotionally starving for it. A few years ago, a Michelob beer ad asked, "Who says you can't have it all?" Life! The culture expects all of it, with endless choices. Choice used to mean making a choice, that there was something you *didn't* get. Now TV tells us you can choose everything.

In winner-take-all cultures the winner gets not just the fortune, but all the fame and happiness, too. Once Americans might have hoped for Andy Warhol's much hyped "15 minutes of fame." Now folks can't even have that because Bill Gates and Madonna have grabbed it all. The same uber-people—Gates, Madonna, Trump, Jordan, Gifford—are displayed over and over again. Of the 6 billion people on the planet, *these* are the only people worth covering? It's only natural to think, "What about me?"

The winner-take-all culture is inescapable. It's everywhere, from the news, recorded music, and movies to video games and the Internet. The average American receives 3,400 hours of information and other media "output" a year, according to a 1996 report by the Census Bureau and investment advisors Veronis and Suhler. That's "40 percent of the hours in our lives," writes *Washington Post* columnist Richard Harwood. Ninety-seven percent of American homes have a color TV. When TV's winner-take-all, perfect people occupy so much of our time, it's no wonder many feel left out.

Americans are not only exiles, but victims, too, according to the producers of TV news and talk shows. The items media producers select as big news are often only the little disappointments we all experience in life. Everyday crises are characterized as unique betrayals and dysfunctions. A new kind of eating disorder or an incidence of chemical sensitivity, for example, is grist for the morning talk show.

Victimhood is hot. A newscaster referred to the death of 100-year-old George Burns as "tragic," for instance. "Tragic" implies drama and surprise, descriptions that don't apply to the natural death of a very old man. At the same time, oddities such as the twenty-three-year-old high-tech millionaire are covered so frequently, many are left with the impression that whiz-kid moguls are everywhere but we aren't among them.

BECAUSE THEY CAN

Attacks, and the uncivilized behavior that accompanies them, proliferate because they are allowed to continue. Being rude used to be considered bad manners. Now it's cool. "What is a parent's plea for 'thank-you,' " wrote Janet Kinosian in the *Washington Post* "amid Internet raunch and mayhem, guns at school and on the freeways, tantrum throwing and spitting sports figures, the drones of trashy misfits exploited on daytime talk shows, TV shows like *Crossfire,* where politicians yell at one another in lieu of civilized discourse?"

There is a new Emily Post *Etiquette* for the Culture of Attack, but shame and self-restraint aren't listed in the table of contents. The new guide says it's all right to be pissed off. It's okay to be rude. Do it. And maybe you'll catch someone's attention. "The first prime-time premature ejaculation sight gag debuted on network TV early one evening last season," James Morris wrote in a 1996 *Wilson Quarterly* article. "And there followed . . . indignation? A crusade? An apology? Nothing of the kind? Nothing at all, really. The black hole of the acquiescent culture sucked the moment in without trace or resonance."

Psychotherapists, the courts, and the media encourage us to let it all hang out. Invoking your pain before the judge will get you acquitted and confronting your sex-addicted spouse on the *Jerry Springer Show* will make you famous. When you spill hot coffee on yourself, sue. It used to be that spilling coffee made you a klutz. Now it can make you rich. "There are few implausible scenarios anymore in America," wrote Morris.

Tonya Harding was allowed to compete after she plotted to whack Nancy Kerrigan's knee prior to the 1994 Olympics. At a news conference, she acknowledged to having "let myself down." Kerrigan's knee is mutilated but Harding let *herself* down. Mike Tyson has earned $142 million since he was released from jail for rape. He celebrated his reformation by biting Evander Holyfield's ear. He said he "just snapped," as if that explained why part of Holyfield's ear was lying on the canvas.

As an adolescent, I watched during the Watergate scandal the first hint of the rudeness to come. During a news conference, CBS News reporter Dan Rather rose to ask President Nixon a question. Nixon jokingly asked Rather, "Are you running for something?"

"No, Mr. President, are you?" Rather shot back.

Though today it wouldn't register on the cultural radar, at the time it was shocking. Fewer than fifteen years earlier, no member of the press dared to breathe in public the fact of President Kennedy's flagrant carousing. This changing sense of respect and decorum (contrary to views held by conservative conspiracy theorists) probably had less to do with the political affiliations of Kennedy and Nixon than the times in which they held office. As Adam Gopnick wrote in the December 12, 1994, *New Yorker,* "The reporter used to gain status by dining with his subjects; now he gains status by dining on them."

Dan Rather's smart-alecking of the president reflected the anti-establishment feelings of the Vietnam and Watergate eras. Adversarial journalism made sense in an extraordinary time of widespread political cover-ups, an unpopular war, and presidential wrongdoing. Now in more peaceful times, it is commonplace. Every news story seems to deserve the community's wrath. The danger is, when every story is Watergate, none of them is. We can no longer tell the difference between appearance and reality.

DEFINING DEVIANCY DOWN

"Outside of the killings, Washington has one of the lowest crime rates in the country."

Washington, D.C., mayor Marion Barry

"We have been re-defining deviancy," wrote Daniel Patrick Moynihan in his 1992 essay, "Defining Deviancy Down." Actions once considered bad are now acceptable, the senator wrote. A culture can only tolerate a certain level of badness in its collective mind, so when social behavior worsens, it redefines "badness." In places like New York City, crime is so prevalent, many people don't report burglaries. They know the police won't investigate and they mentally render the theft a noncrime. New Yorkers surrender to car thieves before they strike, says Moynihan, by leaving helpful notes in windshields reading "No Radio."

A similar force is at work when the schizophrenic and institutionally insane are released from hospitals. Governments and medical officials with authority believe they are doing the right thing by not inflicting their bourgeois morals on others. "They may henceforth sleep in doorways as often as they choose," wrote Moynihan. Policy leaders have also repackaged the issue of madness in the streets by redefining these unfortunate souls "as persons who lacked 'affordable housing.' "

Unfortunately, some "persons who lack affordable housing" can turn out to be evil, too. The debate about how accommodating our society should be to the needs of the insane resurfaced in its most malignant form on January 3, 1999, when a man with a long history of schizophrenia pushed Kendra Webdale, 32, in front of a New York City subway train, killing her instantly. This horror left many sane people wondering when tolerance degenerates into recklessness.

It's hard to miss the new standards. On my drive to work I hear Howard Stern refer to a caller as a "dick"; rock ingenue Alanis Morrissette has a hit about oral sex in a movie theater; I pass school children with pierced noses and bus billboards featuring Calvin Klein models that either look like junkies (known as "heroin chic") or super-studs with the Capitol rotunda in their jockeys. At work, corporate executives have exchanged suits for blue jeans—which were once reserved for counterculture revolutionaries.

When standards are lowered attacks proliferate. Rage seeks the trappings of respectability and the commuter on the freeway cuts the other car off and threatens its driver because our culture tells him that kind of behavior is okay.

I followed the case of O. J. Simpson with professional interest, especially since Simpson claimed he was under attack. The trial hadn't gone far, however, before I was distracted by newscasters referring to Paula Barbieri, Simpson's girlfriend, as "elusive." Barbieri had posed nude in *Playboy*'s October 1994 edition, but now, to the newscasters' chagrin, she was refusing to be interviewed. When I checked the dictionary, I found elusive to mean evasive, hard to see or capture. Posing in *Playboy* is many things, but hard to see is not one of them. The incident told me two things about the new Culture of Attack. It was further evidence of how pliable our definitions have become. But more important was the notion of implied betrayal. It was as if the public was *entitled* to see as much of Barbieri as they wanted.

I see every day in news coverage how it is no longer possible to demand too much information. To the public, discretion is the same thing as covering up. The media sense the public's pique, invoke Watergate, and give my clients the Information Age's most ruthless ultimatum: Tell us everything or you may not like what we turn up ourselves. This is precisely what the *Globe* did to Kathie Lee Gifford.

RAGE AS CONTEMPORARY CULTURAL EXPRESSION

"I've had this feeling ever since I graduated, this kind of compulsion that I have to be rude all the time."

Ben to Elaine, *The Graduate*

There is a threatening undercurrent of violence in America that affects everything from the way our citizens drive to the music we listen to. Grown children whose parents once complained about Elvis and the

Beatles contend with today's rock music groups like Dead Kennedys, Megadeth, Niggas with Attitude, and Rage Against the Machine. Their names are angry. The band Marilyn Manson's principals took their individual names from famous mass murderers.

It is estimated that a child will see over 100,000 acts of violence on television, including 800 murders, before leaving school. Body piercing, certainly an aggressive act, is at an all-time high. Cultural violence existed in earlier eras, but in the form of shoot 'em up western films. In those days Frank Sinatra was singing with Tommy Dorsey, not Switchblade Tommy and the Sucking Chest Wounds.

Given the increase in cultural aggression and the decline in standards and rules of decorum, it's no surprise that communication in America is affected. The attacks I see every day are an extension of America's in-your-face ethic. "Nothing seems astonishing," says Morris in the *Wilson Quarterly,* "only inevitable."

2. *Main Ingredients of Allegation: Plausibility and Resonance*

These days, if it could be true, it is.

"All you have to do is say something nobody understands and they'll practically do anything you want them to."
Holden Caulfield in J. D. Salinger's The Catcher in the Rye

THE TWIN PILLARS OF ALLEGATION

When the target of an allegation comes through my door, the first thing he wants to know is if I think it will stick. The answer depends on two factors: *plausibility* and *resonance*.

I define "plausible" to mean "it could conceivably happen," with the understanding that *most things* could conceivably happen. Take the unsolved murder case of child beauty queen JonBenet Ramsey. The girl's parents have been consistently portrayed as suspects. It isn't known whether they were involved in the murder, but the spectacle of posing a child like a sex kitten is not only resonant, but for many it seems plausible that they might be capable of doing something worse. Some may even *want* the parents to be the killers because of disapproval over how the Ramseys exploited their daughter.

O. J. Simpson was acquitted of double homicide because it was plausible that a police force known for awful race relations might have framed him. Detective Mark Fuhrman's liberal use of the word "nigger" in a taped interview was resonant to the mostly black jury, to say the least. After the tapes were played, all reason was abandoned for the remainder of the trial.

Simpson's defense lawyers were able to leverage Nicole Brown Simpson's libertine lifestyle to raise suspicions with the jury (and the public), the argument being that because Nicole ran with a wild bunch, someone—or something—other than O. J. might explain her death. Dallas Cowboys star Michael Irvin's well-publicized drug trial made it feasible that he could be involved with the gunpoint rape that was later alleged. The distinction between being a wild partier and being a rapist was lost in the whirl of allegation.

The replacement of proof with allegation may be distasteful but it's getting more common. Once bad information is "out there," it is impossible to recall it. Would a woman really ever feel comfortable around an acquitted rapist? Would we leave our children with a vindicated child molester? Did consumers feel safe in Audis—which, they had been told by *60 Minutes*, suddenly accelerated—even after the car had passed safety tests showing that sudden acceleration was impossible?

Today, allegations are supported primarily by emotion-based propaganda. The objective is "hitting the mark," "moving the needle," or getting a reaction. The healthy consumer advocacy movement has mutated into an orgy of claims that have, if nothing else, succeeded in making everybody nervous. In a country that is politically opposed to aging and dying, any message that implies these life events are inevitable is met with resistance.

One of the most effective allegers of abuse is the Center for Science in the Public Interest (CSPI). In recent years, this organization has attacked ground beef; restaurants such as Denny's, Shoney's, and Big Boy; and pastries, breakfast foods, popcorn, Mexican food, and Italian food all for their high fat content. The group referred to the global scourge of fettuccine alfredo as a "heart attack on a plate." CSPI isn't always wrong in flagging dietary concerns, but its extreme characterizations of hazards exaggerates the risks by positioning all consumptive acts as being suicidal. CSPI has also attacked fat replacers for disrupting digestion and artificial sweeteners for being carcinogens. The Food and Drug Administration does not agree, having studied and approved the same ingredients CSPI cites as hazards.

A CSPI news conference announcing things like this is guaranteed to paralyze the food industry because it will be heavily covered. Truth is incidental. Who wants to eat something that might CAUSE A FATAL HEART ATTACK? Rationality takes a backseat to press turnout.

TOOLS OF ALLEGATION

"The great masses of the people . . . will more easily fall victims to a great lie than a small one."

Adolf Hitler, *Mein Kampf*

During the past fifteen years, I have kept a record of the most effective tools of allegation used by attackers to aggravate their claims. Look for these when the next attack erupts.

1. Detailed Analysis of Commonplace Things

The Research Conundrum: Exhaustive research into a subject can validate, rather than disqualify, an allegation. In-depth analyses tend to make people think that if you studied something for a long time, your finding must be worth worrying about.

Food ingredient manufacturers are particularly vulnerable to this technique. When one of my client's food additives neared marketplace introduction, its critics cited the extensive research that had been done as evidence that there must be something wrong with it. If the ingredient were truly safe, the attackers argued, it would not have have had to go through so much testing. Of course, had the company had too little data, it would have been used as evidence of greed and slipshod research.

Pre-Trial Conviction: The American public equates attorneys with guilt. Many of my clients who are under investigation and hire attorneys have been positioned as being guilty *because* they hired counsel. The very act of retaining counsel can be positioned with a barely perceptible roll of the eyes (usually by an on-air reporter) as being a significant development. In the absence of any other evidence in the JonBenet Ramsey case, pundits and reporters alike made quite a fuss over the parents' having hired lawyers.

Class Warfare: Attack targets come under fire for the very act of possessing and expending funds. When debating my corporate clients in the press or in court, attackers often cite the companies' revenues (or the amount they spend on advertising). These impressive figures have little or nothing to do with the debate at hand, but succeed in exploiting a visceral, emotional sense that anyone who possesses wealth should spread it around more.

Listing a target's possessions is a reliable way to provoke resentment. In coverage of the medical competence of a prominent Texas doctor, a local television station repeatedly filmed his expensive cars and real estate holdings. He must have done something really bad to merit these goodies.

2. Selective Portrayals and Nasty Edits

An unflattering visual portrayal of a target is used to communicate the target's corruption. Many of my clients have been surprised by television camera crews who ambush them outside of their homes and offices. A startled person, regardless of his innocence or guilt, does not come across well on camera. The camera interprets jumpiness as guilt.

One of my clients, a corporate executive, was filmed getting into a dark sedan wearing sunglasses. He looked like a gangster. A simple story about a recycling controversy wound up looking like something much worse.

Choosing a clip of an interview subject stammering or equivocating works, especially if it is accompanied by a close-up shot. Lower-end news programs like to film big shots at close range while their victims and vindicators are filmed from further away. Close-up shots of people revealing facial pores and mild eye twitches disturb viewers, which is why they are used. A magazine program used footage of one of my energy industry clients, who had begun to exhibit a facial tic under questioning. There had been plenty of footage of him *not* ticking, but it ended up on the cutting room floor.

After he was grilled, the segment was summarized by the news personality back in the studio, which served as a psychic sanctuary far from the dangers of a nervous businessman who *looked* as if he had something to hide.

In July 1989, a *20/20* news story about Federal Express aired alleging that the company had compromised sensitive documents, mishandled explosives, and ran a morally lax business where workers used drugs and sometimes opened customers' packages in search of drugs. The correspondent, indicating that Federal Express would not comment, pointed toward a Delaware building and said, "The lights are out, the shades are drawn, but they were here a few minutes ago when a producer was here—but not now. They are locked up tight." Viewers were not told that the building was still under construction and hadn't even opened for business. Federal Express had, in fact, invited the network into their Memphis facility but *20/20* did not accept the invitation. The spectacle of a bloodless corporation in a dark and distant building conveyed guilt where the facts didn't.

Similarly, the Texas doctor under investigation for incompetence was photographed surreptitiously, giving the visual impression that he was up to no good when, in fact, he was just meeting an acquaintance. A graveyard was used as a visual in one segment, presumably to underscore where his patients ended up.

3. Tap the Barnum Effect

The phenomenon of people believing what they want to believe while ignoring facts and inaccuracies has been called the Barnum Effect, named after famed ringmaster P. T. Barnum. Attackers and plaintiffs use this sleight of hand to make health hazards resonate. Self-styled victims can link some item to their malady just by verbally making the correlation. The symptom is considered proof enough.

When reformulated gasoline was introduced in several states, a small number of people claimed to become dizzy and nauseated while driving. Publicity of the gasoline's alleged hazards were widespread, including reports by ABC's *Day One* and the *New York Times*. In order to determine if the gasoline was causing this reaction, some consumers began sniffing the gas pump nozzles. Lo and behold, some of them felt lightheaded.

Something was getting lost here: *This was gasoline!* You're not supposed to inhale it from the nozzle. The self-fulfilling prophecies validating the gasoline's hazards were embraced by many media and legislators, who called for a ban on the additive.*

Says Washington, D.C., psychiatrist Robert Litman in an interview: "What you often get is a small group that isolates itself and reinforces the vicious circle of illness because they lack outside input from a clinical, experienced voice. This situation is exacerbated by the tendency of these people to seek out so-called experts who, on the basis of their track records, will validate their [the victims'] pre-existing opinions of exactly what causes their suffering."

In a December 6, 1996, article called "Bad Information," the *Washington Post*'s Joel Achenbach wrote about the dangers of diagnostic information: "You are terribly lethargic and you go see a succession of mental health professionals. One says you are depressed, another says you are not depressed but have chronic fatigue syndrome, another says you have multiple personalities because your mother was a member of a satanic cult. You say you don't remember your mother being a member of a satanic cult, and the therapist says that's a dead giveaway." These kinds of vague suggestions by professionals frighten vulnerable people, not cure them.

On December 16, 1990, attackers linked amalgam dental fillings with multiple sclerosis. An MS patient named Nancy Yost appeared on a *60 Minutes* episode entitled "Is There Poison in Your Mouth?" She reported that she was forced to walk with a cane until she had her fillings removed. Then she was able to go dancing.

This episode falsely gave hope to thousands of MS sufferers despite

---

*The *Philadelphia Inquirer* (July 30, 1996) and *Los Angeles Times* (June 16, 1997), later exposed the activists as having been front groups for the manufacturer of a competing additive.

a statement released by the National Multiple Sclerosis Society saying that there was no "epidemiological evidence which relates mercury amalgam fillings to MS and no sound clinical evidence, gained through controlled clinical trials, which suggests that replacement of dental amalgams leads to any improvement in MS."

4. One-Way Allegation Forums

The best place to launch an allegation is in a forum that offers no resistance. Talk shows and the Internet are ideal because they offer issue-specific topics; access to large, preselected and sympathetic audiences; an anonymous communications launch pad; and minimal chance of being forced to defend the allegation. Talk show audiences can be counted upon to back the victim. The host boldly cheers on the aggrieved minority. The news media are better than the Internet at weeding out bad information because reporters have the journalistic imperative to convey the appearance of objectivity.

The World Wide Web includes allegation forums such as the Electrical Sensitivity Network, for those who claim to have been injured by electromagnetic fields from items such as telephone wires and microwave ovens; sites set up by disgruntled employees of K-Mart and Ford with names like "K-Mart Sucks" and "Flaming Fords"; support groups for people with various genuine illnesses ranging from allergies to AIDS, which allege conspiracies between government and industry; self-styled medical experts with inside dope on the side effects of chemicals that supposedly give men feminine characteristics; sites on chemical sensitivity and immunotoxins, the Zionist control of Hollywood, government coverups of UFO landings, and urine therapy (as in consuming one's own).

5. The Measurement Is the Message

Science has become good at measuring alleged hazards, real and imagined. The very act of being able to measure something can give the impression that if it's quantifiable (e.g., parts per billion), it's dangerous.

As William Clark concluded in his *Freeman* article titled "Witches,

Floods and Wonder Drugs," if a targeted item doesn't test positive in a parts per billion test, it "can always be exposed to a parts per trillion examination. The only stopping rule is the discovery of the sought-for effect, or exhaustion of the investigator (or his funds)." In other words, if an initial hazard cannot be found, redefine the threshold of danger so that any *trace* of the substance, even one-billionth of a particle that could cause harm, can be declared problematic.

In his polemic *Science without Sense,* junk science critic Steven Milloy shares ways that science is distorted to fit the preconceived conclusions of its sponsors. These techniques include the "Texas Sharpshooter Method," in which "The Texas Sharpshooter sprays the side of an abandoned barn with gunfire. He then draws a bull's-eye target around a cluster of bullet holes that occurred randomly. He can then say, 'See what a good shot I am!' " The most popular manifestation of this technique are "cancer clusters," where unusually high incidents of cancer are linked to the presence of heavy industry. Alleged cancer clusters are said to have existed in Woburn, Massachusetts (as featured in the book and film *A Civil Action*), and in Toms River, New Jersey. The melodrama in these cases has overpowered the scientific evidence linking specific substances to specific cancers.

Milloy writes about *data dredging,* in which huge quantities of data are analyzed for a shocking result and, once found, a random correlation can be associated. This method was used in an association between hot dogs and leukemia on the grounds that "children consuming more than 12 hot dogs per month were 9.5 times more likely to develop leukemia than children who consumed no hot dogs." This correlation was supposedly due to nitrites in hot dogs. Unfortunately, according to Milloy, the research "failed to come up with associations between other types of processed meats (including ham, bacon, sausage and luncheon meats) and leukemia. These other meats also contain nitrites and, under the hypothesis of the research, also should have been associated with leukemia."

6. Counterfeit Activists

The Culture of Attack provides great cover to interested parties looking to dress up a selfish agenda as a public hazard. Waste hauler Browning-

Ferris Industries (BFI) learned this when a neighborhood group calling itself "The North Valley Coalition of Concerned Citizens" emerged to oppose one of BFI's landfill projects in the Los Angeles area. BFI became suspicious, according to an exposé by the *Wall Street Journal's* Jeff Bailey, when this underfunded group "submitted to state water officials a highly sophisticated seismic critique" of the planned landfill's liner. The feint came to an end when BFI discovered that the study had been funded by the company's chief competitor, WMX Technologies Inc. WMX had been seeking a landfill permit of its own for the region. The California Regional Water Quality Control Board had been unaware of WMX's support for the North Valley Coalition's study and ultimately found the ruse to be a relevant factor in its decision to award BFI the landfill.

Attack Summary: Browning-Ferris Industries—1996

Victim:	Los Angeles citizens
Villain:	Browning-Ferris Industries
Vindicator:	North Valley Coalition of Concerned Citizens (backed by WMX)
Void:	Anxiety about landfills' impact on health and safety
Vehicle:	Front-group protests, local media coverage
Value:	Environmental protection; public welfare

The counterfeit activist strategy is employed more frequently due to legitimate concern about health and safety issues combined with public gullibility. These efforts are rooted in the premise that if it were known who was footing the bill, the public wouldn't listen. The gamble is that no one will check. It's a good bet; checking requires work and most parties—corporations, activists, the news media—lack the time, energy, and money to conduct the investigations with due diligence.

Legitimate coalitions are built every day. Unions team with corporate management to seek important relief legislation; AIDS activists join with medical researchers to oppose the animal rights movement; university nutritionists advocate certain food products over others, and so on. What is fundamental, however, is how the issue is packaged and presented.

When a coalition does not disclose its funding, it's safe to assume there's something they don't want known. Industry groups have been known to use opaque names. Until recently the nuclear energy industry's association called itself the U.S. Council on Energy Awareness. Today, it's known—rightly—as the Nuclear Energy Institute to more accurately reflect its platform.

7. Validate an Existing Prejudice

One way to spread a false allegation is to circulate it to people who are predisposed to certain kinds of stories so it will "bottom up" (i.e., rise unchecked) to higher-end sources, say from the Internet to the mainstream media. This strategy was used in the late 1980s by American Express to smear its competitor, billionaire Lebanese banker Edmond Safra. The motive was to discredit Safra as he set out to grow his competing Republic National Bank.

Attack Summary: Edmond Safra and Republic Bank—Late 1980s

Victim:	Those doing business with Edmond Safra
Villain:	Edmond Safra
Vindicator:	Assorted international media
Void:	Fear of drugs, money-laundering; anti-Semitism
Vehicle:	International tabloid media
Value:	Protecting business people; exposing criminal behavior

---

The attack was orchestrated by placing false and damaging news stories connecting Safra with narcotics and organized crime in small, right-wing publications around the world. The allegations were considered plausible because Safra was a wealthy, powerful, and mysterious man. The false information resonated because Safra was Jewish, something that appealed to scandal sheets with a history of advocating notions of world Jewish domination of banking.

The objective, according to Bryan Burrough in his book *Vendetta:*

American Express and the Smearing of Edmond Safra, was to instill concern among financial leaders about doing business with Safra. Financial leaders, it was believed, would repeat the story line without checking because international banking is competitive and personal relationships are more important than financial statements and legal agreements.

Burrough explains that the strategy worked for a while. The bad information was ferried around the world by an American Express operative. The rumors hit Safra in the areas that would do the most damage to a financier looking to grow his business with a prestigious international clientele. The Paris-based scandal sheet *Minute* entitled one article "Millionaire of the White Stuff" (August 31, 1988), the implication being that Safra made his fortune trafficking in drugs.

According to Burrough, the smear stories, which were published in France, Switzerland, the United States, Mexico, Peru, Argentina, and Uruguay, dealt with Safra's purported links to money laundering, South American drug barons, American organized crime figures and the Iran-Contra fiasco, which was in the news at that time. The *Minute* story vaguely linked Safra to the murder of a security consultant who was close to proving that Safra masterminded the arms-for-hostages deal.

Another article ran months later in the Buenos Aires newspaper *Cronica*. It stated in part, "According to the DEA, what Republic Bank and Safra are looking for is the total control of the ways to launder dollars that come to banks in Miami, Los Angeles, New York, Luxembourg, France and Switzerland."

Furious, Safra investigated. Among the things he discovered was a fax printout sent to *Minute* with the heading: "FEB 25 '88 21:25 AMEX CORP COMM * NYC." The fax had come from American Express. Safra also learned that an American Express operative had paid newspapers that had printed negative stories. Safra took legal action against American Express and settled for funds given to select charities. Safra's four libel suits against the European newspapers that had published smear articles were successful.

Despite Safra's vindication, a politician in Brazil, where Safra does business and keeps a home, denounced the banker as a drug trafficker on the floor of the legislature. He cited as his proof the media reports from the smear.

"To this day," writes Burrough, "there are businessmen and journal-ists who swear Safra must be involved in criminal endeavors; all that's lacking, they acknowledge, is proof."

The Safra case is an extreme, but chilling, template for how attackers who desperately want an allegation to be true can mobilize seemingly respectable resources to damage a target.

3. *The Need for Witch Hunts*

*Historical "witch hunts" and
today's Culture of Attack have similarities.*

A TV STATION IN BOSTON

January 1987 was a big blizzard month. I was holed up at a TV network affiliate in Boston with a client whose company was in trouble. A woman from Brookline, a suburb of Boston, was alleging that one of the company's lawnmowers had taken off on its own, running into a bush and narrowly missing her child. The woman was in the network affiliate offices at the crack of dawn to confront my client, a corporate executive. The station had already run the promo for the mid-day news.

In addition to the snowstorm, everything else that day started off wrong. The TV reporter began the interview by breaking the ground rules. She wanted the Brookline woman to "debate" my client. A "debate" in my business is little more than a neutral-looking forum where a target can be criticized with little chance of presenting his case. The TV station had agreed in advance that there would be no debates. I didn't want my client facing someone who would shout "murderer" every time he opened his mouth.

The reporter was playing her hand, a hand that figured we wouldn't have traveled all the way from Washington only to refuse to go on camera. During the verbal scuffle that ensued, the reporter told me about the victim's "right" to confront her assailant.

"Her assailant is a lawnmower," I said. "And this is a TV show."

She threw down her clipboard in disgust and pressed me on this "rights" business. I said I'd never heard of this "right" to attack in public, not having gone to law school. She rolled her eyes. I repeated that we would be happy to conduct the interview, but not with the victim in the room.

I lamely added, "You know the product is safe. My client didn't do this." She pointed to the camera lens and said through her teeth, "But they think your client did it." "They" were her viewers!

I was stunned, though I shouldn't have been.

"So, what's important here is that the promo you made this morning be validated. You promised a big event and now you'd better deliver, is that it?"

The reporter huffed at my remark and said something about this being the way things were done. She left the room to speak to her producer. When she returned, I made it clear that my client and I were willing to walk out the door. The reporter agreed there would be no head-to-head "debate" and the alleged victims were not in the studio.

The half-hour interview went as expected. There was no debate, but just enough vituperation to make me feel I had earned my pay. The snowfall had stopped and my exhausted client and I parted ways. I wasn't scheduled to leave until the following morning and was in no mood to brawl at Logan Airport for an earlier flight back to Washington. I'd find something to do.

Back in the hotel room I opened a Boston guide book and saw a feature on Salem, the nearby town notorious for its seventeenth-century witch hunts. A Salem villager was quoted as saying of one of the accusers in the witch trial that "she did it for sport." I embraced this quotation as my own little epiphany. How I would spend the remainder of my day, as well as my career, came into focus. Salem was a half-hour away.

SALEM AND THE DYNAMICS OF BEWITCHING

"It is a shameful thing that you should mind these folks that are out of their wits."

Accused witch Martha Carrier, executed August 19, 1692

Attack Summary: Salem Witch Trials—1692

Victim:	Elizabeth Parris, Abigail Williams
Villain:	Accused witches
Vindicator:	Reverend Samuel Parris
Void:	Explanation for girls' hysterical behavior, economic uncertainty*
Vehicle:	Witch trials
Value:	Protection of village children

I've studied witch hunts ever since that snowy day in Boston. I know one thing for certain: The modern Culture of Attack is a breeding ground for witch hunts. I've discovered that witch hunts, regardless of the era in which they take place, tend to coincide with times of economic and social uncertainty and of perceived helplessness. A witch hunt gives an anxious society the illusion that it is acting decisively to fill a necessary void. The hunt initially focuses on the wealthy and powerful, but ends up preying on those least able to defend themselves. Then comes a highly public torture that continues until either the accused confesses or another definitive conclusion—execution, in Salem—is reached.

The Salem witch hunts were triggered on January 20, 1692, by nine-year-old Elizabeth Parris and eleven-year-old Abigail Williams when they first behaved strangely in front of Tituba, their slave caretaker from Barbados. The girls had been playing a gypsy game, common in those days, of looking into a makeshift crystal ball to determine their futures. One of the girls cried she saw a ghost lying in a casket when she looked into the crystal ball. Panic ensued.

Elizabeth and Abigail were not just any children—and this is critical —they were the daughter and niece of the town minister, the formidable Reverend Samuel Parris. Parris immediately opened an investigation into the cause of the girls' behavior. The town doctor, William Griggs, ruled out medical illness. The girls must then be victims of a terrible crime, said Parris, and he turned to finding and prosecuting the perpetrators. By the

---

*Salem Village was being threatened by competing centers of commerce, including nearby Salem Town.

end of February 1692, the girls had identified three women responsible for their strange behavior: two townswomen, Sarah Good and Sarah Osborne, and their caretaker, Tituba.

In the months that followed, one hundred people were accused of witchcraft and ninety were tried by a jury. Twenty-four were convicted. Nineteen were hanged and four died in jail, including Giles Corey, who was pressed to death by giant stone weights used during his interrogation. Corey had pled not guilty and had refused to stand trial.

During interrogation, Sarah Good also denied being a witch:

Have you made no contract with the devil?
No.
Why do you hurt these children?
I do not hurt them. I scorn it.
Who do you imploy [*sic*] then to do it?
I imploy [*sic*] no body. . . . I am falsely accused.

Good was executed and her four-year-old daughter, even though she had testified against her mother, was jailed in irons for nine months. Like Good, only those who denied being witches were executed; if they confessed, they were shunned, but spared. Accused witch Margaret Jacobs said, "They told me if I . . . would confess should I save my life." Margaret confessed and accused her grandfather and another man, who were hanged on August 19, 1692. In *Salem Possessed,* authors Paul Boyer and Stephen Nissenbaum write, "It is surely no coincidence that not one of the confessing witches was hanged." Confessions fill the attacker's void.

As for the other purported tormentors of Elizabeth Parris and Abigail Williams, Sarah Osborne died in prison several months after her arrest. Tituba, on the other hand, was spared when she identified the family dog as a witch. Reverend Parris decided that Tituba might not be a witch after all, and used his influence to save her. Tituba's rescue was due to Parris's realization that his position would be weakened if other villagers thought witchcraft was going on inside his own home.

WHO WERE THE WITCHES?

Years before the witch trials, Salem Village was known for its political unrest and poorly defined government. Salem farmers and townspeople were also feeling economic competition from neighboring towns.

A few Salem merchants, however, the contemporary equivalent of corporate executives and their influential wives, were very successful. They controlled 12 percent of the total tonnage of shipped commodities in the entire Massachusetts Colony. According to Boyer and Nissenbaum, "the richest 10 percent of Salem's population controlled 62 percent of its wealth—almost three times as much as it had controlled a generation earlier." The winners took all.

As the merchants got richer, the less prosperous farmers of Salem saw their own lot grow worse. By 1690 the average Salem Village landholding stood at 124 acres—about half what it had been in 1660.

Despite popular perceptions that Salem's accused witches were the poor, the truth is that by the spring of 1692, many of those charged were some of the region's most prominent people, including two of the seven men on the town council. The townspeople, under the direction of Parris, had focused their anxiety on those they most resented. According to Baylor University historian Elizabeth Dunn, "a classic witch was a woman that inherited land," someone whose holdings *hadn't* shrunk. But Parris couldn't keep attacking Salem's "haves."

Colonial Salem's well-to-do weren't passive and they had no intention of being stoned, pressed, or hanged. In a witch hunt, *somebody* has to be hanged or else the whole endeavor looks like madness on the part of the vindicators like Reverend Parris, which, of course, it is.

Nearly three hundred years later, I was nose to nose with a TV reporter who saw her job flash before her eyes when I threatened to take away her witch. Without my client on camera, the attack would be incomplete. No witch, no hanging. It was the job of my client, an employee of a large, faceless corporation, to take the hit.*

Reverend Parris made a strategic error in his initial public campaign.

---

*His company, worried about public image, considered fighting his accuser but decided against it because it would appear too heavy-handed.

He targeted too many influential people. Here he was, the colonial equivalent of the Moral Majority's Jerry Falwell, going on *Nightline* and leveling child abuse charges against people who weren't easy to hang. Many of the accused witches would be today's equivalents of the prosperous, but less famous, neighbors of people like Warren Buffett or Katharine Graham—contributors to local churches and shareholders of major local companies. As the Buffetts and Grahams of colonial Salem saw their neighbors being jailed they started asking questions.

So it was, as with most scapegoating, that the villagers of Salem hanged the outsiders, the poor, the unpopular or defenseless. Sarah Good was a beggar and, by most accounts, rude as hell. Sarah Osborne was a crotchety old woman. To be sure, some big shots were executed, but most of them got off long before the judicial system came too close. The Parris family dog, however, named as a witch by Tituba, was executed.

CONTEMPORARY WITCH HUNT PARALLELS

Contemporary America is primed for witch hunts. Like Salem, ours is an anxious society. Family life is chaotic. Americans see a widening schism between themselves and the very wealthy. News of massive layoffs in corporate America increases this anxiety, which will not abate as domestic and global corporations buy one another and consolidate, thereby requiring more layoffs to pay for the buyouts.

It's hard to keep up with the information that spills over us every day. There are new lethal microbes, scientists who clone sheep and may someday replicate humans, and American terrorists blowing up American buildings. Rapidly changing technology is overwhelming: Many people aren't "on line" and are scared by the digital world that almost everyone appears to be embracing. Finally, we have venereal diseases that *kill*, not just inconvenience. The public is so confused, and its priorities are so out of whack, deadly viruses can take a backseat in the media to agonizing over the environmental dangers of using plastic cups versus paper.

How is this anxiety alleviated? A witch hunt. But modern America is enlightened and doesn't *do* witch hunts. The nation has seen Vietnam. It has seen Senator McCarthy and the Holocaust. The country is politically correct and won't fall into scapegoating. Or will it?

True, the twentieth century has delivered Americans from much of human ignorance, but it hasn't delivered everyone from the monsters of anxiety. Though colonial Salem and contemporary America aren't identical, there are enough cultural similarities to be disturbing. Because of greater enlightenment, attackers cloak their fears in social principle and attack in the name of public safety. Witch hunts appear in the guise of "gotcha" journalism and the political nominations process, hidden camera "stings" on TV news magazines and Internet "flaming" (smear campaigns).

Instead of people, attackers often gun for corporations and products, because they don't have human faces that tweak their guilt. Attackers pass laws to ban convenience products like disposable plastic containers, once referred to as the "devil" on the popular sitcom *Murphy Brown*. This "devil" has recently possessed apples, Chinese food, cellular phones, cranberries, dental fillings, diet sodas, fast food, fat replacers, hair dryers, hair dyes, hot dogs, Mexican food, plastic cups, runaway cars, sparkling water, and sweeteners. The Center for Science in the Public Interest broke the shocking news that fattening muffins are fattening, as if the public had mistaken them for a low-calorie health food.

PUBLIC SCRUTINY AS TORTURE

A witch hunt must take place in public. This is true across cultures. Public participation and enjoyment of the witch's torture is essential. In her study of mid–twentieth-century Nigerian witch hunts, "Bloodhounds Who Have No Friends," Misty Bastian describes a witch poisoning in the town center: "The accused had to drink a cup of sasswood mixture at the break of day, just as a nocturnal witch's power was ebbing away, and survive for twenty-eight days. . . . The sasswood poison took rapid effect, causing respiratory failure." If the accused witch survived—and few did—she was vindicated.

In the Culture of Attack, the rec-room TV is the nation's town center, and it is there that the epitome of American wholesomeness, the apple, almost met its demise. The beginning of the end of Alar, a pesticide used on apples, came February 26, 1989, on CBS's *60 Minutes*. During the show, Alar was called "the most potent cancer-causing agent in our food supply." *60 Minutes* produced the piece relying heavily on the Natural Resources Defense Council (NRDC), along with the group's public relations firm, Fenton Communications, as its main source of information about Alar. Other national and regional media outlets immediately ran similar stories.

Attack Summary: Apples and Alar—Winter–Spring 1989	
Victim:	Children
Villain:	Alar, Apples
Vindicator:	National Resources Defense Council (NRDC)
Void:	Fear of chemicals, demand for environmental scare stories, NRDC agenda
Vehicle:	*60 Minutes*
Value:	Protecting children

A classic witch hunt ensued. It was the kind I'm often asked to control. Panic swept the country. Consumers jammed hotlines with questions about the safety of disposing of apple juice. Elizabeth Whelan's book *Panic in the Pantry* describes a mother who persuaded state troopers to follow and pull over a bus carrying her child and her child's apples. Actress Meryl Streep formed a strike force to monitor Alar and similar products.

I can't say I was surprised by any of this. As I followed the Alar scare, I described to myself the inevitable dynamics that made the attack come together. First, there was the Culture of Attack itself, which had provided all the ingredients for panic: The media had recently grown hungry for environmental scare stories (a basic need for news). Fear of chemicals, such as Alar, was fashionable and the ranks of chemophobes were growing (cultural anxiety). Then there were the two powerful symbols of innocence: the American apple and the small children who drink its juice (the helpless victims).

A second development soon followed. It turned out that the scientific facts were as uncertain as the hysteria was overwhelming. In the meantime, apple growers had lost $250 million and produce processors lost an additional $125 million. The Department of Agriculture was forced to buy tons of leftover apples and Alar was discontinued for use on edible produce. Only then did the scientific experts and investigative media—from the World Health Organization and the American Medical Association to the U.S. Environmental Protection Agency and *Science* and *ECO* magazines— conclude that the scientific evidence for the charges against Alar was weak.

I had to look a little closer to pinpoint the attack's real instigators, but it became clear once the produce and chemical industries tried to defend themselves. The National Resources Defense Council, working with *60 Minutes,* was the real culprit. The NRDC immediately counter-charged that industry was funding the defense. Of course the apple industry was, it was the one being attacked. The NRDC gave itself away by using two of Salem's most popular techniques: depicting defense as foul play (How dare you fight back!) and depicting contrary information as trickery (Don't go dragging evidence into this fight!).

What did the NRDC, a nonprofit public interest group, have to gain by attacking Alar? The NRDC is an agenda-driven entity that relies on fundraising and a high public profile to prosper. Fenton Communications is a for-profit PR group, and *60 Minutes* is the most profitable franchise in the multibillion-dollar CBS empire. They all benefited from the controversy. NRDC raised its profile, Fenton pleased its client, and *60 Minutes* got high ratings. If they were motivated exclusively by public welfare they might have waited for evidence before making accusations. As it was, they shut down an industry—the definitive conclusion required of all witch hunts.

BRINGING IT HOME: WHY WITCH HUNTS STOP

Witch hunts are publicly supported activities that stop when the public decides they should. Timing is important. I've seen it over and over again with my clients. The attackers need to have enjoyed sufficient success that they begin to tire, get cocky, or became careless in pursuing their cause. If and when the attack loses momentum, a bold, powerful, and charismatic challenger, who's not afraid of the attackers, often emerges.

The beginning of the end of the Salem witch hunts came when the attackers broadened their list of targets to the general public, including some of the most influential people in the Massachusetts Colony. It was one thing to target a specific subset of the community; it was another thing to target familiar and popular people. Likewise, Senator Joseph McCarthy's madness in the 1950s ceased when the public began to feel that the search for communists was more dangerous than the communist menace. People began to ask, "Am I next?" This was understandably so in Salem—death sentences for witchcraft were being handed down in record numbers in the weeks prior to the ultimate intervention by Massachusetts Colony officials.

A witch hunt, like a virus, also needs to run its course. Efforts to stop them are unlikely to work until people see for themselves the damage done, something (unfortunately) that takes time. History students have asked: Why didn't the accused witches defend themselves or leave Salem? or Why didn't the Jews of Eastern Europe fight back or flee the Nazis? Many tried, but none had the weapon of historical perspective.

Once a society witnesses the destructive power of witch hunts it can understand why such social madness is bad and then develop the courage to act. The society also sees that the (implicitly) promised benefits of the witch hunts do not bear fruit: Economies remain uncertain and spiritual fulfillment does not follow—the society doesn't feel any more secure. In fact, it feels *less* so. The initial feelings of fear and anxiety that helped produce the witch hunts are transformed into feelings of revulsion.

Justice is close at hand when the attackers begin interpreting the quantity of their media coverage with their depth of support. The community senses this as well and begins to resent it. Average citizens also begin looking for a new guru—one less likely to threaten their well-being. This guru, a "knight," recognizes the attacker's grandiosity as a strategic weakness. And, at the right moment, the knight poses *the question* to the community: "Are *you* next?"

A KNIGHT EMERGES

"It were better that ten suspected witches should escape, than one inno-cent person be condemned."
Colonial Massachusetts power-broker Increase Mather

At the height of their power, attackers like Salem's Reverend Parris take on an aura of invincibility. The community is unlikely to challenge them because of the perception that more will be punished. As distressing as the concept of a social hierarchy is to many Americans, some members of the community have more power to stop the witch hunts than others. In Salem, the bold figure came in the form of Increase Mather, one of the most powerful men in Massachusetts and formerly the colony's ambassador to England. Mather led the fight against the witch hunts by raising doubts about the "spectral evidence" used to convict witches. Spectral evidence included things like other people's confessions, unusual physical features, and the testimony of the bewitched little girls. In other words, a witch could be convicted on nothing more than mere accusation. Mather argued that "the evidence . . . ought to be as clear as in any other crimes of a capital nature."

In October 1692, after nineteen people had been executed, Governor Phips of the Massachusetts Colony declared that the spectral evidence was no longer admissible in court. The following month, a special court was created to deal with the remaining witch trials. Under the new rules there were no additional convictions.

THE END OF MODERN WITCH HUNTS

Contemporary attacks are defused for the same reasons as the colonial ones were. Intense personal fears about health, for example, have prompted the current culture to question animal rights groups' attacks on biomedical research. The media have just begun to key in on Hollywood's contradictory support for AIDS research and opposition to animal research. And while consumers may like to see Kim Basinger in the movies, they don't want her having too much influence on the advancement of cures for terrible diseases. Similarly, the end of activist assaults on disposable diapers came when Jane Pauley, then hosting the *Today* show, asked an anti-diaper activist if she had young children. The activist was not a mother. While Pauley didn't tell the woman to shut up, she might as well have. Pauley's question and facial expression brought the issue home by driving a wedge between the activist's assertions and the basic needs of moms and dads who rely on disposable diapers.

No single white knight has emerged in modern times because there is no singular witch hunt like there was in Salem or in Joe McCarthy's day. Today's witch hunts are habitual, not catastrophic, so it's hard to focus and soul search. Contemporary attacks are not seen as being personally relevant. Americans don't feel bad for Kathie Lee.

Business interests are among the most hunted, but the argument that attacks on business ultimately hurt us all in the end (through lost products or higher prices) doesn't fly. The attacks are seen as victimless crimes because no one associates corporations with real people. Corporations are seen as giant, wealthy institutions that play no important role in the community.

Interest in pursuing witch games remains high. Knowing this, today's accused almost always choose to take their beating rather than fight. Many believe they are up against an unbeatable apocalyptic force. A witch hunt, after all, is anchored in notions of salvation—once the witch is dead, the world will be perfect. The truth is much less exciting. As Dorothy learned once she followed the yellow brick road, the witch turned out to be a nasty neighbor, the wizard was a little man from Kansas, and Oz was just a dream she had after some bad weather. Lest we forget, the Salem witch trials began because two little girls flipped out in front of their babysitter.

Like the villagers in Salem, today's attackers also have agendas. The attack's true motive is far more important than its trigger. The trigger need only be something that resonates with the rest of the population. In contemporary attacks, few things resonate better than the pretense of victimhood.

4. *Victimhood and the Scourge of Living*

Everyday life is a tragic mishap.

"Never before in human history were so many acronyms pursuing identity. It's as though all human encounters were one big sore spot, inflamed with opportunities to unwittingly give, and truculently receive, offense."
Robert Hughes, *Culture of Complaint*

PSYCHIATRISTS AND WOODPECKERS

I see a lot of psychiatrists. It's part of my job. I talk to psychiatrists because I need to understand what is motivating my clients' attackers, and psychiatrists are often able to give me an explanation based on an easily overlooked word or expression.

On one occasion, Dr. R came to my office to review a clip from a TV magazine program. His mission was to give me insight into a group of people claiming to have been injured by my client's product. The product, a household cleanser, had been heavily tested and I believed the alleged hazard had been greatly exaggerated. I wasn't certain how to approach the victims or whether to counsel my client to approach them at all.

Dr. R paused the tape, rewound it, and asked me to watch the interview of the victims without the sound.

"You're screwed," the esteemed psychiatrist said. "Now tell me why."

I watched a few minutes of the silent tape and nothing really struck me. Dr. R sped up the tape. We both watched it in faster motion.

"What do you see?" he asked.

I laughed and said, "They look like woodpeckers."

"Why?"

"They keep bobbing their heads forward."

"Exactly. These people don't want to feel better," Dr. R said. "They keep moving forward because they want to be noticed. People in pain don't jump toward cameras, they look for relief." This drama, he concluded, was a desperate plea for attention. The people on the videotape were committed to their grievances. A dialogue, that staple of problem-solving, would not defuse this attack.

Unfortunately, Dr. R's insight applies to many groups I encounter. During the past decade, my cases have increasingly included attackers who have lost the capacity to differentiate between being victimized and being disappointed. The fact that some Americans celebrate unfounded grievances is rooted in the unwarranted proposition that life should be risk-free and, if it's not, *someone* should hang for it.

The same surreal mindscape that allows newscasters to call comedian George Burns's death at 100 "tragic," ignores that at the beginning of this century 3 percent of the U.S. population died of a flu outbreak within two years. In 1918, in October alone, 200,000 Americans died of the flu, prompting neither lawsuits nor hidden camera exposés to ferret out the perpetrators.

Attackers assume that if their lives cannot be described in a string of superlatives, somebody stole from them. Attackers don't believe in bad luck, nature, or "bad breaks" and attribute bad things to mismanagement or malice. Civilization has made so much progress in so many areas that a core group of malcontents attribute their disappointments to spite and conspiracy. I remember flipping through the TV channels at the time of the January 1996 Los Angeles earthquake and nearly dropping my remote control when a reporter asked a rescue worker "what went wrong?" A tectonic plate beneath the earth's surface just moved the whole continent is what went wrong!

Most of the victimization claims that I see are alleged illnesses or threats to the attacker's physical well being. A victim of a true tragedy has no choice. In my cases, loneliness and desperation, not actual physical misfortune, are often driving the process. Edward Shorter, in his book on psychosomatic illness, *From Paralysis to Fatigue,* writes that in post-modern life the "disaffiliated, having lost their faith in scientific medicine and unable to interpret body symptoms in social isolation, seek out alternative forms of cure." Some of these cures are marketed by charlatans whose main pitch consists of communicating that they *believe* the patient's self-diagnosis and are on their side.

Victimhood gives attackers relief from the loneliness. They use evidence of commonplace frustrations and anxieties as leverage to get attention. Maybe they jump in front of cameras as a painkiller of some kind. The question then becomes, "Is greater exposure the kind of relief they need?"

THE VICTIM'S SEDUCTION

In modern times, the diagnosis—the catch phrase—comes before all else. Writes Wendy Kaminer in *I'm Dysfunctional, You're Dysfunctional,* "What's remarkable about our notion of victimhood today is its inclusiveness and its spread beyond the courtroom's structured exchange of accusations. Smokers are the victims of tobacco companies, troubled teenagers are the victims of rock and roll, alcoholics are the victims of their genes, and a support group for the 'Victims of Plastic Surgery' claims 3,500 members." *Time* magazine art critic Robert Hughes wrote in his 1993 best seller *Culture of Complaint,* "Since our new-found sensitivity decrees that only the victim shall be the hero, the white American male starts bawling for victim status too."

One staple of modern crisis management is the "victim's network," an affiliation of torment groupies united in their persecution by products ranging from breast implants to German automobiles. In 1986, the "Audi Victims Network" sprouted in New York and around the country to protest the phenomenon of "sudden acceleration," a syndrome that supposedly sent cars crashing through living room walls—on their own. The centerpiece of the attack on Audi was a devastating *60 Minutes* story on November 23, 1986, in which victims recounted their horror stories.

Membership in the Audi Victims Network once included a T-shirt, as if having been in a runaway car were an achievement. Audi was vindicated in a 1989 report by the National Highway Traffic Safety Administration (NHTSA) and the phenomenon of sudden acceleration was discredited. NHTSA experts believed that the drivers had inadvertently pressed the accelerator instead of the brake. Vindication occurred *after* the company's U.S. market was virtually destroyed by the allegations. By the time the NHTSA report was issued, Audi's annual sales had dropped from their pre–*60 Minutes* peak of 74,000 to about 20,000.

Attack Summary: Audi—1986

Victim:	Audi drivers, innocent bystanders
Villain:	Audi of America
Vindicator:	Audi Victims Network
Void:	Explanation for "sudden acceleration" syndrome
Vehicle:	*60 Minutes*
Value:	Consumer safety

Effective victims' networks tend to be associated with a scientific-sounding "syndrome." The syndrome is preferably something that has happened to or could happen to anyone. In other words, there's a manifestation you can choose or be talked into, especially if you are vulnerable and prone to suggestion. (Question: "Did you ever notice that you're tired at night?" Answer: "Why, yes, now that you mention it.")

To better understand victimhood and the motive for my meeting with psychiatrists like Dr. R, imagine a gardener named Ralph, who founded a victims network in response to a bad reaction to Grass-alot,* a fertilizer. It makes him sick. It's the beginning of gardening season, but he's had to stop gardening. He can hardly work anymore and has applied for disability. He found information on the Internet that described similar reactions to products like Grass-alot. A local news program covers him. Dr. Van Wick, a retired toxicologist, sees Ralph on TV and calls him. He

---

*This is a fictitious name. I know of no fertilizer by this name.

wants to work on the protest. He asks Ralph questions. Does he feel dizzy? Does he sweat? Does his throat hurt? He thinks he knows what ails Ralph. Together they form the Grass-alot Patrol.

Dr. Van Wick believes Ralph suffers from a chemical reaction caused by an ingredient in Grass-alot. Dr. Van Wick has hit Ralph's symptoms right on the head. It's uncanny. Ralph feels relief that his illness has an explanation—it's a "chemical reaction." The cure Dr. Van Wick recommends is to rid the world of Grass-alot. They pass along their local coverage to the national media, hoping that the bigger players will recognize the potential of their story. The network magazine show, *America Betrayed,** runs a hostile segment on Grass-alot. Dr. Van Wick's description of Ralph's symptoms hits a nerve with the audience. *America Betrayed*'s telephones light up. The Grass-alot Patrol has found other sufferers who will be heard from again in a form that will be hard to ignore.

BOUTIQUE DISABILITIES

"Political extremism involves two prime ingredients: an excessively simple diagnosis of the world's ills and a conviction that there are identifiable enemies back of it all."

John Gardner

In the search for somebody to blame, victimhood, labeled with a nasty-sounding syndrome, makes belligerence acceptable. Victimhood is the opposite of responsibility. It is psychic income, a mental form of compensatory damages because the attackers didn't get all the things that they believe were owed to them as citizens of a robust nation. *Culture of Complaint* author Hughes writes, "As our 15th-century forebears were obsessed with the creation of saints and our 19th-century ancestors with the production of heroes, from Christopher Columbus to George Washington, so are we with the recognition, praise and, when necessary, the manufacture of victims."

Nowhere have the effects of affliction chic been felt more acutely

---

*To my knowledge no such show exists by this name.

than in the disabled community. In a 1995 op-ed piece in the *Los Angeles Times,* disabled activist William Bolte wrote that the Americans with Disabilities Act, for which he fought, "makes no distinction between severe disabilities and disabilities that cause inconvenience. . . . When the benefits and advantages disappear for the opportunistically disabled, millions will experience miraculous cures."

America is in the throes of disability inflation, perhaps best exemplified by a vogue phenomenon called multiple chemical sensitivity (MCS), a condition where patients link uncomfortable symptoms with specific chemical exposures. "MCS" sounds serious. The use of the word "multiple" conjures up images of multiple sclerosis, a devastating neurological disease. The use of the word "chemical" is guaranteed to scare a healthy segment of the population that equates chemicals with carcinogens.

Suffers of MCS cannot distinguish between a preference and a disease. According to media reports and information contained in various MCS pamphlets, the cauldron of items that people with MCS react poorly to includes the following:

> acid, after shave lotion, air fresheners for rest rooms, ammonia, artificial colors, astringent cleaning products, bananas, beer, being tired, black insulation under the car, blowing out a match, books, bug spray, candle smoke, car exhaust, copy paper, carpets, cats, cellulose products, chemicals used in art, chemicals used in treating new fabric, chlordane, chlorine bleach, cigarette smoke, citrus products, cleaning solvents, cleaning supplies, cleaning the coffee machine, climbing stairs, colored pamphlets, concrete buildings, copy machine exhaust, corn, crying, deodorants, detergents, disinfectant, dogs, dry cleaning solvents, dust, electrical appliances, essential oils, exerting oneself, fabric softeners, fibers in walls and clothes, fireworks, flea shampoos, floor wax, flowers, fluorescent lighting, food flavoring, food preservatives, formaldehyde, fragrances (perfumes, cologne), fresh tomatoes, freshly felled trees, furniture, furniture wax, garlic, gas stoves, gasoline fumes, ginseng products, glue, guinea pigs, hair gel, hair spray, holding something frozen, house rabbits, humidity, ink, ironing clothes, kerosene, kitty litter, laser printers, laughing, lawn fertilizer, lawn pesticide, lotion, makeup, mercury, mold, natural gas lines, new clothes, newspapers, organophosphates, paints, perfumes, personal care products,

pesticides, petrachlorophenal, petrochemicals, photocopier ink, photo-copies, photography chemicals, plastic food wrap, plastic garbage bags, polyester, polystyrene picnic products, powder, roach sprays, room deodorizers, roses, sap, shampoo, synthetic fabrics, tires, toothpaste, Weed-b-gon, wood preservatives, leather, lighting a match, lubricating oil, magazines, milk products, new rubber, newly mowed grass, news-papers, opening the freezer, paper napkins, paper tablecloths, particles left in the air after spraying, pea pods, pets, pollen, raw onions, salty licorice, scraping potatoes, shoe polish, silicone products, smoke from frying, smoke from soldering, talking too long, tennis shoes, tobacco smoke, too much cold, too much heat, vinegar, walking down the street, white out, white spirit/oil of turpentine, and wine.

Virtually every one of us could opt in to this disability. A colleague once showed me a report on the Internet from an MCS sufferer who claimed that she developed a Jamaican accent whenever she came in contact with someone wearing clothing that had been laundered in a particular detergent.

There is little question that what many MCS sufferers feel is genuine. Furthermore, people really do have allergic reactions to certain chemicals. These reactions, however, can be validated by clinical research. What makes MCS unique, according to Drs. Stephen Barrett and Ronald Gots in *Chemical Sensitivity: The Truth about Environmental Illness*, is that "the range of sympotms is virtually endless; the onset can be abrupt or gradual and may or may not be linked to any specific exposure or causative factor; and symptoms can vary in intensity, can come and go, and typically do not correlate with objective physical findings and laboratory results. . . . It exists because patients believe it does and doctors validate those beliefs.

VICTIM RECRUITING

Dr. Van Wick and Ralph continue their campaign against Grass-alot. Lisa, one of the new members of the Grass-alot Patrol, has an idea. She knows how to do a home page on the Internet and asks Dr. Van Wick and Ralph what they think. They go for it. Lisa does freelance work part-time out of her home. She has plenty of free time. In about a month, she has a home page set up with a list of symptoms caused by Grass-alot and what those who view the home page can do to help ban it.

The Internet has become a menu of scourges that reinforce each other's visions of misfortune. The websites inevitably propose as a cure some form of punitive action. Once you find your affliction on line, the "search engine" prompts you to "Go Get It." Some MCS sufferers have created at great expense their own Internet home pages devoted to sharing their torments with the rest of us. They become celebrities in cyberspace for their ailments.

While many attackers are truly suffering, the "problem arises," writes New York University professor Carol Iannone in *Commonsense,* "when this pattern [of victimhood] becomes the key to the whole identity, narrowing individuals' sense of accountability, and causing them to lose sight of the facts that moral choice is possible even in difficult circumstances, and that no life is perfect, without pain, trauma, grief, and loss." Illness, disability, and discrimination are permission slips to let rage fly. They are weapons for people seeking not relief from suffering, but power or vengeance. There has been a blurring of the genuine disenfranchised and those "boutique" forms who engage in victimhood for ulterior motives.

The words "severity" and "choice" have lost their meaning. A person cannot choose to be diabetic. A person can, however, choose to show up for work on time and remain faithful in marriage. Nonetheless, "Chronic Lateness Syndrome" was recognized by a court as an excuse for one worker's tardiness. A *Ladies' Home Journal* article on "stress-induced-straying" reported, "We all know that stress can make us do crazy things. Now, according to a groundbreaking theory, it may be the reason more and more wives are cheating on their husbands. How stressed-out—and vulnerable—to infidelity—are *you*?"

These new syndromes can offer their victims a strategic advantage. Comedienne Roseanne, for example, claimed she was a battered wife when she was seeking a divorce from Tom Arnold. Her accusation received a lot of media coverage. After the two reconciled, however, Roseanne said, "I signed an uncorrected, unread copy of a letter from my divorce lawyer in anger and haste. . . . He never beat me. He never abused me."

THE MEASUREMENT IS THE MESSAGE

Dr. Van Wick now has a test that can measure levels of Grass-alot in someone's blood. He demonstrates the test on a follow-up segment of *America Betrayed*. A person holds a bottle of Grass-alot up to his nose and breathes in for a moment. Ten minutes later, Dr. Van Wick draws blood. Indeed, some of the chemicals in Grass-alot can be detected. The skeptics are wrong, Dr. Van Wick says. This is the proof. The host is fascinated. A state legislature considers a bill to ban Grass-alot. One local town council has accepted that the reaction caused by Grass-alot will be recognized as a disability.

Today, misfortunes are graded on a curve. Both multiple chemical sensitivity and quadriplegia are treated as disabilities in some communities. The result is that if everybody's disabled then the term loses all meaning. We will have to make minute distinctions between kinds of disability. Attackers confuse dislikes with diseases so there are "epidemics" of codependency, sex "addiction," multiple chemical sensitivity, recovered memory and chronic fatigue syndromes. Carol Showalter, in her book *Hystories*, uses as an example health reporter Neenyah Ostrum's speculation on PBS's *Frontline* that comedienne Gilda Radner might have died from fashionable chronic fatigue syndrome, not lethal ovarian cancer. One person's discomfort is another's terminal illness.

What makes victim assessment even trickier is technology's stunning ability to detect and measure the presence of substances, regardless of whether or not they are hazardous. As with Dr. Van Wick's Grass-alot test, science can quantify chemical elements in *billionths* of the quantity that would be necessary to cause harm. That science can identify traces of an offending chemical at all is leveraged proof that the chemical correlates with the hazard being alleged.

In April 1997, Nathan Zohner, an Idaho junior high school student, got forty-three out of fifty people he surveyed to support a ban on the chemical dihydrogen monoxide. They supported the ban on the grounds that it caused excessive sweating, vomiting, acid rain, and had been found in the tumors of terminal cancer patients. What Zohner did not inform his respondents until after his award-winning science project was complete was the familiar name of dihydrogen monoxide: water.

BACK TO THE MAINSTREAM

"In this pattern, a growth in deviancy makes possible a transfer of resources, including prestige, to those who control the deviant population."
                          Daniel Patrick Moynihan, *Defining Deviancy Down*

Giving people options that work in the real world is what good doctors,
counselors, and friends attempt to do. Says Washington, D.C., psychiatrist
Sally Satel in an interview, "The goal of psychiatry is to get people back to
the mainstream. Embracing victimhood keeps them out on the fringes."

Of particular concern to Satel is the "consumer" movement in psychiatry, whereby patients are characterized as "consumers" or "clients."
Satel writes in *Psychiatric Times,* "How can a psychiatrist set limits with
an individual whose attitudes and behavior have been shaped by a client
mentality that has adopted the consumerist credo, 'The customer is
always right'?"

Attackers love a good scourge. A scourge validates their self-image
as wretched and projects witchery onto a third party. America has a president who feels its pain and campaigns proudly on this. Whether it's
Michael Jacobsen of the Center for Science in the Public Interest or, on
the capitalist side, some weight loss guru, Americans are not lacking
prophets who can perform miracles or otherwise heal them.

Messiahs inevitably betray those who applaud them because salvation
isn't a job for Washington operatives and shrewd capitalists. Americans
become angry that they can't eat hamburgers with impunity and angrier
still when their weight loss goals are not easily met. The public is also put
off by the deprivations that go hand-in-hand with artificial plagues. Consumers want their freedom to use cellular phones, automobiles, convenience products, freedom to pig out on junk food once in a while, and
freedom to listen to Howard Stern talk about lesbians. When the attacks
amuse, Americans tune in; when they restrict, Americans tune out.

As the number of sad sacks has multiplied, it's hard to tell who really
needs help anymore. Tragedy used to be an inevitable part of life—now
it's a recreational sport. Our society once believed it could clear unfair
barriers and give others an opportunity to improve their lot. These tenets

built America and launched needed movements like Civil Rights. The Culture of Attack operates under different rules. The culture no longer wants to *protect* victims, it wants to *recruit* them.

Dr. Van Wick, Ralph, and the Grass-alot Patrol are foundering. Autumn is approaching and their Grass-alot pitch has peaked.

"We get the point," the producer of a TV news show tells Ralph, a little agitated. Ralph reminds the producer about the "smoking gun" blood test.

"Of course you'll find it in your blood—you're sniffing fertilizer," the producer says, annoyed. No sale this time. The producer has just received word that a major political figure was killed in a car accident. The horror of the paparazzi takes precedence over Ralph's plague. Fresh news cycle, new scourge.

OF ALTAR BOYS AND RECOVERED MEMORY

> "To be a victim, you don't need to remember your abuse, you need only imagine it."
>
> Wendy Kaminer, *I'm Dysfunctional, You're Dysfunctional*

Some folks collect stamps, I collect pop-syndromes. Some are pathetic (Chronic Lateness Syndrome), some are libidinously convenient (Stress-Induced Straying), but one is lethal: Recovered Memory Syndrome. Recovered memory usually consists of someone recalling incidents of sexual abuse years after the trauma actually occurs. The memories are supposedly "recovered" through methods including psychotherapy, "art therapy" (drawing pictures of one's childhood), "age regression" interviews (being asked to imagine one is five years old), and upon review of old family albums.

According to Elaine Showalter in *Hystories*, by the mid-1990s, more than three hundred cases involving recovered memory were filed in U.S. courts. Perhaps the most famous case involving recovered memory was the accusation of sexual molestation that was leveled at the late Cardinal

Joseph Bernardin by former altar boy Steven Cook. In late 1993, Cook came forward and accused the powerful prelate of molestation. The accusation was accompanied by a $10 million lawsuit against Bernardin and others. Cook, who was thirty-four at the time, claimed that he remembered being molested by Bernardin when he was a teenager. He said that the revelations came as a result of hypnosis by a psychotherapist and, separately, in a flashback, while talking on the phone to a friend.

Attack Summary: Cardinal Joseph Bernardin—Late 1993

Victim:	Steven Cook
Villain:	Cardinal Bernardin
Vindicator:	Media, Cook's lawyers
Void:	Validation for rash of priest/child abuse incidents
Vehicle:	Lawsuit, media coverage
Value:	Protecting children, altar boys

Cook's lawsuit came equipped with top billing in network news and major print and radio media. The extensive coverage had been sparked by the molestation trial of a former Massachusetts priest named James Porter, who was ultimately convicted. During that period, CNN devoted an entire segment to molestation by clergy, which lent a credible backdrop to the charges against Bernardin.

Bernardin's position required that he show dignity and grace throughout his ordeal. We crisis managers are under no such divine mandate. As Cook's case moved closer to trial, I was thrilled to see Bernardin's crisis managers—in this case his lawyers—shift into full throttle. Through their relentless efforts, according to the March 1, 1994, *Chicago Tribune,* they determined that one of Cook's therapists was, in fact, a graphic artist who was unlicensed to practice hypnosis. In a deposition, another one of Cook's therapists said that he had hypnotized Cook in the late 1970s and into 1980 and Cook never mentioned instances of abuse.

From my foxhole in an attack, the moment I discover that the guerrilla is something other than he purports, he forfeits his victim status. I empathized with Bernardin's lawyers, who were in the tough position of taking on an altar boy. Priest-as-molester and altar-boy-as-victim fit the media's template wonderfully. The press couldn't get enough creepy priest stories at the time of Cook's charges.

The media would only have defended Bernardin if they had been held at gunpoint. Bernardin's lawyers uncovered the proverbial "smoking gun" when they found that the altar boy wasn't such an altar boy, after all. The holes in Cook's story, said reporters Michael Hirsley and Jan Crawford in the *Chicago Tribune,* "coupled with prodding by defense attorneys and the prospect of heavy sanctions against Cook's lawyers, helped convince Cook that 'the memories of sexual abuse by Cardinal Bernardin which arose during and after hypnosis are unreliable,' according to Cook's motion to dismiss the charges against Bernardin." Media reports of Bernardin's vindication were considerably more subdued than the initial allegations.

ALLEGATIONS ARE IMMORTAL

Bernardin's vindication was no cause for celebration. He was vindicated only after becoming universally known as a child molester. Not even hardened convicts are kind to child molesters in prison and slipping in "alleged" does little to help. When Cardinal Bernardin died in November 1996, his obituaries cited Cook's allegations.

In 1990, wrote Showalter in *Hystories*, George Franklin was convicted of murder and sentenced to life imprisonment. The evidence used against him was the testimony of his daughter, who had suddenly recalled seeing her father kill another child many years ago. The conviction was overturned by a federal judge primarily because of the dubious scientific support for Recovered Memory Syndrome.

A prominent California man was ruined after his daughter remembered during a hypnotic procedure that her father had forced her to perform sex acts on the family's dog. The man was ultimately vindicated and awarded damages when the stories did not pan out, but he will never again enjoy the status he had achieved prior to the charges.

JUDGING VICTIMS

"In the penumbra between absolute obscurity and worldwide renown there exists a shadow region filled with a seething horde of pan flashers, egotists, dime store magicians and Holiday Inn cover bands hoping for a big slice of the adulation quiche. And while most of us are content to rubberneck the carnage on the berm of the road, too many people are desperately striving to actually be the car wreck, and I'm not sure we should feel compelled to recognize them."

Dennis Miller, *The Rants*

Decent human beings are instinctively disarmed by allegations made by victims. When we see someone fall, we automatically ask, "Are you all right?" It's hard to judge anyone who claims to have been harmed for fear that judging them is insensitive.

Questioning a victim just *feels* wrong, which is why attackers habitually pepper their rhetoric with references to the ultimate wrongdoers: Nazis. It's their way of saying, "By withdrawing your support for me, you will open the floodgates of intolerance and, the next thing you know, it's Treblinka all over again." This is heavy stuff and no one wants the Third Reich on their conscience. I have heard opinion research subjects conclude that those who claim to recover memory and other malcontents are so pathetic that it won't hurt to "throw 'em a bone" once in a while. This position is dangerous. These self-styled victims are not a harmless minority. They are America's guerrillas. My partner and I have built a business out of the bones of men like Cardinal Bernardin.

When victimhood is used to manipulate, it becomes raw power. I marvel at how the same mighty corporations that lay off thousands with a pen-stroke will not challenge guerrillas out of fear of looking ungentle. Acceptance of emotional blackmail fogs society's ability to recognize a real tragedy when it sees one.

As Dr. R, my visiting psychiatrist, concluded our "session," a tearful woman appeared on the screen. She explained how when she used a certain product, something made her "ions reverse."

"She's so sad," I said, watching the network anchor, who was listening to her on bended knee.

"That," Dr. R concluded, "is her power."

The vast majority of my cases where terrible allegations are made never become fodder for houshold discussion. This is either because the attacks are quietly resolved or get limited attention when they do go public. There is my friend, the corporate vice president, who lost her job because she questioned the veracity of product safety claims that were made by a media-savvy group of plaintiffs. It is easier to fire her than confront the plaintiffs on *Good Morning America*. There is the automobile model that vanished from the marketplace when government regulators, activists, and the media leveled an allegation that was too lurid for the manufacturer to fight, even though it was later proven to be false. Jobs were lost, careers ended.

None of these things would have happened had the attackers not mastered the dual arts of emotional extortion and media manipulation.

5. *The Attackers*

Attackers and their causes are proliferating and wreaking havoc.

"One fifth of the people are against everything all the time."
Robert F. Kennedy

THE GUERRILLA'S ADVANTAGE

Luke does public relations for attackers. Like me, he has his own business. Unlike me, his clients include plaintiffs, protesters, and altar boys, real and self-invented. He didn't always do this. He used to work with me. Now his clients attack my clients.

Despite the divergence of our worlds, Luke and I remain close and over a recent lunch he said that working for our firm had been daunting. "These days, I just pick up the phone, tell a producer at the morning shows that some yahoo is protesting at Independence and 17th, and four camera crews show up. I couldn't do that with your clients," he said.

No, he couldn't. In a public fight, Luke's guerrilla clients have one big advantage over their targets: They are not constrained by rules. My celebrity and business clients are crippled by them. Effective guerrillas will say anything, allege anything, attack anyone—and it's okay. They will invoke the Holocaust, cancer, and illusory "higher truths" to justify their zeal.

Luke's expertise is "packaging" attacks. He exploits the Culture of Attack's confusion about who's a victim. He knows if he can position his clients as victims, it will be hard for their targets to fight back; after all, what kind of person attacks the vulnerable? If Luke can position his clients as victims, he can be audacious and justify almost anything his clients say or do under the mantle of "public good."

Attack targets are hamstrung by deep cultural prejudices against them. When Bart Simpson pushes the stuffy corporate chief Mr. Burns into the swimming pool, it's funny. When Mr. Burns pushes Bart into the pool, it's mean. Luke understands this. Celebrities and businesses understand this, too, which is why many opt to do nothing when attacked—they don't want to look mean.

Attacks are easy to launch these days because there is an apparatus in place to support it, namely a news media clamoring for the story lines that Luke peddles, an Internet that welcomes all allegations, and special interests in search of a new grievance. He says most of the stories he "places" with TV magazine programs he does on behalf of somebody suing somebody else.

Luke is deeply committed to some issues. On others, he acknowledges that he is not a "true believer." Luke calls the whole game "warped." My concession is to acknowledge that Luke's clients aren't always evil or insane, that sometimes there are legitimate differences of opinion and competing agendas. Nevertheless, Luke is, at root, an entrepreneur, a gifted adrenaline junkie who likes being where the action is. The action is in attacks.

After the waiter takes our order, Luke asks my opinion on the most effective attackers. "Who really amazes you?"

"The animal rights movement, definitely."

"Why?"

"Because they've positioned their movement so that only a moral monster could disagree with them."

THE GORILLAS' GUERRILLAS

"It is characteristic of all movements that the psychopathic element rises to the top."

Robert Lindner

To understand how clever attackers manipulate public opinion, look closely at how the animal rights movement exploits the culture's confusion about who's a victim.

Many of us support animal welfare programs. I know I have. How could any sane person support anything that brings discomfort, pain, or death to another living thing? This ultimatum is at the foundation of the animal rights movement's attacks on biomedical research—research on animals to find cures for humans. Either you like to torture animals (you're a bad person) or you like helping them (you're a good person).

The issue, of course, isn't this simple. To the activists, however, it is. The greatest achievement of animal rights activists has been to sever the link in the public's mind between animal research and human cures. This achievement is largely the work of People for the Ethical Treatment of Animals (PeTA). They have positioned their crusade as being strictly about animal cruelty so that you're either for animal cruelty or against it. The movement's genius is having created a moral campaign of compassion while hiding its contempt for human life.

Attack Summary: Animal Rights versus Biomedical Research

Victim:	Animals
Villain:	Pharmaceutical, heath care companies
Vindicator:	People for the Ethical Treatment for Animals
Void:	Desire to test products for human benefit without harming animals
Vehicle:	Protests, media events featuring celebrities
Value:	Animal welfare

While few would oppose compassion for animals, not many people would want to punish humans; that is, if they were aware that humans were getting hurt. When attacking biomedical research, the trick is to overwhelm the public's emotions with spectacle so that no one ever sees the human price.

The animal rights movement began its modern crusade in the early 1980s with terror. Activists have successfully sabotaged biomedical research efforts using tactics such as destruction of property, theft, death threats, personal harassment against researchers, and lawsuits. In its "Report to Congress on the Extent and Effects of Domestic and International Terrorism on Animal Enterprises" the Department of Justice cites firebombings, arson, and malicious destruction of property by individuals and groups associated with the Animal Liberation Front (ALF).

According to the Foundation for Biomedical Research (the leading advocates of animal research) specific instances of terror in recent years have included the theft of animals with experimental pacemakers from UCLA; a break-in at the University of Pennsylvania to steal animals and years of data being used in arthritis, sudden infant death syndrome, and head injury research; theft of equipment and animals used in cancer and emphysema research at California's City of Hope Research Institute and Medical Center; theft of chimpanzees being studied for AIDS and hepatitis from a Washington-area laboratory; arson causing $4.5 million in damage to a diagnostic lab under construction at University of California/Davis; the freeing of cats with potentially harmful bacteria from a U.S. Department of Agriculture facility; placing a radio-controlled pipe bomb in U.S. Surgical Corporation's Connecticut headquarters; releasing mice infected with cryptosporidium in a break-in and major fire at the University of Arizona. Obviously, not all animal rights advocates are harmless bunny-cuddlers.

One of the latest fashions among the radical activists is sending sympathy cards to researchers that reference the impending deaths of their children. Typical excerpts from letters to researchers include the following:

"We know where you live, where your cars are parked, and how to get to you. Be careful when you start your cars up!"

"The only punishment that you are entitled to is to have your eyes gouged out and be bolted to a frame through your penis, then be smeared all over your body with cat food and turn all the hungry cats in Berkeley loose on you, to tear you limb from limb . . . slowly."

"Now I am the slaughterer and you are my cattle who I sentence to death. . . . Revenge is sweet so is your blood as it trickles down my fucking throat."

"I'm glad you like experiments. I have a few of my own to perform."

Terror was a shrewd first step. It told attack targets that the movement meant business. You cross us, we hurt you—a lucid message to be sure. However, in the late 1980s, animal rights activists realized that violence alone wouldn't accomplish all of their objectives due to events that had nothing to do with them. The airwaves became saturated with coverage of murderous international terrorists. Viewers watched the evening news in horror as Americans were being kidnapped, tortured, and murdered around the world. The nation witnessed a navy officer shot dead on a tarmac and a marine colonel set swinging from a noose. In one unimaginable incident, an elderly and handicapped tourist, Leon Klinghoffer, was killed and thrown off a cruise ship into the sea. When his body was found, sharks had eaten much of him.

Americans rightfully hated the terrorists. To tap into this outrage, Hollywood released a spate of features like the *Die Hard* series that inevitably concluded with a red-blooded American restoring a sense of control by killing terrorists.

The anti-terror fervor presented a problem for animal rights activists. *Anyone* who stole, made death threats, and blew things up would run up against public opinion. Americans do, after all, see themselves as compassionate people who are exquisitely sensitive to the plight of the helpless. The activists had to, at least on the surface, get out of the terror business.

The cloak of compassion provided the activists with their strategy. All they had to do was determine the vehicle for tapping the culture's emotions. They found one in celebrities. Terrorists are repulsive, celebrities are seductive. In a society that equates celebrity with salvation, it is hard to associate glamorous people with anything inhumane. This strategy (mobilizing famous people to get attention) earned PeTA and its allies unprecedented favorable media coverage and funding.

The new celebrity apostles of animal rights didn't look like attackers. Their numbers included such well-known figures like Alec Baldwin, Kim Basinger, Sandra Bernhard, Cindy Crawford, Woody Harrelson, Chrissie Hynde, k.d. lang, Rikki Lake, Mary Tyler Moore, Alicia Silverstone, and Oliver Stone leading the cause in advertisements, protests, and press conferences. Some of PeTA's advertisements featured scantily clad (or unclad) supermodels.

BEHIND THE STARS

"I am shocked, shocked, to find that gambling is going on in here!"
Inveterate gambler Captain Renault to Rick in *Casablanca*

Despite its sexy sheen, the real power of animal rights remains in terror. While actual acts of violence have tapered off in the late 1990s, the threats have not.

PeTA claims on its Internet site to have "no way to contact the liberationists and no way of knowing if we will ever hear from them again." (The liberationists are the faction believed to use violence and property damage to "liberate" animals.) Like gambler Captain Renault in *Casablanca,* who claims to be "shocked" to see games of chance taking place, the activists would have us believe they are clueless about the muscle end of their crusade. But on the same website, PeTA urges its members to support its "Activist Defense Fund, which helps pay the legal fees of individuals accused of liberation-related activities."

The movement has plenty of funds to spend on defending—and denying—terror. Animal rights activists comprise one of the few movements that are actually richer than their industry adversaries. Between 1993 and 1995, animal rights activists operated with collective budgets of $134 million according to public documents such as I.R.S. Form 990. During the same time period, organized proponents of biomedical research had operating funds of less than $5 million.

Some assume that the pharmaceutical, medical, and research industries are better funded than the animal rights activists. They are not. These industries are not spending their multiple billions fighting for biomedical research. More and more of the institutions that use biomedical research are, in fact, distancing themselves from it publicly for fear of violence and consumer boycotts of their products. They figure it's better to let someone else fight the fight. Said differently, PeTA and others have been quite effective.

In the late 1990s, a backlash began against Hollywood celebrities who simultaneously support AIDS and breast cancer research *and* animal rights. There is no earthly way to avoid that the most critical aspects of this medical research is done using animals. Hollywood retorts by tapping into our belief in special effects by assuring us that computers can be used instead of animals. This was true in the movie *Jurassic Park* but not in real life. In the December 12, 1996, *Wall Street Journal*, renowned heart surgeon Michael DeBakey wrote to PeTA and their Hollywood supporters, "Leave your AIDS ribbons at home. The patients, activists and families, as well as your fans—and the scientists working hard on cures—deserve to know precisely where you stand."

Slick diversions or not, support for animal versus human rights is a choice that society has to make. It's not an easy choice given the latest strategy of the activists: Providing elementary schools with curricula containing animal rights messages. Try explaining to your six-year-old why something that hurts animals may actually be a good thing.

Nevertheless, the animal rights movement is clear on where it stands: PeTA's Ingrid Newkirk has said that even if animal research produced a cure for AIDS, "We'd be against it." And, of course, they drag the Holocaust into it: Newkirk remarked in the November 13, 1983, *Washington Post*, "Six million people died in concentration camps, but six billion broiler chickens will die this year in slaughterhouses."

The danger to humans has not registered in the heartland, where record numbers shell out millions to animal rights groups. The movement taps into a human need to be considered decent by associating a cause with goodness, but it obscures the price. When humans catch wind that the price is *other humans,* activists exploit the culture's penchant for fantasy and reference illusory computer models that can supposedly be used instead of animals. In reality, computer models cannot duplicate real world medical conditions.

More than 40 percent of those surveyed in a Foundation for Biomedical Research poll said there "must be alternative methods" to animal testing; 59 percent said they would be against "using dogs and cats in experimental tests" even if those tests had "a 50 percent chance of resulting in a new medicine to treat some types of life-threatening illnesses or disease"; and 68 percent believed it would still be possible, although more difficult, to develop new treatments without animal testing.

"It's impossible to quantify how much the animal rights movement has obstructed research for human diseases," said Frankie Trull, president of the Foundation for Biomedical Research. Animal research has been fundamental in the development of breakthroughs ranging from the polio vaccine to coronary bypass surgery. The foundation reports that, "During the 40 years between 1920 and 1960—a period when biomedical research contributed to remarkable progress in medicine—life expectancy jumped from 54 to nearly 70 years."

VICTIMS GROUPS AS CULTURAL TERRORISTS

"We live in a wondrous time in which the strong is weak because of his moral scruples and the weak grows strong because of his audacity."
Otto von Bismarck

Some of the most effective attackers are little-known operatives who use nonviolent terror to accomplish their goals. A core group of organized "Multiple Chemical Sensitivity" (MCS) activists intimidate doctors and research institutions that won't diagnose MCS and other boutique disabilities. These groups also serve as litigation support and harassment services for prospective toxic tort plaintiffs.

Among other activities, one group publishes the complaints it levels against researchers whose studies do not validate the existence of MCS. The complaints need not have been accepted by any noteworthy institution; they just have to be lodged in order to imply that researchers have committed ethical or other violations.

<table>
<tr><td colspan="2">Attack Summary: Multiple Chemical Sensitivity (MCS)</td></tr>
<tr><td>Victim:</td><td>Sufferers of MCS</td></tr>
<tr><td>Villain:</td><td>Doctors who won't diagnose MCS</td></tr>
<tr><td>Vindicator:</td><td>"Clinical ecology" support groups and expert witnesses</td></tr>
<tr><td>Void:</td><td>Explanation for discomfort</td></tr>
<tr><td>Vehicle:</td><td>Lawsuits, filing complaints against doctors</td></tr>
<tr><td>Value:</td><td>Protecting the disabled</td></tr>
</table>

Dr. William Daniell of the Department of Environmental Health at the University of Washington wrote the following in *Regulatory Toxicology and Pharmacology*: "Researchers' records can be seized without notice and without proof of sufficient cause, and researchers can be denied rights of due process, expedient review, legal representation, rules of evidence, confidentiality, or protection against multiple jeopardy. Scientists who are accused of misconduct can suffer interim or permanent damage to their professional reputations, particularly if 'gagged' from public discussion during a misconduct review, and even if ultimately exonerated." Under the current scenario, the attackers have all the rights; the researchers have none, effectively making subjective greivances more valuable than scientific expertise.

Dr. Daniell, along with several associates, was attacked by activists who filed a complaint with the government's Office of Research Integrity (ORI) and other institutions with which the authors were affiliated, alleging "misconduct and intentional conspiracy to misrepresent." The attackers conducted a letter-writing campaign against Daniell, and circulated and marketed the complaint materials that were used against him. During this time period, Daniell (and his co-defendants) were restrained by an ORI "gag" request until the review was completed.

According to Dr. Daniell, "Without doubt, the professional reputations of accused researchers and the credibility of the research in question face the risk of substantial and possibly permanent damage from such a public debate, particularly when it is done unilaterally while the researchers are gagged from response because of the very process triggered by the complainant, and even if the allegations are ultimately determined to be without foundation."

Virtually all of the institutions to which complaints had been filed against Daniell and his colleagues concluded that "the allegations lacked foundation and that formal investigation was not warranted." Despite this, medical professionals have backed away from studying MCS for fear of similar attacks by activists. Dr. Gregory Simon, who worked with Daniell on the MCS research, abandoned his work according to the April 17, 1997, *New York Times.* Said another doctor interviewed on this subject, "Who needs the trouble?"

During the time period when complaints were being filed against MCS-doubting doctors, media coverage and Internet communications skyrocketed, contributing to protests outside of the doctors' offices. Attackers can take comfort in knowing that if they lose in the laboratory, they can still win out in the public forum because the Culture of Attack will entertain their claims.

Timothy Kapshandy, with the Chicago-based law firm Sidley & Austin, cited for me the proliferation of MCS suits in the last ten to fifteen years, specifically, "a growing dichotomy between scientific knowledge and the average layman's understanding of science." He says

> The vast majority of people (including jurors) make conclusions based upon inductive reasoning. . . . Con men over the centuries have exploited this flaw peddling panaceas such as snake oil, magnetic therapy, and liver pills to whomever will buy them. Sir Francis Bacon declared in the 17th Century that scientific truths must be tested rather than observed. . . . Jurors, however, do not follow the scientific method in deciding whether to touch a hot motor (or wear a pair of lucky shoes). They are mistrustful of the unfamiliar, scientific method and do not appreciate its limitations. . . . They thus opt for the more familiar inductive reasoning making themselves prey for 20th Century snake oil purveyors with simple explanations for all that ails them (or the plaintiff).

CRUISIN' FOR A BRUISIN'

Our culture is awash with warnings about unsafe products and practices. When a client has been accused of perpetrating some hazard, my first question is, "Did you?" If the answer is no, my second question is, "Who benefits from attacking you?"

On the surface, this question sounds cynical and conspiratorial, but, as Henry Kissinger remarked, you can be paranoid and still have enemies. It's hard to tell the difference between attacks based upon genuine hazards and those based upon agendas because the media and the courts are increasingly vague about the difference. The most common agenda for alleging hazards is legalized extortion—suing companies with the threat of widespread negative publicity if they don't pay up.

Nowhere have victimhood's guerrillas been given greater incentives than in the area of health and insurance fraud, where alleging unsafe practices is big business. Worker's compensation cases are booming. The Coalition Against Insurance Fraud estimates that California leads the way in worker's comp fraud to the tune of $502 million per year, followed by Pennsylvania ($180 million) and New York ($166 million).

There is a simple economic reason for the success of insurance fraud. Private investigator Alan Hart told me, "It's cheaper for the insurance company to pay off the perpetrator and keep him quiet than to fight him in court." Hart is frequently hired to demonstrate that the purported victims do not, in fact, suffer from the problems they claim. He then shares the story of a man who claimed to have been disabled on the job due to poor working conditions. The man filed a lawsuit against his employer. Hart's client had doubts. Hart and his associates looked into the plaintiff and found him, of all things, engaging in a passionate tango with a bridal shop mannequin, a pretty suave maneuver considering his disability. Hart got him on videotape.

Most con artists are more subtle. On a National Insurance Crime Bureau (NICB) videotape, "Confessions of an Insurance Fraud Offender," former insurance fraud perpetrator David B. informed an NICB audience that "the insurance company is just like the great gold rush in California." David B., who agreed to cooperate with authorities after his arrest, said, "We know that the claims adjuster is in business for only one reason: to settle claims. . . . We take advantage of that fact."

When asked by one of the seminar participants how he could easily fake documents like birth certificates and drivers' licenses, which are needed to make fraudulent claims, David B. responded, "The seals for the State of Illinois are available to the public. You can buy 'em."

Apparently, David B., who has since expressed remorse for his crimes, was not alone in his belief that faking claims isn't such a bad thing. A study by the Insurance Research Council showed that 19 percent of those surveyed believed it was okay to continue "to go to a doctor for treatment after the injury has healed, in order to get a larger settlement." Said David B., "At any given date, I can go out within three months and make $200,000. Today. Right now."

Among the most popular targets of hazard-oriented attacks are the cruise lines, where an increasing number of bunko artists go out to sea for the purpose of injuring themselves so they can sue. Investigator Hart shared with me a trend of cases where cruise revelers claimed to be severely injured while on vacation and file suit upon reaching land with great fanfare. Hart says these scam artists are increasingly adept at using the media to publicize their cases. These schemes are especially popular among foreign nationals eager for their cases to end up in the shakedown-friendly U.S. courts. In some cases, Hart has captured the injured parties playing sports and hauling boxes while they waited for the cruise lines to pay off.

A Texas law firm proudly advertises about its litigation services for maritime injuries. The firm says it will "create custom-tailored compensation packages that yield superior results in the area of maritime accidents."

The next time you see an allegation that a popular product is a hazard, consider this: The National Council Against Health Fraud (NCAHF) estimates that fraudulent goods and services worth $15 billion are marketed to people facing health concerns every year. Many of these products are sold immediately following a public attack on the competing product. The consumer media's bread and butter are these scares. These media are reluctant to look "under the hood" of the allegation to see what's really driving it.

According to Dr. William Jarvis, in *Consumer Health: A Guide to Intelligent Decisions*, the U.S. government's General Accounting Office estimated that in 1995 fraud consumed about 10 percent—$100 billion— of expenditures for America's health care. The NCAHF conducted a study that showed 58 percent of those identifying themselves in the Yellow Pages as "Nutritionists" were "spurious" or "suspicious." The Arthritis Foundation alone estimates that arthritis sufferers buy "quack" remedies worth $1 billion each year. According to the *Mayo Clinic Health Letter,* one in four Americans will use a quack health product or service.

Quacks are rewarded for playing fast and loose with the facts. Chutzpah is a core component of fraud, which is why the perpetrators are called "confidence men." Their blue-chip targets, perpetually under siege, are risk averse, a quality big companies reward. That's why they are targets.

ATTACK SEQUELS

Sometimes activists who make their names on issues of consequence become garden variety attackers when their initial, often worthy, crusade runs its course. They leverage the goodwill earned during earlier campaigns to promote new and less worthy causes in order to stay in the center of the action and keep their organizations afloat. Lois Gibbs, founder of the Citizen's Clearinghouse for Hazardous Waste (CCHW) became famous for her role in the Love Canal affair of the late 1970s and early 1980s. The controversial location in upper New York state was thrust into the national spotlight when residents began complaining of chemical odors from a nearby hazardous waste site that were linked to birth defects. At the height of her activism, Gibbs, as head of the Love Canal Homeowners Association, was meeting with notables including actress Jane Fonda and even President Jimmy Carter. The drama was so intense that on May 19, 1980, Love Canal residents detained EPA officials in the association's offices. Later, Gibbs was hailed in 1982 by *People* magazine as a heroine. Actress Marsha Mason portrayed Gibbs in a two-hour CBS drama called *Lois Gibbs and the Love Canal.*

In an environment that encourages attacks, what would CCHW do for an encore once Love Canal became old news? The organization began attacking the highest-profile business target it could find—McDonald's. CCHW identified a marginal but emotionally resonant target: the polystyrene plastic packaging that McDonald's used at that time for its hamburgers. I was active in this fight, representing plastic manufacturers. The attack began with an old but resonant argument. First, CCHW claimed that plastic packaging was excessive and unrecyclable. Media coverage of this message in 1988 and 1989 was exhaustive and roundly antiplastic. References to the country being "buried" in garbage were commonplace. I knew this would be a tricky issue when spontaneous fistfights broke out at public meetings over garbage.

McDonald's and the plastics industry were able to defuse some of the criticism on the solid waste front by committing to recycling. I was pleased to see the hostility toward polystyrene diminish when consumers learned that this plastic was recyclable—and that there were plans under way to recycle it more broadly. Recycling facilities were built and my industrial clients felt, for once, like they were the environmental good guys. The media, to their credit, began paying attention to the industry's recycling efforts. This was bad news for the activists.

CCHW (and other antipolystyrene activists) then changed strategy. They turned the issue into a "fugitive," that is, shifted the debate from attacks on plastic's lack of recyclability to frightening allegations that plastics were a toxic threat to the children who ate from the containers. CCHW cleverly entitled their campaign "McToxics" and launched protests against the company around the country. In two hundred different grassroots actions driven by visibility tactics similar to those used at Love Canal, CCHW protested against McDonald's use of polystyrene.

By leaving the allegations murky but scary, the attacks drew significant nationwide media coverage because they forced the industry to prove a negative—that polystyrene plastic *didn't* do all these bad things. McDonald's soon decided to curtail its use of polystyrene because the attacks became relentless, including the physical destruction of a West Coast restaurant. Said McDonald's president Ed Rensi of the plastic, "Our customers just don't feel good about it."

McDonald's decision had less to do with CCHW's actions than recommendations made by the Environmental Defense Fund (EDF), the powerful group with which McDonald's had conducted an audit of its waste management policies. Underscoring the competitive nature of the activist business, CCHW's Internet site material reports,

In the warm glow immediately after the November 1 announcement, the major media essentially "blacked out" any significant mention of the role of the hundreds of local grassroots, student, and church groups in winning this fight, preferring instead to credit the major national environmental groups. EDF head [Fred] Krupp was all too willing to take the credit. "The task force helped to persuade McDonald's that they could do business without the clamshell [plastic container]. . . . McDonald's has seen the future and it is green." . . . But you know who really made this victory happen and, we're confident, so will history.

Knowing who made the victory happen says a lot about how modern activism works. *Knowing* means publicity, visibility, and money. The group that made its fame on a very seminal issue—hazardous waste disposal—needed another "hit" to perpetuate its public role. The fastest way to do this was to launch a high-profile attack on the most famous quick service food company in the world and its highly symbolic plastic "clamshell" regardless of the merits of the attack.

ADVANTAGE: ATTACKER

"The enemy in blue will undoubtedly pursue
For that's what you depend upon an enemy to do."
"War Is a Science," *Pippin,* Steven Schwartz

To win, attackers don't have to prove their points. They just have to stun their targets, which isn't difficult, because the targets are reluctant to fight back. Despite all that's said about ruthless big shots and businesses, I encounter far more timid players than tough guys. Attacks are often viewed by targets, especially businesses, as being beneath them. I have heard many top executives say things like, "We sell widgets, not fight malcontents." They relegate the fight to the public relations office, which attempts to finesse its way back into the sights of top management. Once the PR folks get management's attention again, they often annex the issue to a trade association. Action won't happen immediately because the association will need to get consensus on how best to respond. Consensus goes to a committee where decisive action dies a slow death.

In the meantime, the attackers have used their lead-time to seize the agenda and force their targets to prove a negative proposition:

"Can you prove that Tasty Salad Dressing* *doesn't* cause lupus?"

"No."

"Aha!"

To hear Luke tell it as we conclude our lunch, his guerrilla clients are well aware of their targets' weaknesses and they exploit them. "While your guys are out interviewing consultants to figure out how to respond, my guys are pitching reporters in the network cafeterias. When will your clients ever learn that?"

"Many have learned it."

"Then why don't they move?"

"Because they are paralyzed. They are paralyzed by their own rules of engagement, by a fear of how an aggressive response would *look,* and by the different standards they're held to. Can you imagine what would happen if a drug company doing animal research debated a bunny-cuddling child? They figure that it's better to let the kid win. They say it's good PR."

"That's what we're betting on."

Luke's bet on his target's paralysis is a safe one. The extent to which his attack succeeds, however, will depend heavily on factors beyond anyone's control. As there are different kinds of diseases, there are different kinds of crises—two to be exact. The original diagnosis is the best predictor of whether a target will survive or perish.

---

*This is a fictitious brand name.

6. *The Two Breeds of Crisis*

THE SOURCES OF CRISIS

My friend, a reporter, called me as the media were breaking stories across the country about syringes showing up in cans of Diet Pepsi.

"Do you have your hands in this Pepsi thing?" he asked.

"No."

"Who's handling it?"

"From what I know, it's all internal."

"You've done soft drink stuff though, right?"

"Right."

"I need some background. I won't quote you. Pepsi's screwed, aren't they?"

"No."

"Seriously?"

"Seriously. They'll be fine," I said.

"Why?"

"They didn't do it."

"So all these people with the syringes are lying, that's what you're saying?" he asked.

"Every one of them."

"You're cynical."

"I'm right. You don't have to be brilliant or well coordinated to hurt somebody. You just have to do it. Why don't you do a story about that?" I added that I had spent a lot of time in bottling plants and that it was practically impossible for tampering to occur in the plants. Because I did not believe that Pepsi caused the problem, I didn't believe they would be seriously damaged by the syringe news. I gave my reporter friend my spiel on who gets hurt in a crisis, who doesn't, and why:

The single most important predictor in the resolution of a public image crisis is who is believed to have caused the problem. Who the public roots for is determined by who it thinks the good guys and bad guys were in the onset of current events. Who's the aggressor? Who's the victim? Who will audiences like? There are, then, two types of crises: *character* and *sniper-fire*. A *character crisis* is one in which the inherent trustworthiness, quality, or competence of an individual, organization, product, idea, or behavior comes into question. A *sniper-fire crisis* is one caused by an outside force—not the entity under attack.

Examples of character crisis include the breast implant controversy, the Exxon Valdez oil spill, and the 1996 ValuJet airline crash. Sniper-fire crises include the Johnson & Johnson Tylenol poisonings of 1992 and the Pepsi-Cola syringes-in-cans scare.

It is much easier to recover from a sniper-fire crisis because audiences understand that the target didn't cause the problem. In sniper-fire crises, the target is perceived to have been a victim. Audiences tend to sympathize with true victims and hold others responsible for their misfortunes.

Despite the outside catalysts for sniper-fire crises, they are inevitably considered by laypeople to be the best-managed. The general public—and many in business—think that all crises are created equal. They are not.

In the Tylenol case, the crimes were so bad that no reasonable person would have believed that Johnson & Johnson could have caused such a tragedy. Seven people, including three in one family, were killed when they took Tylenol tablets laced with 65 milligrams of cyanide. It would take only five to seven micrograms to kill a person. The killer emptied more than twenty capsules in each bottle and completely refilled them with potassium cyanide. The Chicago-area crimes remain unsolved.

In a sniper-fire crisis, if the targets act responsibly and invest in a solution, they will probably recover. It didn't take public relations wizardry for Johnson & Johnson to convince people of its fundamental message: *The company was not responsible for the wicked act.* Yes, they could be taken to task for packaging safety, but that is very different than having a Johnson & Johnson employee murdering people.

In the Tylenol case, Johnson & Johnson strong but neighborly chief executive James Burke stepped forward and demonstrated the company's empathy by directly handling major media inquiries and appearing in advertisements highlighting what the company was doing about the crisis. He validated this with tangible actions, including recalling and destroying 31 million Tylenol capsules at a cost of $100 million. This swift action meant that the product would not suffer. Tylenol rapidly bounced back close to the level where it had been prior to the tampering.

In situations like the Tylenol tamperings and the Pepsi syringe scare, the public wants to know if they are going to be all right. Johnson & Johnson effectively assured the public that they were safe and showed them the path to safety. The companies acted like good people who shared their consumers' values. Consumers liked that. More importantly, the company didn't poison anyone.

CRISIS VARIABLES

Despite Johnson & Johnson's exemplary handling of events, it should not be held out as a case study for all types of crises. If an obstetrician delivered one hundred babies in a month and an emergency room surgeon lost one hundred patients during the same time frame, would one conclude that the obstetrician was a better doctor? Of course not. The variables were different.

The Culture of Attack doesn't evaluate things this way because it doesn't fit the fantasy-driven template for characterizing events. Given that the world should be perfect, many feel that anything that didn't turn out well was botched or part of somebody's wicked scheme. The conclusion: Handling of Tylenol tamperings = GOOD. Handling of ValuJet Crash = BAD. Just because a tragedy such as the May 1996 ValuJet crash occurs, it doesn't mean its *handling* was poor; plane crashes are called "disasters" because everyone loses no matter how things are "handled."

Consumers also don't factor in elements of chance. No one could have anticipated that a supermarket security camera would catch someone putting a syringe into a Pepsi can. That visual image shut down the crisis. Brilliant crisis management? Yes, in some respects, but the existence of that camera was lucky.

Those on the receiving end of a character crisis don't have it quite so easy. In these situations, the public doesn't think that something bad happened *to* the target but that the target did a bad thing, which may in fact be true. These are visceral reactions based on values and personal experiences. Breast implant manufacturers were accused (and later vindicated) of making a product that hurts women. In 1986, the Audi 5000 was said to spontaneously accelerate. Both of these products have been vindicated by prestigious authorities, but it didn't change who was perceived to have been the source of the problem.

The following case studies highlight the complexities of managing character versus sniper-fire crises.

Sniper-Fire Crisis

This Won't Hurt a Bit: The Pepsi Syringe Hoax

> "I'm 70 years old and I've been drinking Pepsi for a number of years. I haven't found a cotton-picking thing in it yet."
> Consumer calling into Pepsi-Cola hotline during syringe crisis

On Thursday, June 10, 1993, Pepsi-Cola's Washington-state bottler was told that a Seattle resident had found a syringe in a Diet Pepsi can. The company alerted the Food and Drug Administration (FDA) and set its

---

Attack Summary: Pepsi-Cola—June 1993

Victim: Consumers
Villain: Pepsi-Cola
Vindicator: Consumers who discovered syringes
Void: Attention, money, confirmation that big companies do
               bad things
Vehicle: Media coverage
Value: Public safety

---

crisis management team into motion. Pepsi had a natural ally in the powerful FDA and its crusading chief David Kessler. Had syringes found their way into the nation's food supply, it would have been a disaster for not only Pepsi but for FDA as well. Said Pepsi's safety chief Jim Stanley in the company's summary report of the crisis, "The Pepsi Hoax: What Went Right," "As the nation's protectors of the safety of all foods and beverages, the FDA can't afford to make a mistake."

While skeptical that a syringe could have gotten into a soft drink can, "We had to operate under the premise that the tampering could have happened in our plant until we could prove differently," said the local bottler's chief, Carl Behnke, in Pepsi's report. During the course of Pepsi's FDA-assisted inspection, the company allowed the news media to film the plant in action. This was especially important because the bottling and canning process itself renders it practically impossible for tampering to occur. Cans whiz around a filling device at great speed (1,200 cans per minute) and actually are upside down for a time, allowing jets of air and water to clean and fill them. All of this occurs within nine-tenths (0.9) of a second. Said Pepsi's public affairs chief Becky Madiera, "What was happening with syringes was not occurring inside our plants."

As this footage was being filmed, however, more reports of syringes in Diet Pepsi cans were surfacing across the country. Pepsi and the FDA issued consumer advisories on the weekend following the first syringe report. The FDA's advisory specifically recommended that people pour their Diet Pepsi into glasses before drinking it. *Good crisis management is about giving the audience control over the situation. When control is returned, anxiety diminishes.* By encouraging people to pour their drinks into glasses, FDA and Pepsi shifted power from the alleged saboteurs to consumers.

On Monday, June 14, all four major television networks led with the syringe scare story. Pepsi had activated its toll-free hotline and produced media materials, including video footage of Pepsi's manufacturing process and the actions that were being taken to address the scare. Pepsi-Cola North America CEO Craig Weatherup was personally handling network TV interviews while his staff was working with the thousands of other inquiring media. "A can is the most tamper-proof packaging in the food supply," said Weatherup. By week's end, Weatherup had appeared on a variety of network news programs and Pepsi spokespersons had participated in 2,000 interviews with a variety of media.

The scare was swiftly becoming part of the popular culture with late night talk show jokes and newspaper cartoons. The tenor of the comments were mostly lighthearted and skeptical, including a joke about one man finding a power drill in his Diet Pepsi can.

Smoking Gun

A "smoking gun" surfaced on Thursday, June 17, in the form of a video-tape showing a supermarket customer in Colorado allegedly dropping what appears to be a syringe into her Diet Pepsi. Pepsi described frame 4:08:32:39 in the company's report: "The woman places the can back on the counter, then asks the clerk for a cup into which she pours the Diet Pepsi and allegedly discovers the syringe." Pepsi released the videotape nationwide via satellite. FDA Commissioner Kessler publicly declared the tamperings to be a hoax. The surveillance footage not only vindicated Pepsi, but it was communicated in a way that the public likes: video. The footage explained the crisis and it was also, well, kind of cool, with Pepsi playing the role of sleuth and superhero.

Why Pepsi Won

Pepsi fared well due to excellent management and external factors that were beyond the company's control.

Internal Factors

- *Soft drink manufacturing is a familiar process.* For years, soft drink companies like Pepsi have been active members of the community. Cub Scout and Brownie troops, Kiwanis Clubs and the media (cameras and all) have been touring bottling plants for decades. There is nothing exotic or mysterious about the soft drink industry. Consumers have a hard time believing that someone they know—and a process they've seen—could be responsible for something bad.

- *The chief executive officer was the chief crisis officer.* The visibility of the CEO is not the act of a guilty party. People want the boss to be human, to show leadership and a little pain. Pepsi's Weatherup was out front from the beginning. Because he believed in his company, consumers were inclined to as well. Moreover, Weatherup's demeanor was that of a popular social studies teacher or softball coach, as opposed to a corporate power player. Consumers liked him.

- *Pepsi used visuals to communicate.* The company knew that people are persuaded by video footage. It's a "show me" culture. Pepsi was fortunate enough to have the "goods" on camera and knew how to use them.

- *Pepsi didn't make the crisis about them; they made it about consumers.* Pepsi's actions were focused on safety, not clearing its good name. Pepsi reasoned that by looking out for the consumer, vindication would follow. Pepsi showed us that it knew who was ultimately in charge of its success—consumers.

- *Managing the crisis was a core priority.* The Culture of Attack has put big shots, businesses, and institutions in the line of public fire and managing attacks is a part of the responsibility, not an exception to it. If fate decides you're in the fight, you're in the fight. Pepsi accepted its role.

External Factors

- *Pepsi had no motive to do something bad.* Why on earth would a company with a century of consumer goodwill allow syringes to get into its product? What motive could the company possibly have? No reasonable person could conclude that the company willfully inserted—or allowed the insertion of—syringes into its product. Because Pepsi was not perceived to be responsible for a malicious act, the crisis was relegated early on to the sniper-fire category.

- *Nobody got hurt.* When people are injured or killed, the public is outraged. When there is damage, the need for a scapegoat increases, especially because aggrieved parties emerge to extend the life of the crisis. There were no true victims in the Pepsi case to raise hell and put the company on the defensive.

- *An unanticipated smoking gun emerged.* The supermarket video apparently depicting tampering was Pepsi's saving grace. Very few entities in crisis enjoy such good fortune.

- *The media didn't want to be used in a hoax.* The media hate—HATE— being used. They are well aware of their vulnerabilities, not to mention the chances of being sued if they run with something bad.

- *The public doesn't like to be conned either.* The scam artists were not just shaking Pepsi down, they were hustling consumers, too.

- *Pepsi had a powerful partner in the government.* Both Pepsi and the FDA had something to lose in the case of a nationwide tampering. The two unlikely allies made a formidable team. That Pepsi had a well-established working relationship with the FDA only helped matters. Said Pepsi's product safety boss Stanley of the FDA, "The fact that they are so cautious serves us well." Echoed President Clinton: "I was pleased to see that [the FDA] so effectively resolved a potentially harmful situation."

Said Congressman Hamilton Fish (R-N.Y.) of the Pepsi hoax, "This was no simple scam, but a challenge against the security of the nation's food supply." It's better to have third-party experts championing a position than a party with a blatant profit motive.

Pepsi estimates that it lost $25 million in sales during the week of the scare with sales dipping 3 to 4 percent during the week of the crisis. Sales returned quickly. The company reported that Americans bought "800,000 more cases of Pepsi products than the week before the hoax. July 4th proved to be Pepsi's strongest sales week of the year, as millions stocked up for holiday parties."

Pepsi CEO Weatherup offered this concluding remark in the company report on the hoax: "Our strongest allies during the crisis were honesty and openness. We believed that if we invited America inside a Pepsi plant—via video—and showed them a behind-the-scenes look at the speed and safety of our production processes, as well as other key events that shaped the crisis, their good judgment and reason would prevail . . . and the scare would end."

CHARACTER CRISIS

Playing the Hand That Was Dealt: The ValuJet Crash

> "When a trout rising to a fly gets hooked on a line and finds himself unable to swim about freely, he begins with a fight which results in struggles and splashes and sometimes an escape. Often, of course, the situation is too tough for him. . . . His struggles are all that the world sees and it naturally misunderstands them. It is hard for a free fish to understand what is happening to a hooked one."
>
> Karl Menninger

"Got Something Out There"

Shortly after 2:00 P.M. on Saturday, May 11, 1996, pilot Candalyn Kubeck, 35, and co-pilot, Richard Hazen, 52, pull ValuJet flight 592 into Miami airspace over Biscayne Bay. Jesse Fisher, 36, directed the DC-9's flight path from his post at the airport's control tower. The plane was referred to as "Critter 592," a nickname that came from the happy-faced airplane cartoon logo painted on the fuselage.

The plane flies over North Bayshore Drive and is redirected to the north by the tower. It then makes a broad swing past Joe Robbie Stadium,

---

Attack Summary: ValuJet—Spring–Fall 1996

Victim:	Passengers
Villain:	ValuJet
Vindicator:	Federal Aviation Administration, National Transportation Safety Board
Void:	Explanation for senseless deaths
Vehicle:	Public hearings, media coverage
Value:	Public safety

---

the Palmetto Expressway, and the Florida Turnpike—all routine vistas en route to ValuJet's Atlanta hub.

Co-pilot Hazen turns on the radar and observes, "Got something out there, about 80 miles out. That must be that thunderstorm." As Hazen remarks upon this exterior challenge, a much worse one is generating beneath Critter 592's passenger section. Oxygen canisters in the forward cargo hold, by most accounts, are igniting. At twenty seconds past 2:10 P.M., six minutes into the flight, Captain Kubeck is stunned by an explosion. "We're losing everything," she says. Shouts of "fire" are audible. From the tower Jesse Fisher attempts to redirect the plane. He calls for a supervisor. A flight attendant can be heard entering the cockpit requesting oxygen.

Above the Everglades, seventeen miles northwest of Miami, fire has overwhelmed the cabin. Controller Fisher can hear the words "You can plan" from the cockpit and then nothing for one minute and twelve seconds. Co-pilot Hazen returns abruptly: "One-four-zero." Then nothing again.

Back on the ground, Fisher and others stare at the radar screen. The blip denoting ValuJet 592 pulses X-X-X, indicating the plane has disappeared from tracking. It is four minutes after the explosion.

Two private planes are flying near the Everglades. One reports a crash. Moments later, the other one does, too. "It's scary," one of the pilots says, adding that the plane "broke up into a million pieces."

What Came Out

> "ValuJet just had another one."
> Elizabeth Marchak of the *Cleveland Plain Dealer*

The crash of ValuJet flight 592 represents the quintessential character crisis. Not only were the inherent ethics and competence of the company under siege, but the tragedy validated existing beliefs that a fear of flying is not a phobia at all, but a rational aversion to something dangerous. To these jittery ends, this crash let loose a flood of negative information about ValuJet. Initially, the Federal Aviation Administration (FAA), the government agency that regulates air travel, stood behind ValuJet. As with the Food and Drug Administration in the Pepsi case, the FAA had something to lose if it were discovered that it allowed people to board unsafe planes. After the crash, however, FAA investigators unearthed thirty-four violations, including failure by ValuJet to repair jammed landing gear and cabin doors. The FAA also discovered that some of its investigators had known about these problems for months and had been looking into ValuJet at the time of the fatal crash.

ValuJet's safety troubles appeared to mount in step with the company's swift expansion. In 1994, the airline made fifteen emergency landings, in 1995, there were fifty-seven. "From February through May of 1996, ValuJet would have an unscheduled landing almost *every other day*," wrote Mary Schiavo, former Department of Transportation Inspector General, in her book *Flying Blind, Flying Safe*.

ValuJet's troubles were sufficiently well-known among industry watchers that when reporter Elizabeth Marchak of the *Cleveland Plain Dealer* called Schiavo three months before the crash, she opened the discussion by saying, "ValuJet just had another one." According to Schiavo: "Landing gear collapsed on a plane coming down into Nashville; the same plane's landing gear had collapsed in December. When the plane hit the ground this time, the right main landing gear collapsed, the belly slammed onto the concrete, the crew lost control, and the aircraft skidded off the end of the runway. Was the FAA going to do anything about it? Marchak repeated."

Some of the passengers who had traveled on Flight 591, which immediately preceded the crash, described the DC-9 as having the "smell of an old, dirty airplane," according to Schiavo. Said another passenger, "The seat that I faced when I sat down: the fabric was literally coming apart. I could see the aluminum inside." To make matters worse, ValuJet's planes were an average of twenty-six years old, as compared to TWA's twenty years, U.S. Airway's twelve years and Southwest's eight years. Wrote Schiavo:

> ValuJet bought used or reconditioned planes for cheap—nine from Turkish airlines, ten from SAS, eighteen from McDonnell Douglas (planes which had been previously owned by Delta Airlines) and ten others from various sources. Five spare engines and about 4,000 parts were bought from Turkey, too. All maintenance was farmed out to repair stations, freeing ValuJet of the need for costly repair facilities, parts bins, and mechanics of its own.

Training for ValuJet's employees also appeared to be shoddy. Two of those who stored the canisters aboard the doomed aircraft had little or no training. Some of the employees working at ValuJet were temporaries who had been hired by a company controlled by company president Lewis Jordan's daughter. The give and take between one of the ValuJet ramp agents and an aviation investigator was disturbing, according to partially published transcripts in the *Miami Herald*:

Investigator:	"When did you first get your training as a ValuJet ramp agent?"
Employee:	"The first day I started working at ValuJet."
Investigator:	"What kind of training was that?"
Employee:	"I had a manual."
Investigator:	"Was that the extent of your training?"
Employee:	"I don't know."

Said another ValuJet employee under questioning about the oxygen canisters, "I didn't have a hazardous material tag. We trust in the people who bring the boxes."

Confidence in the company was further shaken by the publicized low salaries of ValuJet's pilots. At the time of the crash, pilots were earning about $45,000, less than half of what pilots from other airlines earned. Furthermore, wrote Schiavo, "pilots were paid only for the flights they completed, a policy that encouraged them to fly rather than delay or cancel flights for maintenance or bad weather." These things were cited as possible evidence that the pilots might have been under pressure "to overlook seemingly minor problems and adhere to schedules," as a *Miami Herald* article speculated. An FAA study made public in the weeks following the crash named ValuJet as having more accidents than its competitors, which lent credence to the corner-cutting theory.

The National Transportation and Safety Board (NTSB) said that the fire began by faulty oxygen generators in the plane's Class B cargo hold. The generators, which had been loaded by ValuJet's vendor, SabreTech, did not have the required safety tops, which were valued at $1 each. SabreTech admitted, according to the *Miami Herald,* "that its employees failed to protect the devices with safety caps, mislabeled them, and erroneously described them as 'empty' on a shipping form."

Outrage resulted when inspectors and the media—rightly—noted that a ban of these devices had been proposed by the NTSB in 1988 and had been rejected. The reason: The proposal was not cost effective.

Air Jordan

As ValuJet's terrible track record came out, Lewis Jordan became the company's chief crisis officer in addition to being its president. This became especially necessary when, on June 17, 1996, a little over a month after the crash, the FAA grounded ValuJet.

Former pilot Jordan recognized that the very survival of his airline was at stake. The public could see the strong but visibly concerned executive hustling to attempt to make things right. He personally directed the crisis both behind the scenes and in front of the camera. Jordan set realistic goals in light of the gravity of the tragedy. The most essential objective was to get the airline flying again, even if that meant flying fewer planes to ensure safety. ValuJet sold some of its airplanes, a sign that it understood how very perilous the company's future was.

To demonstrate a commitment to long-term viability, ValuJet hired the former president of TWA to help run the company, as well as a former

TWA maintenance and engineering chief. ValuJet also hired a four-star air force general to serve as the company's "safety czar," and an outside consulting firm to evaluate the company's safety procedures.

ValuJet cooperated vigorously with the FAA. In May and June of 1996, all of ValuJet's planes were combed over by an average of 1.2 FAA inspectors. Schiavo wrote that "sixty inspectors working around the clock performed the equivalent of four years' inspection activities in four weeks." Anxious to operate again, the company paid $2 million to the FAA to cover the costs of special inspections.

When ValuJet re-opened for business in September, the company's manpower for safety was four times greater than that of any other airline its size. Industry publication *World Airline News* reported, "ValuJet has made a Herculean effort since the crash to beef up its safety office and its maintenance oversight. Indeed, it has been one of the industry leaders in flight testing a cargo hold smoke and fire detection system."

Despite its commendable campaign to commence operations, ValuJet made post-crash mistakes, too. According to a November 11, 1996, Associated Press story, ValuJet vice president David Gentry publicly blamed its contractor SabreTech for putting oxygen generators without safety caps aboard the aircraft. He said at an NTSB hearing that the vendor should have fastened the $1 caps on the canisters before loading them, adding, "We don't tell them what to do with it. They have been in business for a long time." Trashing SabreTech in this tone came off as a callous attempt to dodge responsibility. The NTSB's Gerald Loeb felt that way, too. He angrily asked Gentry, "Are you responsible for making sure that a plane is air worthy, and therefore are you responsible for what your contractors do?" Gentry answered yes.

The Lessons

ValuJet survived, which was the best that was doable given the tragedy. The number of employees dropped from 4,200 to 2,000. Its stock was 60 percent lower than it had been prior to the crash ($7 a share versus $17.88). The company showed losses for the five straight quarters following the accident.

The impact that the ValuJet crash will have on the discount airline industry as a whole remains to be seen. Right now, the prognosis is not good. According to aviation consultant Mort Beyer, as reported in Bloomberg Business News, small airlines made $55 million in 1995 as compared to a net loss of $196.4 million in 1996. "Those airlines have already lost $75 million in the first quarter of 1997 alone," Beyer said.

The airline industry may very well be a business with operating costs, deadlines to meet, and so forth, but nobody cares. It is held to a higher standard because lives are at stake. Airline accidents are catastrophic, as opposed to auto traffic accidents, which are unfortunate but are not interpreted as landmark events the way plane crashes are. No one ever says, "Do you remember where you were when that car ran into a telephone pole?" People in Washington, D.C., on the other hand, still talk about what they were doing when Air Florida slammed into the 14th Street bridge and sank in the Potomac in 1982.

Different entities have different burdens. Outsiders and pundits can never completely understand what "hooks" may be dragging others down, even if some of those wounds might have been self-inflicted. By almost all public accounts, ValuJet brought much of the tragedy of flight 592 on itself. That the company has not roared back to its prior levels of success does not mean that Lewis Jordan and his team did not respond impressively once the crash occurred.

Unlike with Pepsi, ValuJet had no telltale video to make things right. Had ValuJet had a better safety record prior to the crash, the public would have been more likely to view the tragedy as an aberrant lapse of divine grace, a fluke. Instead, ValuJet's safety history was held against it because it was so violently at odds with the industry standards.

The combination of the loss of life with a perceived indifference toward safety landed ValuJet well outside the bounds of likability. In 1997, ValuJet merged with another airline and changed its name to Air-Tran, which is performing solidly.

In the ValuJet case news media coverage was deservedly harsh. Not all events, however, are of equal gravity. The media find it hard to spread out events along a continuum of significance, tending to concentrate them in the same neighborhood of malfeasance. There are simple reasons for this that have more to do with business than any social or political agenda. These will be discussed next.

7. *How the Media Pique the Culture's Rage*

The media cultivate attackers for business reasons.

"I should go so far as to say that embedded in the surrealistic frame of a television news show is a theory of anticommunication, featuring a type of discourse that abandons logic, reason, sequence, and rules of contradiction. In aesthetics, I believe the name given to this theory is Dadaism; in philosophy, nihilism; in psychiatry, schizophrenia. In the parlance of the theater, it is known as vaudeville."

Neil Postman, Amusing Ourselves to Death

RETAILERS OF BERSERK

When Sam Donaldson has a camera a few inches from a client's face, it doesn't matter whether or not he's got a liberal bias. I am constantly asked by clients and friends how big a role personal politics play in who and what the media attack. The short answer is that politics are usually incidental to media coverage. To understand who gets attacked, don't think about politics, think about business.

News, like entertainment, is a product that needs "hooks"—appealing attributes driven by market demand—to grab consumers. To do this, the news cannot operate independent of the Culture of Attack, away from shock rock music, body piercing, in-your-face sneaker ads, and ear-biting prize-fighters. With annual revenues of about $200 billion a year, media companies do well because they exploit social trends like other pop-merchants.

Since the culture is increasingly driven by rage, the news media have been lurching toward the berserk for more than a decade. This is true of "respectable" news programs as well as the talk shows that have been over-the-top for some time. Even though individual reporters may resist it, the news media, as a whole, have adapted the "Whatever" ethic that defines the times. There is market pressure to supply hateful targets to consumers who are interested in their world to the extent that it amuses or enrages them.

With fierce competition, declining journalistic standards, and a new generation coming of age, contemporary news coverage now mimics entertainment. Dramas and comedies have always tapped into existing human impulses, which include the desire to see bad people punished. Because there is a market in victimhood, the media stock their shelves with the villains who are believed to have caused misfortune. These villains tend to be people or institutions of means, just as they were in 1692 Salem.

"WE NEED VILLAINS"

The haves, increasingly personified by business leaders, tend to be "establishment" types, which is why the media are thought to have a liberal bias. "If they're nailing a white guy in a business suit," the reasoning goes, "they must be lefties."

It's really not liberal bias as much as it is resentment bias. The haves get nailed in news shows in the same spirit that they have long gotten nailed in entertainment programs. It's burlesque.

Media coverage of issues isn't much different from Tweety Bird tripping up the priggish Sylvester the Cat; the Road Runner meep-meeping the anvil onto Harvard-educated Wile E. Coyote's head; Dennis the Menace running through the fastidious Mr. Wilson's garden; Bart Simpson setting the repressed Mr. Burns's pants on fire; or the Three Stooges smashing the Countess in the face with a pie.

In the 1993 release of the movie *The Fugitive,* the antagonist is not just the murderous "one-armed man," who killed Dr. Richard Kimble's wife; he is the murderous one-armed man who works for a pharmaceutical company that knowingly markets a drug that doesn't work. Then there are animated features like *FernGully,* where adorable pixies battle a timber concern that is in cahoots with a satanic spirit named Hexus.

While watching *FernGully,* I tried to explain to my children that humans need trees to live. They cocked their heads in disbelief at my lame explanation as Hexus oozed out of the engine of a colossal tree-eating machine. A cartoon villain handily beat the glib crisis manager in our debate, hands down. More and more children's programming is of the enraging idiom. The message: Strike back at those who are conspiring to destroy you.

A June 1997 study by the Media Research Center confirms that the entertainment media are going full-throttle positioning the businessperson as the *villain du jour.* In a study of prime time network television over twenty-six months, including 863 dramas, TV movies, and sitcoms, the study showed that:

- *"TV businessmen commit more crimes than those in any other occupation."* Of the criminals portrayed, 29.2 percent were business executives, 9.7 percent were career criminals, 4.1 percent were doctors, 3.9 percent were government officials, and 3.5 percent were police officers;

- *"TV businessmen murder more than others, too,"* with 30.4 percent being business executives; 9.8 percent career criminals; and doctors, government officials, and police officers rang in with 4.2 percent of the murders each;

- *"TV businessmen are more likely to cheat than to contribute to society,"* with 28.7 percent of the businessmen cheating to get ahead and only 25 percent shown addressing societal concern through their work.

The entertainment media are just confirming existing prejudices that resonate with their audiences. In a July 7, 1997, *Fortune* article on the Media Research Center study, reporter Marc Gunther wrote, "The networks cite another reason why they portray businessmen as heavies: they're credible in that role. If viewers didn't accept the idea that CEOs lie, cheat, and steal, they wouldn't be shown doing so. 'We need villains,' says an unrepentant network insider. 'And if we portray businessmen as not caring about society or their employees, would we be all wrong?'"

THE "HOLY SHIT!" STORY

The media's pie-throwing ethic is especially true for television, which must prioritize and translate current affairs in order to effectively compete with entertainment programming. Audiences now have a choice between watching news programs and cop shows like *NYPD Blue,* whereas news programs used to only compete with other news programs. How do you make the news better able to compete with *NYPD Blue*'s detectives Sipowicz and Simone? You make the news more *like* them—sexy, tough, confrontational, and conclusive.

News shows, especially the "magazine" programs that directly compete with entertainment, use a proven formula of suspicion, interrogation, and punishment in pursuit of what some reporters call the *Holy Shit!* story. The *Holy Shit!* story stuns the public with the venality of the perpetrators. They feature furious (but effective) reporters like Brian Ross of ABC, whose *modus operandi* is skewering. This style is why there are more adjectives than ever to describe contemporary journalism. Larry Sabato identifies some of them in his book *Feeding Frenzy* as bloodsport, character cop, cheap-shot, food-fight, gotcha, hit-and-run, jugular, keyhole, paparazzi, peek-a-boo, peeping-Tom, skinhead, soap opera, tabloid, totalitarian, trash, and voyeur. Hyper-aggressive media coverage has also been called "reporting with attitude."

Wrote the *Washington Post*'s Howard Kurtz, " 'what works on television' began to compete with more serious forms of journalism. The profession's center of gravity shifted from those who ask questions to those who seem to have all the answers. Writing a long, thoughtful piece was fine. Spending weeks poring over documents was a public service. But television didn't care." What television does care about, however, is the *spectacle* of serious journalism, which is equated with bullying, embarrassing, humiliating, or appearing to perform a public service by "nailing" a target who doesn't have the public's best interests at heart. These histrionics oblige television to short-circuit the investigative process, which is not entertaining, and proceed immediately with the punishment phase, which is.

Aggressive reporting is the style of the times in the same spirit that martial artist Steven Seagal can achieve world peace in the movies by throwing a nuke-happy psycho off of a moving train. People don't leave a Seagal movie saying, "Gee, Steve articulated a trenchant paradigm there about controlling our nuclear arsenal." Viewers see brooding valor, abject evil, and a much-welcome smashed head on a stone underpass.

The news purports to be sharing critical information for the public's welfare. It is intended to be taken seriously and is packaged for this purpose. Serious subjects are given Hollywood endings that validate the anger that now defines us. Only extremes resonate. Coverage is deliberately polarized so that targets are positioned at their most flagrant.

In news terms, the message is no longer a bo-*ring* "watch your diet" but "hamburgers are bad" (Detective Sipowicz slaps the handcuffs on Mayor McCheese). A profiled chief executive is either a "genius" or is "embattled." Dissatisfaction is repackaged as disease. Kathie Lee Gifford is not a chirpy nuisance, she is evil. An earthquake is no longer just a geological tragedy, it was "mishandled." Cultural anger makes Americans relate better to a botched job that hurt people than to shifting tectonic plates that held no malice.

The broadcast media are notorious for embracing the absolute because the forum encourages it. The print media are resisting the trend toward absolutism as hard as they can but are under a cultural imperative to deliver a sequel to Watergate, the mother of all *Holy Shit!* stories.

THE BUSINESS OF ATTACK PROGRAMMING

"It's a Small World News Tonight"
A joke new name proposed for the evening news
after Disney bought ABC

The popularity of outrage-driven programming continues to rise. Television magazine shows like *PrimeTime Live,* CBS's *48 Hours,* and NBC's *Dateline* are one step down the media food chain from hard news shows like the *CBS Evening News.* They routinely attack high-profile targets with stories about unsafe products, bad government policies, and overall rotten behavior. Financial considerations attendant to programming are largely responsible for making magazine shows so hostile.

Magazine shows became more popular because they are cheap to produce. Even a failed program—and many of them do fail—is no big loss to the networks. According to *Broadcasting* magazine, "they generate millions in revenue at about half the cost of licensing entertainment programs from outside suppliers, thus providing significantly higher profit margins."

One-hour magazine shows cost about $500,000 each to produce. An hour-long drama program (e.g., *Homicide*) costs about $1 million per episode. The formula for a garden-variety attack requires only that the producers locate a victim (vulnerable person who is suffering), a villain (someone who *caused* the suffering), and a vindicator (reporter or activist who valiantly confronts the villain). Putting a package like this together is a lot easier than negotiating with big-name stars to do a sitcom or choreograph high-priced chase-scenes through mid-town Manhattan for a cop series.

Magazine shows are produced internally, which means that if the show is a success, the network won't have to compensate outside producers. Outside production companies can fetch fees ranging from $500,000 to $2 million for blockbuster programs.

The revenues of low-overhead magazine programs can be staggering if they make it. *60 Minutes* has generated well in excess of $1 billion for CBS in its thirty years on the air. *60 Minutes* can bring in $200 million for CBS and *20/20* generates more than $120 million for ABC annually. In some years, according to a *New York Times* report, *60 Minutes* has "accounted for as much as half of CBS's entire broadcast revenues."

YAK ATTACK

> "TV is an invention that permits you to be entertained in your living room by people you wouldn't have in your home."
>
> David Frost

The talk show lies in the nether region that separates hard news from raw entertainment. No one on either side of this murky border wants to claim the talk show, so low are they in everyone's esteem. Never mind that the same people who hold their noses at *Oprah* and *Sally* watch them. The little sense of decorum remaining demands a sneer at the very mention of their names.

Talk shows are by far the cheapest to produce, which is why so many of them spring up. All that's really needed is a host with a pulse, a few working cameras and some chairs to sit on (or throw). These programs are notorious for outrageousness and are problematic because they bypass journalism and allow allegations and subjective grievances to masquerade as "issues." It's easier to have ordinary citizens allege on *Oprah* that "Mad Cow" disease is a concern in the United States than it is to have a seasoned health reporter set out to prove it.

While people tend to think of talk shows as focusing exclusively on freak show extravaganzas, some of the most serious public panics have been launched or aggravated by these programs. The cellular phone cancer scare was launched on *Larry King Live,* lynch mob attacks on silicone breast implants originated with talk shows, as did some of the attacks on food additives aspartame and monosodium glutamate (MSG).

Without the berserk element, a talk show will have trouble getting off the ground. In *TV Guide,* one producer conceded, "When you're booking guests, you're thinking, 'How much confrontation can this person provide me?' " Nicholaus Mills, in his book *The Triumph of Meanness*, quotes veteran talk show producer Martin Berman: "For a show on rape, it used to be enough to interview the victim. Now you need the victim and the perpetrator. You need her to come face to face with her rapist."

Talk shows guarantee a lynching. If a viewer pushed the "mute" button on the remote control, it would still be very clear who the villains, victims, and vindicators were. The host and the studio audience can be counted on to back anyone who claims to be the victim. Not doing so would be off-strategy, the equivalent of Arnold Schwarzenegger accidentally killing the cute kid being held hostage instead of the swarthy terrorist.

COMPETITION

Competition between media is largely responsible for declining journalistic standards and marketplace pressure to enrage. During the past fifteen years, the United States has gone from having three media networks to about thirty-five. According to one survey by the Pew Research Center for the People and the Press, network news viewership dropped from 47 to 42 percent during the measured period between 1995 and 1996. In the "under thirty" age range, however, viewership dropped from 36 to 22 percent during the same time period.

This is frightening for news executives. Said Andrew Kohut, director of the Pew Research Center in the *New York Times*, "The networks are facing a serious problem, with increased competition within their industry and with a decreased appetite for news, especially among younger people." In response, the media are scrambling to launch magazine programs that "report" news using entertainment-style visuals, often staffing them with unseasoned producers. Said one TV producer in *U.S. News & World Report*, "These are the vidkids who know much more than us about filming, editing, and graphics. But they aren't very familiar with the basic rules of journalism. If you don't vigilantly supervise, they'll come back with stuff that sets your hair on end."

When I walk through media production operations, I am thunderstruck by the extraordinary youth of the people who work there. Their ages are relevant because they are more driven by entertainment than journalistic standards due to when they grew up. Because of competition, marketing wizards continue to replace journalists, especially in the broadcast media.

The standards of decorum in the news media reflect the values of the time. Decades ago, this standard was conservative. There were stories that reporters didn't touch based on "gentlemen's agreements" (such as presidential carousing). This changed after Watergate, when aggressive questions became commonplace because the scandal richly justified them. Bob Woodward and Carl Bernstein, print reporters, may have discovered this trail but broadcast reporters like Dan Rather and Sam Donaldson blazed it in search of WATERGATE: THE SERIES. Gentlemen's agreements don't occur anymore because competition has killed all the gentlemen. It's Dodge City now and decorum is obsolete in the media, as it is in the rest of society.

MEDIA PIE THROWING TECHNIQUES

"In the past twenty years, the American press has undergone a transformation from an access culture to an aggression culture."
Adam Gopnick, *The New Yorker,* December 12, 1994

The American impulse to pelt the haves with their desserts is as old as the revolution that launched the republic. It's just that there are fewer inhibitions about spiteful actions. There is the added benefit of state-of-the-art pie-throwing techniques that pose as journalism: A hidden camera or ambush interview is just another angle for capturing someone catching a pie in the face. Look out for these aggressive tricks, which are used mostly by the broadcast media:

- *The prime time subpoena* consists of handing an unfamiliar document to a target and requesting that it be reviewed while the camera is rolling. The prime time subpoena visually implies an indictment and the recipient looks like a caught thief. It also makes dazed targets look illiterate because they don't know whether to read the document, listen to the interviewer, or impale themselves.

- *The Placido Domingo* consists of shouting down a "debate" adversary as if in the concluding scene of an opera and/or using hyperbolic, emotional examples. (I recall one activist repeating the mantra "We're being buried alive in our garbage!" during a "debate" about recycling.) This is used by activists or protesters who sometimes show up to interviews unannounced to surprise a target. This technique makes whoever is being shouted down look weak, ineffectual, and guilty.

- Garden-variety attackers effectively use the *Godzilla meets Bambi* technique of listing horrors committed by fanged giants against vulnerable populations. The very act of Godzilla questioning Bambi violates a sense of fair play, even if Godzilla is right. In 1988, Bryan Gumbel, then of the *Today* show, pitted a chemical industry executive up against a few Brownie Troop school children in a "debate" about the environment. Guess who won? The Godzilla meets Bambis derive from a new-age method of data collection known as the *icky feeling hypothesis*, as in "I've got an icky feeling that Tasty Salad Dressing causes lupus."

- The *Connie Confessional* is used to attempt to get an unsavvy target to slip "off-the-record," an arrangement that is practically extinct. The technique includes play acting that a special bond exists between the interrogator and the target that warrants the sharing of something intimate. Connie Chung employed this effectively against Newt Gingrich's mother, who had a few observations about First Lady Hillary Clinton.

- The *Dr. No* is used to negatively portray a target by filming him walking into an office building wearing sunglasses (he must have something to hide); driving away in a dark car after a media ambush; or filming a target's place of business from a distance so it looks cold and scary.

- Conducting "independent," "scientific" tests, or the *Einstein,* can be used to refute whatever a villain/target claims. Einsteins are routinely used by magazine programs to make the target look like a liar, even though there's no reason to believe that the media's consultant is any more independent than the target's. Industries under fire pull Einsteins, too.

- The *Sweaty Al technique* consists of obtaining and using a video clip of a target stammering, brow wiping or just looking awfully uncomfortable, usually after being peppered with hostile questions. The Sweaty Al, named for Albert Brooks's tragic and moisture-laden attempt at news anchoring in *Broadcast News,* was made famous by *60 Minutes* and is used less frequently nowadays because it is considered rudimentary. Furthermore, the other techniques listed here represent a new generation of superior pie-throwing techniques.

- The *Marie Antoinette* incites revolution by demonstrating that the target has money and status, often by filming material goodies. The Marie Antoinette was used against televangelists like Jim and Tammy Faye Bakker, whose gold toilet seats were displayed for the nation. *Spy* magazine is the master of this approach, having turned vilification of society figures such as Donald Trump into an art form with repeated physical descriptions (Trump was described as a "short-fingered vulgarian") and superlative assessments of possessions (his "super-spectacular" yacht).

These are among the tricks the media use to tweak rage. At the same time audiences support the skewering, they are outraged at the media for exploiting them. The media are blamed not because they are seen as a vicious, external virus, but because they are an intimate part of the culture that Americans cannot accept.

The media know what human beings really are: curious, flawed creatures who like gossip and amusement and find comfort in the misfortunes of others, especially those who are suspected of mugging the public. The media are America's id, so what audiences get is sex, violence, and other titillation. That's what ids do: fornicate and attack. The media are the ultimate manifestations of democracy. They are the public.

A central concept rests at the magnetic core of the Culture of Attack, which assures attackers that they will not be alone in their crusade against a target. *Schadenfreude*, in fact, guarantees accomplices.

8. Schadenfreude and Its Four Stages

Humiliating others is its own reward.

OTHERS MUST FAIL

"A party is never given for someone. It is given against someone."
Guest at Truman Capote's Black & White Dance, 1966

The attackers I battle believe that if they can't seize the American Dream they can make damned sure that somebody else can't either. It's a perversion of the pursuit of happiness where the goal is to knock others down rather than lift oneself up. Sometimes the attack targets deserve it. More than ever they don't. I haven't found there to be a substantial difference in rage against my clients who are guilty of wrongdoing and those who become targets for other reasons. When I can't find malfeasance in my client's actions, I am forced to identify other motives for the attack.

The motive I find most often is *schadenfreude* (pronounced *"shadd'-in-froyd"*). It means the enjoyment of someone else's misfortune. It derives from the German words *schaden,* meaning damage, and *freude,* meaning joy. Author Gore Vidal once handicapped *schadenfreude* perfectly: "It's not enough to succeed, others must fail."

When the much-loathed Columbia Pictures chief Harry Cohn died in 1958, his funeral was attended by thousands. When asked why such a hated man's send-off was so well attended, one of the attendees (either Joan Crawford or Red Skelton) said, "It only proves what they always say—give the public something they want to see and they'll show up to see it." This is *schadenfreude* at its nadir.

Eli is one of those persons whose funeral people seem to want to attend. He grew up in poverty, served honorably in World War II, began his career in construction doing demolition work and built a successful real estate development company. Too successful, Cassius thinks, when he leaves meetings at the house Eli designed and built himself.

After twenty-five years working for Eli, Cassius thinks he "made" his boss. He marvels at the injustice of Eli's success. "Were it not for me," Cassius says, "Eli would still be blowing up buildings, not building them." Never mind that Eli started his company when Cassius was just a toddler. Resentment isn't rational.

Cassius leaves Eli's company. He is appalled at Eli's insensitivity. Eli wants to build an apartment building on land that the people of Meadow Brook want to remain undeveloped. Cassius worries for the people of Meadow Brook. His conscience bothers him that he could have been a part of Eli's scheming for so long. Cassius becomes a whistleblower hell bent on getting Eli.

In the Culture of Attack, tripping up others is an easily met goal. The peculiar mission of President Bill Clinton's former friend Cliff Jackson is a case in point. Jackson, a native Arkansan who studied with Clinton at Oxford, has made a crusade out of attacking Clinton. Jackson, an attorney, represented the two Arkansas state troopers who claimed they arranged trysts for Clinton. He recalled for Republican operatives how a desperate Clinton attempted to evade the draft in 1969 and appeared briefly as a player in Paula Jones's sexual harassment suit. It is hard to determine what Jackson gained other than making Clinton's life more difficult.

The desire to see bad things happen to noted people is ancient. In the Old Testament, God told Jonah to warn the people of Ninevah that unless they improved their behavior, the city would be ruined. When the people repented, God decided not to destroy Ninevah. Jonah felt betrayed. He had been hell-bent on destruction and didn't get to see any.

Contemporary Americans aren't unique because they have mean impulses; they are unique in the delusion that society has come a long way from Ninevah, that today's attackers are somehow nobler than silly prophets and witch-chasing ministers.

Nevertheless, the current Culture of Attack accelerates *schadenfreude*. Tearing somebody down is the height of fashion. Resentment-driven, an attack can be launched without shame. Years ago, if someone said they wanted a house like Eli's, people would laugh. "Who doesn't?" they'd say. Had Jonah lived in the millennial United States, he might have sued God for violating his "right" to see Ninevah destroyed and e-mailed a computer virus to make sure they suffered anyway.

Nowadays, coveting is not a sin because it can be called something else that sounds vaguely Jeffersonian. There is a loose affiliation of attackers who have little to lose by attempting an attack. They've got the tools, too, which include the media, the Internet, and the plaintiff's bar.

Attackers never cite *schadenfreude* as their motive for attack. There's still a part of human nature that believes there is something wrong with enjoying the humiliation of others. Fear not, there's a loophole: Attackers can convince us that they are acting on principle. This principle dictates that the target warrants the assault, after all, attackers are not resentful, they *disapprove*.

DISGUISING SCHADENFREUDE

"Sometimes we like to see the mighty fall, because it makes our pallid, boring lives seem decent and OK. Sure, we don't have a yacht and *Playboy* centerfold girlfriend, but at least we're not serving time in some jail for looting an S&L or checking into a drug rehab clinic."

Rudy Maxa

At the next Meadow Brook town meeting, Cassius takes the microphone. He announces he has left Eli's company. He is starting his own construction firm and would like to work with the people of Meadow Brook in opposing Eli's project. He is applauded. Cassius tells the packed room how Eli plans to con them into allowing him to build his apartment building. He's going to try to buy them off. He'll throw money everywhere, promise them everything. Don't be fooled, Cassius warns them, skyscrapers are coming.

Eli called me up one night at home. He has a traitor in his midst who is threatening a big project he has worked on for years. The aging developer sounds tired and shaken. He worries about what Cassius might say about him. He asks if I can meet him and his "team" out at his house the following day. He wants to know what I think about a news broadcast that is running about his Meadow Brook project. I know where Eli lives. A friend once pointed his place out during a run through the suburbs. It is some house.

I am greeted at the end of the driveway by a camera sitting atop a brick post holding one of Eli's two wrought iron gates. The gates swing open and a man in muddy construction boots directs me to a parking space next to a pickup truck. The elegant brick house rising next to the muddy man and pickup truck are a strange sight.

The man greets me as I step out of my car. He introduces himself. The muddy man is Eli.

"You seem surprised," he said as I shook his hand.

"I guess I didn't think you would be the one to greet me."

"Bullshit," Eli says. "You were expecting some jackass in a smoking jacket and slippers."

I nodded. "I guess I was."

"Young fella, I'm seventy-five years old. I've been wearing muddy boots my whole life. Muddy boots built this house."

In C. S. Lewis's book *Screwtape Proposes a Toast,* an elderly devil makes recommendations at a banquet in Hell to younger devils about how to corrupt humankind. The old devil Screwtape suggests that "Democracy is a word with which you must lead them around by the nose." He explains that it is difficult to inspire people to destroy each other based on Envy, "the most odious, and also the most comical, of vices." Democracy must be invoked "purely as an incantation; if you like, purely for its selling power."

Screwtape explains that democracy is an effective cover because it makes people confuse the "political ideal" of equality with "a factual belief that all men *are* equal."

My clients are an unequal lot. They really do have more than others, not always as individuals, but as organizations. Tearing them down may not elevate the attackers, but it will at least put them at parity for a moment.

Enjoying the failure of others is not restricted to people. Products and concepts such as "workplace sensitivity training" are attacked for *schadenfreude*, too. Resentment is easily piqued by anything that attackers feel is being inflicted upon them, be it government-mandated waste reduction program or a presidential news conference that interrupts prime time television programming.

There are four stages of *schadenfreude*. During the first stage, *discovery,* the public identifies a target that seems to easily explain complicated situations. It may be a person with great charisma who comes along during perilous times or a product that works wonders when others have failed. Once the target is identified, it goes through a second stage, *coronation,* where it gets extraordinary attention at the expense of other things. In time, attackers realize that the target isn't all that was promised. I call this third stage *flaw-detection.* Once the target's flaws are known, it is savaged during the *humiliation/settling* phase, in which it is either destroyed or evaluated more critically.

When a winner takes all, he takes it from the public troth. Attackers take the perceived theft more personally than most. The winners make attackers feel helpless. Smart attackers know how to tap into widespread public resentments. Many Americans despise the oil companies and Microsoft because they hate themselves for becoming dependent upon them. Consumers secretly enjoy technological failures like the communications satellite that shut down pagers nationwide in 1998 because they can't stand being beholden to the monoliths that shot their lives into orbit. Audiences resent overhyped TV shows (*Friends, Barney*), overplayed songs (Elton John's "Candle in the Wind" tribute to Princess Diana), ubiquitous drugs (Prozac), and even environmental improvement methods like recycling because they are unable to control the frequency of which these things intrude into their lives.

TRASHING RECYCLING

Recycling is a classic example of an idea that cycled through the four stages of *schadenfreude.* In the late 1980s, the environmental ethic was recycle or die. This was a response to a perceived shortage of landfill space. While recycling had been discovered long ago, it received its coronation in 1988, when a garbage barge began circling the globe under the watchful eye of network media cameras looking for a place to dump its belongings. It wouldn't have to be dumped, environmentalists argued, if it had been recycled, used again. Recycling was characterized in quasi-religious and moral terms by environmental activists and the news media. Setting a box full of recyclables out at curbside became a social litmus test about whether or not you cared about humanity. This was supported by an Environmental Protection Agency "hierarchy" of disposal options, including (in order of desirability) recycling, composting and waste-to-energy incineration and, finally, landfilling. Mandatory recycling rates were set and products with low recycling rates were banned in certain localities.

One of my firm's first big projects was counseling industries under attack for making products that were not easily recycled. The craze was so intense that it was hard for companies to ignore the public's demand that their products be recycled even if it didn't make sense. At one point, even major disposable diaper manufacturers began experimenting with recycling: unappetizing to be sure, but it was recycling.

My partner, Nick, and I encouraged clients to proceed with recycling programs cautiously. We believed that not all of them would succeed because recycling is a commodity business and some materials are inherently more valuable than others. Aluminum and steel, for example, which had long established markets for scrap, were more valuable than, say, used baby diapers.

By the early 1990s, municipalities began having trouble financing their recycling programs. The flaw-detection stage of *schadenfreude* had set in. Communities found it was easier, in some cases, to landfill their waste or send it to waste-to-energy incinerators. The media began to report recycling's flaws by showcasing incidents of materials supposedly destined for recycling facilities being sent to landfills—a sacrilege by the day's standards.

When it became clear that recycling alone wouldn't solve the solid waste problem, the media savaged it during the humiliation stage with the same force that they had once canonized it. The headlines by the mid-1990s included "The Recycling Boondoggle," subheads like "The Folly of Recycling" and leads like "In the good old days there was no recycling problem because there was no recycling." A landmark *New York Times Magazine* cover story was titled "What a Waste."

Despite attacks on the *Times* by environmentalists, the paper had its facts straight. *Times* reporter John Tierney wrote, "Collecting a ton of recyclable items is three times more expensive than collecting a ton of garbage because the crew picks up less material at each stop." He added that by sending a ton of glass, plastic, and metal to a private recycler, New York City spends $200 more than it would if the material were landfilled.

Recycling showed good results, too. Companies like Wellman, Inc. and Browning-Ferris Industries have huge businesses in recycling materials such as plastics, steel, aluminum, and paper. *E Magazine* reports that curbside recycling programs have grown from only two in 1970 to 7,000 today. Nearly a quarter of the nation's municipal waste is now diverted to productive uses.

Then why all the sudden hatred for recycling? Recycling posed as a panacea. If they recycled, the public was told, they would be making the world a better place. If they didn't, they were slobs. Recycling seemed to disapprove of consumers personally. If they didn't put that bin out by the curb, their politically correct neighbors would snarl at them. Indeed, I recall one job applicant at my company expressing displeasure that the recycling program in our office building had been cancelled. Could she work for people like us?

As information came out about recycling's disappointing results, latent resentment bubbled to the top. The public began venting its rage against recycling's inconvenience and costs. Many sneered back at their goody-two-shoes neighbors who had judged them for their environmental indifference. Recycling's humiliation was its critics' psychic reward.

The great error made by recycling's proponents was to position it as a form of salvation as opposed to just another disposal option. In the end, recycling is a business like any other. It has social and environmental benefits, but these things are incidental to the operation of a business. Some things sell under certain conditions, others don't. By tying recycling so closely to society's moral worth, it was set up for a *schadenfreude*-based stoning. The public was happy to be among its assailants. Recycling is far from dead; however, its popularity has been greatly diminished and its growth has dramatically slowed.

THE EMPIRE STRIKES BACK

Eli steps out of his boots and slips on a pair of loafers once we enter his house through a side door. He introduces me to two men. One is a lawyer and the other is a contractor. As we walk to Eli's study, the lawyer remarks that the house should be in *Architectural Digest.* Eli stops.

"I don't want it in *Architectural Digest,*" he says angrily. "Why the hell anyone would want to see where I eat and sleep is beyond me."

Action News comes on Eli's TV. It features parts of Cassius's speech at the town meeting. Cassius says that the Meadow Brook development "just isn't right." The citizens of Meadow Brook agree, including children who fret that their favorite place to play will be lost to jackhammers.

"That's what I am," Eli mumbles. "I'm a playground wrecker."

At the end of the segment, Eli is identified by name. A camera pans his house. Eli recoils. Standing before the iron gates, the Action News reporter concludes that Eli "refused to comment." "Back to you, Barbara," the reporter says to a concerned looking woman at the studio news desk.

Eli rants for a while about Cassius the traitor. I stay silent. I'm used to this. Eli is livid that his house was shown. He knows what "they" are trying to do and he's right. The big house alone will rile the people of Meadow Brook who don't live like this.

I ask Eli and his team to tell me everything they know about the new project. Eli proudly describes every feature of the new building, including special measures to make it blend in with the natural surroundings at Meadow Brook. The lawyer throws in a word or two about zoning. The contractor talks about the landscaping and the new civic center. I perk up.

"What civic center?" I ask.

"The building I promised to put up with recreation and sports activities," Eli says, as if I hadn't been paying attention. "Everybody in Meadow Brook could use it."

"I don't know anything about a civic center," I said. "Is it possible that the people who live there don't know?"

"It was on the notices," the lawyer said.

"Nobody reads notices and Cassius is going to make sure they don't," I said.

Cassius had been framing the debate. He was making references to "buying off" the community, which was an offensive characterization designed to aggravate resentment toward Eli and make people discount the civic center.

The community may not have even been aware of the civic center offering. Eli had assumed that people knew about it. He saw the civic center as a part of a deal rather than a personally relevant benefit to the people of Meadow Brook. He was an old timer, a craftsman who thought in business and aesthetic terms. He never factored in emotions. He viewed them as touchy-feely distractions from enterprise as opposed to a core element of business.

I lay out an informal plan to persuade the people of Meadow Brook to listen to Eli's proposal. He wants to think about it for a while.

In the meantime, the residents of Meadow Brook are protesting. About twenty of them show up in vans and hold placards outside of Eli's house. He is mortified, even depressed. Cassius has taken his battle to Eli's neighborhood.

We plead with Cassius to move his protests elsewhere. He eventually takes his crew to Eli's office. Eli's depression converts to rage. He authorizes the aggressive program we had discussed earlier.

We begin communicating on two levels. First, we publicize the civic center, laying out its blueprints and capabilities in mailings and advertisements. We also inform the people of Meadow Brook that since they don't want the civic center, Eli was being forced to look at locations in another community.

Cassius came under fire at the next town meeting for glossing over the prospects of a civic center. His line about the people of Meadow

Brook being "bought off" still resonated with some. For the most part, however, his hostile actions toward Eli were increasingly seen as a personal ax to grind rather than being a community crusade. Cassius looked devious and petty and his coalition began breaking apart.

Meadow Brook eventually voted to allow Eli to build his development. It cost him a lot more money than he had expected, but he needed to promise a bigger civic center to close the deal. The community had not passed the project because it had suddenly identified with Eli. The personal benefits of the civic center overpowered any resentment that they had held toward him. Besides, they had gotten him to pony up more money, which gave them a sense of control over Eli and their own destinies.

NAILING THE ADMIRAL: MISSION ACCOMPLISHED

"It's inconceivable to me that it was a mistake. It may be a real puzzle to civilians. But it would be a major embarrassment for someone to be caught doing this."

Retired Marine Lt. Col. Roger Charles,
National Security News Service

In 1995, the National Security News Service first raised questions about the efficacy of Admiral Jeremy Boorda's wearing of a "V device," a military decoration for heroism in combat. Boorda had worn two V devices in addition to other decorations earned during Vietnam. Years earlier, former Chief of Naval Operations Admiral Elmo Zumwalt had authorized Boorda to wear the V devices. Upon the 1995 inquiry, however, Boorda stopped wearing them.

The little-known news service hammered away at the Boorda story in 1996 and obtained his records through the Freedom of Information Act. The story bounced up to *Newsweek* when decorated veteran Colonel David Hackworth, a military affairs correspondent, successfully pitched his editor. Hackworth argued that falsely wearing combat medals was "the worst thing a military man can do."

Shortly before *Newsweek* arrived for its 2:30 P.M. interview, Boorda

---

Attack Summary: Admiral Jeremy Boorda—May 1996

Victim:	U.S. Navy
Villain:	Admiral Boorda
Vindicator:	National Security News Service
Void:	Validation of a string of Navy scandals
Vehicle:	*Newsweek*
Value:	Military integrity

---

entered his house at the Navy Yard in Washington, D.C., located his .38 caliber sidearm, stepped into his backyard and shot himself through the heart. In one of his suicide notes, he characterized his use of the V devices as an honest mistake. He was not afraid that he had done something wrong as much as he was afraid that the media would "blow it out of proportion," according to the *Washington Post*.

There were things in the news at the time of Boorda's death that lent plausibility to the notion that funny business could be going on in the navy. The Tailhook sexual assault controversy that forced the resignation of Boorda's predecessor, drug-related arrests of sailors, allegations of cheating at the Naval Academy, and unexplained crashes of navy jets. Boorda himself had not been under fire for any of these matters.

Despite this, the hunt for Boorda's scalp was very important to some. The *Detroit News* reported that Hackworth "mused to an assistant in his office in Montana that if it were known that Boorda wrongly wore such medals, 'He might put a gun to his head.'"

The explanations concerning the appropriateness of Boorda's wearing the medals are confusing at best. In the past, ruthless investigations weren't launched into gray areas; they were launched to uncover bad things.

While the media's motives in the Boorda assault will never be known for certain, sport seems to have been a major element. Boorda had stopped wearing the medals, which had been authorized by Admiral Zumwalt. The only thing that hadn't been achieved was Boorda's humiliation. What other objective could his attackers have had?

The objective of the attack on Boorda was to blow him apart while his career was at its zenith and watch the pieces fall to the ground. This was quintessential *schadenfreude*. Given the continuum of genuine villainy that exists, it is hard to find an honorable principle or probable cause for the attack. Suicide was Boorda's strategy, and no one else's, for defending himself. But he didn't fire the first shot. The debate about the validity of Boorda's medals and the circumstances surrounding his death still rages on the Internet.

In a military era that delivered the My Lai massacre, wearing undeserved medals probably isn't "the worst thing that a military man can do." In the Culture of Attack, however, there are no proportions. Justice is a beard grown to cover the jaws of *schadenfreude*. All actions, especially those that accrue medals, deserve savage penalties when nailing someone is the real mission.

Before a target like Admiral Boorda can be torn down, he (or it) must be built up. Only through the process of initially overestimating a target can the culture guarantee—and thoroughly savor—a long, dramatic fall.

9. *Power, Prozac, and the Four Stages of* Schadenfreude

Some attacks are based more on resentment and visibility than wrongdoing.

"Hollywood is a place where everyone wants to see you fail and if you die in the process, it's even better."

Jeffrey Katzenberg

Most objects of *schadenfreude* are attacked for more than one reason, some of them legitimate. Were it not for the saturating degree of their target's success, however, these other factors would never reach public consciousness. Two unrelated targets that cycled through the four stages of *schadenfreude* at the same time include Hollywood power broker Michael Ovitz and the antidepressant drug Prozac.

DISCOVERY

In the late 1980s and early 1990s, it was hard to read an article about the entertainment business that didn't contain a reference to Michael Ovitz, former Creative Artists Agency (CAA) chief, as the most powerful man in Hollywood. Ovitz appeared on the cover of the *New York Times Mag-*

azine in 1989, followed up in more recent years by covers on *Newsweek* and *Business Week*. His name was almost always accompanied by nouns like "Godfather," "king," "shogun," "uber-agent," and "super-agent." Ovitz earned these titles through a combination of vision, talent, good luck, and the need of the Hollywood and business media to explain a rapidly changing entertainment business.

Attack Summary: Michael Ovitz—1995–1997

Victim:	Entertainment community
Villain:	Michael Ovitz
Vindicator:	Other Hollywood leaders
Void:	Explanation for changing dynamics in Hollywood, need to redistribute power
Vehicle:	Business and entertainment media
Value:	Exposing a monopolist

During the 1980s, when Ovitz's rise achieved its greatest momentum, Hollywood was in the throes of revolution. Once-great studios were collapsing and merging while new, innovative companies were sprouting up. "Special effects" outfits that had not even existed a few years before, like Industrial Light & Magic, were making men like George Lucas very wealthy.

The only thing that was stable in Hollywood was the need for big-name stars to make movies and TV shows. These stars, largely through agents like Ovitz, began demanding—and getting—unprecedented fees and percentages of the gross. In 1989, Jack Nicholson was paid a reported $50 million to play the Joker in the first Batman film.

The big names like Louis B. Mayer and Sam Goldwyn were long gone. Even MCA's indomitable Lew Wasserman was aging and sharing power with young talent like Steven Spielberg, who had produced some of the studio's greatest blockbusters like *Jaws*.

As a revolution brewed in Hollywood, another one was percolating in the nation's psyche. Mental illnesses, which were once considered character flaws, were becoming increasingly identified as treatable, chemically based disorders. Pharmaceutical giant Eli Lilly introduced the drug Prozac at the end of 1987 to treat depression. Within roughly a year of its approval, sales of Prozac hit $350 million, "more than the total amount previously spent annually by Americans on all antidepressants combined," according to Dr. Peter Breggin, author of *Talking Back to Prozac.*

Attack Summary: Prozac—1990s

Victim:	Sufferers of mental illness
Villain:	Eli Lilly
Vindicator:	Prozac victims groups, Church of Scientology
Void:	Controversy over chemical component of mental illness, bad side-effects
Vehicle:	Lawsuits, media coverage
Value:	Protecting the mentally ill

U.S. News & World Report estimates that 24 million people in 107 nations take Prozac, 18 million in the United States alone, contributing to more than $2 billion in sales for Lilly. Given the millions who suffer from depression, the drug's introduction has been, by most accounts, a godsend to sufferers who either took less effective medication or were subjected to other treatments that didn't work. Today, Prozac is the most popular psychiatric drug and the second best selling of all drugs (behind stomach-acid reducer Zantac). One million prescriptions of Prozac are filled each month. The social stigma of depression began to dissolve as more "normal" members of society found relief with Prozac.

CORONATION

"Is It Peace or Is It Prozac?"
Song title by folk singer Cheryl Wheeler

In addition to Prozac's performance, it gained popularity as a low-maintenance drug. Before Prozac, many antidepressants needed to be monitored and regulated with blood tests, hospital stays and special diets. No prior medication for depression had ever been as effective with so few side effects as Prozac.

Prozac's use quickly expanded to address other indications, as magazine covers boldly announced. It has helped many of the five million Americans who suffer from obsessive-compulsive disorder (OCD), which is especially significant given that "90 percent of medicated patients relapse when the drugs are withdrawn," according to *Discover*. Prozac also addressed mood disorders in children, something that couldn't be said for competing drugs.

Almost overnight, Prozac became, well, the Mike Ovitz of pharmaceuticals—the drugfather, the uber-antidepressant. While its success alone would have been enough to trigger *schadenfreude*, its mass media positioning as a wonder-drug that cured practically everything—including depression, anxiety, arthritis, bulimia, anorexia-nervosa, migraine headaches, obsessive-compulsive disorder, shyness, hypersensitivity, chronic fatigue syndrome, premenstrual syndrome, postpartum depression, drug and alcohol addiction, impulsiveness, and poor concentration—contributed to the attacks.

One of the most famous incidents that contributed to Ovitz's godfather mystique, as recounted by Robert Slater in his book *Ovitz*, was his conflict with screenwriter Joe Eszterhas, who left CAA in 1989 for another agency. Eszterhas wrote a letter to Ovitz, which was ultimately leaked to the media, that stated, "You told me that if I left, 'My foot soldiers who go up and down Wilshire Boulevard each day will blow your brains out.' "

Ovitz's coronation came in the form of the rosters that were published by entertainment magazines such as *Premiere*. These lists are notorious for their concise, bulleted, unequivocal approach to who's "in" and "out" of power. *Premiere* published its first Power List in 1990. Ovitz topped the list with the following description: "Despite recent defections and l'affaire Eszterhas, the CAA uber-agent still has more A-list talent at his fingertips than anyone else in town and can package pricey projects to the studio of his choice." MCA's Lew Wasserman was number two on the Power List.

Ovitz headed the *Premiere* Power List in 1991, too. Next to the listing "Rank last year," *Premiere* stated "Take a guess." Under "Weaknesses," it stated "What do you do as an encore when you're Ovitz? Maybe even he's not sure. Does he want to run MCA?" Finally, in the "What to watch for" epilogue, *Premiere* concluded of Ovitz: "Whatever he wants you to watch for."

In 1992, Ovitz commanded the Power List yet again, with references as to how he was taking over Madison Avenue.

During his coronation, references to Ovitz inevitably mentioned things like how feared he was, his Zen-like aura—even his martial arts workout schedule and how he carefully planned his life in five-year increments. No one would comment on-the-record about him. Compounding this was Ovitz's penchant for mystery. People wanted to know what magic was being worked behind those curving I. M. Pei–designed walls that housed CAA on Wilshire Boulevard. Absurdly, most of the media attention focused on Ovitz's low profile, something that's hard to maintain from magazine covers and power lists.

There were business benefits to Ovitz for positioning himself as the ruthless and pre-eminent power-player. It gave CAA a competitive edge over other agencies because stars would want to stay with the shop with the most clout. They might also be reluctant to part with CAA for fear that they might lose clout, be run out of town—or worse.

Ovitz linked CAA clients such as Tom Cruise and Dustin Hoffman with director Barry Levinson to take over struggling movie projects like one called *Rain Man*. The movie went onto become the top-grossing film of 1988 and won Dustin Hoffman a Best Actor Academy Award. Hoffman thanked Ovitz by name when he accepted his Oscar, catapulting the once *sub rosa* role of the agent into America's living rooms.

As Hollywood sought a template to help explain the new pecking order, talent agencies had grown from being lubricants in a big system to being pistons in the engine. It is hard, however, to discern which pistons drive what part of the engine. So a very confused media simplified things by anointing Ovitz Hollywood's king.

FLAW DETECTION

After a while the fawning characterizations of Ovitz became ridiculous. It was hard to imagine the news media dragging the "low profile" agent kicking and screaming onto magazine covers.

This *one guy* is single-handedly running the entertainment business? The backhanded implication was that men like Lew Wasserman, Barry Diller, Michael Eisner, David Geffen, Steven Spielberg, Terry Semel, Bob Daly and many others didn't have what it takes.

"I always thought it was a funny thing to anoint the middleman as king," said an unnamed entertainment industry executive to *Fortune*. Nevertheless, wrote the magazine, "the press needed someone to symbolize the forces reshaping the entertainment industry, and Ovitz, with his Zen aura and his ominous mien, was more an obvious choice than any of the studio heads, none of whom towered over their competitors the way he did."

The first real chink in Ovitz's armor came when he was negotiating for the top job at MCA, a post held by his idol, Lew Wasserman. After intensive negotiations, the deal fell through in June 1995. This was attributed to the size of the compensation package Ovitz was seeking (reportedly $250 million), and his having to report to MCA owner, the youthful Edgar Bronfman Jr. of Seagram's.

Hollywood influentials and the media began wondering why the super-agent couldn't close his own deal. Could Ovitz have overestimated his power? Why would the most powerful man in Hollywood go to work for an untested figure like Bronfman? And isn't Ezsterhas, the writer, still alive, well, and pulling down millions for scripts?

Strangely enough, the fissure in Ovitz's mystique deepened when he agreed to accept a bigger job than the MCA position several months later. In August 1995, the Walt Disney Company announced that Ovitz would be joining the company as the number two in command under CEO Michael Eisner. The perception of Zeus job hunting didn't square with the Ovitz mystique. Why would Ovitz work for someone else? By the time he accepted the Disney job, his critics were emboldened.

One source gave Ovitz's tenure at Disney a year. Another "major Hollywood figure" commented in the *Washington Post*, "I told him that he was making the mistake of his life when he took that job. I told him, 'You're going from a king to a vassal in someone else's kingdom.' . . . I don't think Michael Eisner realized that Michael Ovitz didn't have the equipment for that particular job. Running an agency has little to do with running a company as big as Disney."

On Friday, December 13, 1996, sixteen months after he joined Disney, Ovitz's departed.

Not everyone was impressed by Prozac the uber-drug. Soon after it reached the height of its profile, the victims' and plaintiffs' lawyers surfaced. In a 1992 Securities and Exchange Commission annual report, Eli Lilly stated that in "approximately 170 actions, plaintiffs seek to recover damages as a result of the ingestion of Prozac." Of greatest concern were allegations, based largely on a study by doctors at Harvard, that Prozac routinely led to violent and suicidal behavior in patients.

In Peter Breggin's intensely critical 1994 book, *Talking Back to Prozac,* he mocks a competing book's title, *Listening to Prozac,* with sub-chapters titled "Listening to Cocaine." The implication, of course, is that Prozac is potentially as dangerous as abused narcotics. In a section titled "The Floodgate of Prozac Horror Stories," Breggin cites the following examples (among many others):

- In 1990 the Prozac Survivors Support Group asked the Bucks County, Pennsylvania, coroner to reopen the investigation into political activist Abbie Hoffman's suicide to see if it was driven by Prozac.

- The *New York Times* reported that El Dayyid A. Nosair was taking Prozac for depression at the time he allegedly murdered Rabbi Meir Kahane, the controversial founder of the Jewish Defense League.

- A woman reported withdrawing into herself while on Prozac and plotting the death of her four children, while another woman on Prozac acted on her feelings and killed a friend and herself.

- A woman who held her psychiatrist "hostage" with a razor to her own wrist sued Lilly concerning self-mutilations inflicted while taking Prozac.

- A depressed woman became hostile while taking Prozac the first time and, when placed on it again, committed suicide.

Writes Breggin, "Reports linking Prozac flooded the media during 1991, the year of the FDA hearing. . . . Violence perpetrated while taking Prozac was the most common theme."

Most of the attacks addressed Prozac's side-effects, not its effectiveness. Few critics were more vociferous than the Church of Scientology, which reported in its magazine *Freedom* that Prozac manufacturer Eli Lilly has been aware that "there had already been 15 suicides linked to it—six by overdose, four by gunshot, three by hanging and two by drowning."

Freedom cited an FDA review showing that "Lilly had failed to report information about the onset of psychotic episodes in people during Prozac's testing." Reporters Thomas G. Whittle and Richard Weiland added: "As early as 1986, in other words, long before Prozac was approved for public consumption, evidence existed which linked Prozac to worsened symptoms of depression and the onset of psychotic episodes—a fact underscored by the 1,089 suicides as of September 16, 1993, along with many episodes of senseless violence, homicide and even multiple murder." A whiff of cover-up was in the air.

In the extraordinary case of Joseph Wesbecker, who in 1989 murdered eight people and wounded thirteen others, attorneys for the victims contended that Prozac caused Wesbecker's violent spree. A jury ultimately found no link between Prozac and Wesbecker's actions.

Breggin further explains the mysterious underpinning of *schadenfreude*-based attacks by asking "How could the FDA—and a majority of its pychopharmacological committee—exonerate the drug in regard to suicide and violence?" Breggin believes it was due to a powerful "psycho-pharmaceutical complex." He concludes: "The answer to these questions lies in the intricate web of connections among the FDA, the drug companies, and the psychiatric community."

HUMILIATION/SETTLING

"Foot soldiers! Can you believe it? The guy was out of control. Now the past has come back to haunt him, and all these guys want to kill him."
Bernie Brillstein

People began losing their fear of Ovitz well before his uncomfortable departure from Disney. When Ovitz was blamed for recruiting a popular executive away from NBC to Disney's ABC network, NBC West Coast chief Don Ohlmeyer remarked in *Time* magazine, "Michael Ovitz is the Antichrist, and you can quote me on that." Other news coverage and gossip made petty references to Ovitz's numerous aides, his alleged needs for personal aircraft and a place to nap, not to mention his "gesture of whispering in Eisner's ear—both in meetings and at public events."

Reported the July 7, 1997, *Fortune,* "By the late 1980s, some studio executives were feeling abused by Ovitz and hoping he would fall." The perfection with which Ovitz was alleged to have run the world tweaked the resentment that already was boiling within the imperfect majority in Hollywood. Resenting him and abhorring contradictions, the assault on Ovitz become an all-or-nothing proposition. After he left Disney, people began wondering whether Ovitz had been a paper tiger all along.

In an industry where there are a handful of dukes but no one king, Ovitz was just one of the bigger dukes. Being known as a god in an industry where *everyone's* mother told him he was God (David Geffen's mother called her son "King David"), provoked deep resentment. And some of these people, who bristled at the notion that one man (not them) "runs Hollywood," were mean enough and powerful enough to act on it.

Ovitz's humiliation was brutal. According to his biographer, Robert Slater, "His critics, long silent and long eager to take Ovitz on, sensed that he was in trouble at Disney, that he was growing weaker by the minute, and moved in for the kill. For years Ovitz had made it oh-so-clear to Hollywood's movers and shakers, especially the studio chiefs and some senior producers, that he knew how to conduct business more expertly than they did. And every time, during the CAA years, that he put together a film package and used his talent-heavy client list as leverage against the studios, he rubbed more salt in their wounds."

Fortune magazine declared "plumbing the psychic hole left by his diminution" the "top parlor game in town." Said one Hollywood figure, "People took it until they didn't have to and then they gave it back."

Ovitz had said at the funeral of Frank Wells, his predecessor at Disney, "If I died tomorrow, there'd be 25,000 people at my funeral. Why? Because everyone would want to know that I was dead."

Ovitz is far from dead. He is young, gifted, very rich, and is active once again in the entertainment business. His reign *atop* the power list, however, has been passed to the leaders of the show business conglomerates who, in reality, probably held those elusive top spots all along.

Unlike Ovitz, Prozac thrives because people need medical help more than they need talent agents. Some objects of *schadenfreude* survive because they are grounded in reality. The awful reality of mental anguish brings Eli Lilly $2 billion a year in sales.

Nevertheless, in the Culture of Attack, many suspect that anything that is spectacularly successful was ill gotten. When Prozac's alteration of brain chemistry is thrown into the mix, a script worthy of Oliver Stone emerges. That the drug had been extensively studied by more than seventy scientific and regulatory bodies worldwide did not neutralize the attacks. If the company underwrote clinical tests to prove its point, it was controlling things; if it didn't, it was negligent and trying to hide something.

Like Ovitz, many parties had something to gain by bashing Prozac. The drug's introduction was accompanied by an entire subindustry of supporters, opponents, journalists, publishers, and others with shtick for sale. Much of it was anti-Prozac. There are dozens of books on the market about Prozac. As of this writing, there are at least 6,000 Internet sites that deal with the drug. And, of course, the requisite victim's network, the Prozac Survivors Support Group, surfaced.

Prozac's success—and vulnerability to attack—were tied to its effectiveness. It treats disorders that injure those who previously had little or no relief, and were often considered pariahs to boot. In attacks, whether it's cellular phones, disposable diapers, or antidepressants, when the target's benefits outweigh its risks, the target will survive.

With millions of people taking Prozac, there are bound to be poor reactions and even tragedies. In a culture that sets fantasy as its baseline for living and rejects all forms of risk, all of Prozac's attackers may never be satisfied.

Ironically, it was the merchant of fantasy, Ovitz, who was humbled by real-world forces. Ovitz's apparent belief in the supremacy of his own legend nailed him. Apparently, there were other powerful people in Hollywood, too.

While *schadenfreude* springs from a darker side of human nature, its origins are not wholly illegitimate and mean-spirited. People and institutions have been known to provoke hostility in ways that make the kindest of us root for their fall. Whether it's through naked avarice, outlaw conduct, or stunning violence, the desire to humble those who don't play by society's rules reflects a rational impulse to restore order.

10. *Legitimate* Schadenfreude

Some targets had it coming.
***Schadenfreude** just made matters worse.*

"Dwayne Orville Andreas runs the world."
Mother Jones magazine, July/August 1995

GUNNING FOR ARCHER DANIELS MIDLAND

Some corporate clients love my *schadenfreude* theory of attacks for all
the wrong reasons. Some interpret it to mean that all attacks are without
merit and based purely upon resentment. On the contrary, sometimes the
enjoyment of someone else's misfortune makes sense, especially if there
are other, legitimate reasons to attack that person. The attacks on agribusiness
giant Archer Daniels Midland (ADM) are a classic case.

I first sensed something was unusual about ADM in the mid-1980s,
when I worked on an agricultural public affairs project. I showed a colleague
a list of people I was supposed to call for more information. One
of the names on the list was a representative of ADM. My colleague got
a deer-in-the-headlights look and shook his head.

"ADM," he said. "Don't ever mess with them."

139

I found the presumption odd.

"I don't want to mess with them. I want them to send me information," I said.

I called the company in Decatur, Illinois, and was referred to a very nice woman who dropped the information I had requested in the mail.

When I showed my ADM-phobic colleague the material, he asked me how I "snagged" it. I told him that I used the Machiavellian technique of calling directory assistance, getting the company's telephone number and calling them up.

"Man, that means they know who you are," he said.

ADM. Other than CIA, KGB and Shin Bet, never have I seen initials conjure up so much fear. When I asked other friends in Washington about ADM, many of them went silent. "Don't ever mess with those guys," someone else echoed, as if I were planning a hostile takeover. "Somebody ought to nail those bastards."

I didn't know why anyone would want to "nail" ADM. To me they were a smart collection of farmers. What was the big deal?

GOVERNMENT-BACKED SUCCESS

"Did somebody dream there is some way that the government doesn't need us?"

Dwayne Andreas, *Mother Jones*, July/August 1995

On July 14, 1996, ADM's chief executive, Dwayne Andreas, appeared on the cover of the *Washington Post Magazine* against the backdrop of a chessboard. Andreas was depicted as the king with an oversized head, reminiscent of a *Star Trek* villain. In the distance, a chess piece lay on its side, vanquished, presumably by the guy with the big head. The story's title was "The Player: Dwayne Andreas and the American System." One did not have to be a Washington insider to get the point: Andreas was portrayed as a villain, secretly moving pawns around the chessboard to his advantage. The photo represented why people feared and disliked ADM: The company had too much power.

Andreas's adventures on magazine covers and in headlines were comparatively recent for the octogenarian. He had built an empire by conducting business discreetly. Whatever ADM had been doing to gain power and influence over the years, it worked. When Andreas took over ADM in 1966, it was a struggling regional agribusiness concern like many others. By 1980, the company's sales were $2.8 billion; by 1990, $7.7 billion. Today, sales are around $14 billion and the company refers to itself in advertisements as the "supermarket to the world."

Much of ADM's success is tied to government policies that provide a tax subsidy for ADM's corn-based fuel additive ethanol and price supports for sugar. The *Washington Post* reported that profits from these two policies yielded the company "40 percent of ADM's bottom line."

The U.S. Department of Agriculture's sugar program has been described as a "mini-OPEC." It regulates manufacturing and determines prices at a cost of $1.4 billion per year, says the General Accounting Office. ADM is in the corn sweetener business and has minimal direct interest in cane sugar. Its objective is to prevent soft drink manufacturers and other users of corn sweeteners from going back to using cane sugar.

The government provides a 54-cent-per-gallon credit to ethanol refiners. ADM manufactures between 60 and 80 percent of the ethanol in the United States, which means that the government contributes more than two billion dollars to the company. Writes *Mother Jones*'s Dan Carney, "No other subsidy in the federal government's box of goodies is so concentrated in the hands of a single company."

Andreas has done little to contradict perceptions of ADM's extraordinary power. He once said to *Mother Jones*, "We're the biggest [food and agricultural] company in the world. . . . How is the government going to run without people like us? We make 35 percent of the bread in this country, and that much of the margarine, and cooking oil, and all the other things."

According to Peter Carlson in the *Washington Post*, Andreas

chatted with Stalin, then sold the Soviets 150,000 tons of vegetable oil. He touted Franco on the glories of soybean oil. He took Castro to dinner in New York. LBJ called him down to his ranch. He bought Jimmy Carter's peanut warehouse. He rode on Air Force One with his friend Bill

Clinton to the funeral of his friend Richard Nixon. He sold his friends Bob
and Liddy Dole a condo in the high-rise in Bal Harbor, Fla., where they
work on their tans. . . . Such huge deals. Such high connections.

Former senator and presidential candidate Bob Dole owns a condominium that is managed by one of Andreas's companies. Other tenants of
this building have included former senator and White House chief-of-
staff Howard Baker, Speaker of the House Tip O'Neill, ABC newsman
David Brinkley (who became an ADM spokesman), and high-powered
Washington attorney Robert Strauss.

"He's like Zelig, the Woody Allen character who keeps popping up in
newsreels with the movers and shakers of the twentieth century," wrote
Carlson.

"WE DO NOT LOBBY"

"For more than two decades, Mr. Andreas has reigned as the prince of
political influence."

Wall Street Journal, July 11, 1995

At the 1992 Gridiron Dinner, one of the highlights of the Washington
social season, the leaders of the city's press corps were dressed in out-
landish costumes to parody the Washington establishment. At the head
table were President Bush, Secretary of State James Baker, Joint Chiefs
of Staff Chairman Colin Powell—and Andreas.

The *New York Times* once called Bob Dole "ADM's staunchest ally
on Capitol Hill," noting Dole's use of ADM's private plane. Andreas once
managed the late Hubert Humphrey's blind trust, financed the schooling
of one of his children, and gave $72,000 during the 1970s to Humphrey's
chief of staff. Andreas insisted to Carlson of the *Washington Post,* "We do
not lobby." The reason for Andreas's generosity, he says: "I just consider
it a part of good citizenship."

According to the Center for Responsive Politics, in the most recent
election cycle, Citizen ADM placed third among givers to the Democratic
party and first among givers to the Republican party.

James Bovard of the libertarian Cato Institute selected ADM as "A Case Study in Corporate Welfare" and "the nation's most arrogant welfare recipient." He reported: "At least 43 percent of ADM's annual profits are from products heavily subsidized or protected by the American government. Moreover, every $1 of profits earned by ADM's corn sweetener operation costs consumers $10, and every $1 of profits earned by its ethanol operation costs taxpayers $30."

TRIGGER FOR CASCADING ATTACKS

ADM's adversaries could complain all they wanted about the company's power, but it came off as being petty and self-serving. All of that changed on the evening of June 27, 1995, when the FBI raided ADM's Illinois office to gather evidence that ADM conspired to fix the prices of citric acid and lysine. ADM had gone into the $600-million-a-year lysine market a few years before the raid and, practically overnight, was producing two-thirds of the world's supply.

The FBI raid freed the company's once-timid critics. Within weeks, everybody, it seemed, had problem with ADM. "They are vulnerable," NatWest Securities analyst David Nelson told Bloomberg Business News when ADM paid its record-breaking fine. "Whenever there's blood, vultures circle."

Hostile coverage of ADM surged after the FBI raid. News of the government's price-fixing investigation opened a cascade of attacks on ADM in other areas. It became fair game all of a sudden to pillory ADM for its political influence, hardball business tactics, family-dominated management system, pollution woes, and shareholder revolts. Said Matt Aiello of the Council of Institutional Investors to the *Journal of Commerce*, "The makeup of the board—with seven of the directors related by blood or marriage—is comical."

Attack clusters began to assemble, including media on all ends of the political spectrum and think tanks of all political persuasions. Even former employees formed an Internet home page called "ADM Island," which, among other things lists fellow employees who died in workplace accidents.

Reported Bloomberg, "While it's only coincidence that ADM's chairman bears the name of California's famous fault line, the San Andreas Fault, the company's stock has ruptured and shareholders are feeling the aftershock." News of the antitrust investigation knocked $2 billion off of ADM's market capitalization in the days following the announcement. The company's misfortunes were not helped by ADM director F. Ross Johnson's abrasive comments about the government raid in a speech at Emory University. Johnson said that the FBI "have got some good scumbags in there, too—it's almost a criminal mentality."

As the attacks mounted, ADM was even linked to the granddaddy of all political conspiracies, Watergate. Reported *Mother Jones*, "In a recently released deposition, Richard Nixon's secretary, Rose Mary Woods, recalled a 1972 personal visit from Andreas in which he delivered an unmarked envelope containing $100,000 in $100 bills. The cash spent a year or so in a White House safe before Nixon, with the Watergate investigation closing in around him, decided to give it back."

In April 1996, ADM agreed to pay $25 million to settle one of the lawsuits by customers. In October of that year, the company agreed to pay $100 million and plead guilty to federal charges of price-fixing, the largest criminal antitrust fine in American history.

More than a dozen separate shareholder lawsuits were launched in association with the company's legal troubles. One shareholders group, the "ADM Shareholder Watch Committee" began sending threatening faxes to Andreas such as the following, which was reprinted in the *Washington Post*:

> Dwayne, relinquish the reins and jump from the chariot as you can't control the horses anymore. . . .
> Dwayne, you are the turkey, the government has your files, and the FBI has been recording your crime family for three years. . . .
> Dwayne, we hear you are in Bal Harbor. You do not need a change of climate, you need a change of soul. . . .

The hostilities caused a dramatic shake-up in the company's management, with Dwayne Andreas stepping down as CEO in April 1997.

UNBRIDLED SUCCESS

As with Michael Ovitz, the mystique surrounding ADM was filled with such sorcery that it is hard to separate truth from legend. In the same way Ovitz never single-handedly ran Hollywood, it's hard to believe all of the nefarious things attributed to ADM. Regardless, the news that came out after the FBI raid lent credence to longstanding whispers about ADM's venality.

Two entities didn't fear ADM at all: law enforcement and the news media, the only two categories of people I have ever known that actually *like* being threatened. Once the law and the media swung into action, the resentment toward ADM by competitors, customers, regulators, think tanks, and investigative reporters bubbled to the surface. While the law determined ADM's guilt, the visceral desire to see the company fall fueled the public attacks.

As the attacks took hold, even the company's "supermarket to the world" positioning became a liability. The underside of this slogan is the specter of domination by one company and, perhaps, even one man. "Supermarket to the world?" one of my young colleagues wondered aloud. "I guess that means we can't we get food from anybody else?" Once *schadenfreude* set in, the neighborly tag line became fodder for antagonism.

ADM did more things right than wrong over the years, especially building its political influence. ADM's active sponsorship of public affairs broadcasts and other civic activities were brilliant public relations efforts that certainly staved off attacks. For a while. ADM's error was mistaking its power with invincibility. Arrogant people believe they are smarter and stronger than everyone and can treat people like morons with impunity. When ADM did things like deny that it lobbied while simultaneously lobbying relentlessly, all bets were off. Andreas was asking the public to suspend belief. The public hates contradictions and being patronized. Americans equate stealth with evil. And there will always be somebody brave—or crazy—enough to take a shot at a big target.

Today, the supermarket to the world shares its aisles with an emboldened group of competitors.

THE DON WE DESERVE

"We only kill each other."
                    Benjamin "Bugsy" Siegel

"This is a huge mistake," I told Terry, a friend who worked in law enforcement. It was October 1986 and we were looking in amazement at an Andy Warhol–painted *Time* magazine cover of mob boss John Gotti. The silver-haired don stood purposefully in a precisely cut European suit and hand-painted tie. Warhol had worked his magic with quivering lines and colors that made the new boss look electric, as if he were stepping out of the magazine.

"I suppose you would have counseled Mr. Gotti against this photo opportunity," Terry asked me sarcastically.

"Hell, yes. Where I grew up, these guys stayed out of the press. If Andy Warhol ever showed up in South Jersey or Philly, they would have thrown him off a bridge."

A few years later, after multiple acquittals earned Gotti the nickname the "Teflon Don," Terry and I discussed his conviction and the public's enduring fascination with Gotti. He had finally been jailed for life for the murder of his boss and others. While I didn't doubt that the government had a strong case, I maintained, to Terry's horror, that a personal dislike for Gotti drove much of the law's obsession with getting him.

"I don't think he was innocent," I said. "All I'm saying is that had he not baited law enforcement, he might still be free. I'm raising a strategic issue, not a moral or legal one. There's a lesson here for a lot of people, not just wiseguys."

Terry, who, to my knowledge had no involvement in the Gotti case, laughed at my subversive thinking. "All right," he said, "Say that Gotti's successor had a sharp underworld crisis management consultant. The new boss asks him to prepare a memo on what went wrong for Gotti. What does it say?"

The proverbial memo follows.

Sir:

Per your request, I have prepared an analysis of what went wrong for your predecessor, Mr. Gotti. By understanding the mistakes made by the administration, it will help inoculate your organization ("the Borgata") against future attacks by law enforcement.

Outside of the Government's (the "G") disapproval of the Organization's practices, Mr. Gotti's greatest vulnerability was something called *schadenfreude*. It means that the G hated him personally and wanted to hurt him—respective and irrespective—of the Borgata's business practices.

By avoiding offensive behavior, I in no way guarantee you complete protection from the law. I do, however, believe that you will be able to avoid much of the scrutiny that engendered misfortune to Mr. Gotti and the Borgata.

Recommendation

Stay the hell out of the papers.

Discovery

Mr. Gotti's superstar status was launched by his Andy Warhol-painted *Time* magazine cover, nine months after the .38 caliber management succession program was implemented on the sidewalk outside Sparks Steak House. According to former New York FBI Chief Jules Bonavolonta in his memoir *The Good Guys*,

> The new Gambino family boss had captured the popular imagination. The don's suits, it was advertised, cost an easy $1,200 each, the shirts a few hundred a throw; ditto the ties. The TV cameras waited in ambush for guys like Mafia bosses on courthouse steps. Guys like Tony Ducks Corallo and Fat Tony Salerno had been powerful men, but they were gray figures, shunning the media spotlight, preferring dim haunts like the Palma Boy or some other dump with ripped Naugahyde seating. . . . Not so Gotti.

Coronation

In the early years of Mr. Gotti's reign he habitually beat the law. He was acquitted of numerous crimes, even though there were allegations that he corrupted jurors and embarrassed hostile witnesses. You may recall one witness against Mr. Gotti suffered a memory lapse as he took the stand, which led the *New York Post* to run with the winning headline "I FORGOTTI."

Mr. Gotti became law enforcement's mythical "white whale," an elusive creature who kept getting away and splashing debris on the authorities to boot. "Three to one I beat the case," he challenged the G. The authorities resented how they were looking in the publicity game, getting out-spinned by Mr. Gotti. Writes the FBI's Bonavolonta,

> After each of Gotti's two acquittals, the news media had talked end-lessly about how Gotti had beaten "the government." In that context, I thought, any reference to the government translated immediately to the FBI, and to be perfectly blunt about it, I was getting goddamned sick and tired of being asked why "we" had lost to John Gotti not once but twice.

Flaw Detection

The G wanted Mr. Gotti so badly that they made an extraordinary deal with the Borgata's former chief operating officer, Sammy "The Bull" Gravano, who violated the blood oath of *omerta* and "ratted" on Mr. Gotti and others. In exchange for the Bull's testimony against Mr. Gotti, the Bull, who confessed to participating in nineteen murders, was released after spending five years in prison. The Bull recounted for author Peter Maas Mr. Gotti's preoccupation with his public image, an unusual strategic concern for a man in his occupation:

> He don't want to hear the truth. He's not looking for it. He's looking for people to say what he wants to hear. Not only was the media having a love affair with him, he was having it with himself. He was always talking about his "public." He was completely and totally in love with himself.

The Bull said that Mr. Gotti's penchant for publicity aroused the ire of the Borgata's old timers. "It wasn't the life," the Bull said. "John didn't realize this was going to blow up in his face." Mr. Gotti felt sufficiently invincible that he spoke freely of his activities within earshot of the G's listening devices.

Despite the Borgata's displeasure with the Bull, we must respectfully agree with his analysis. For what strategic business reason did Mr. Gotti need a "public"? None that would benefit the Borgata.

Your predecessor was stage-managed to fit the media age and provoke *schadenfreude*. He was attractive, glib, charismatic, and always had a better cast of characters within camera shot than Martin Scorcese. This is fine for the movies but not real life. We recommend against behavior that leads to books entitled *Mob Star* and a "tribute" home page on the Internet.

Schadenfreude is so powerful that it overwhelmed the G's better judgment and freed a man who was, perhaps, more dangerous than Mr. Gotti. Wrote DeWayne Wickham in *USA Today* of the Bull:

> For what he did, Gravano got off easy. Afterward, he went into the witness protection program for a time before deciding he could do a better job protecting himself. That decision was made easy by the money Gravano's bad deeds have brought him. . . . Sure, Gravano's testimony put Gotti away for life. But what we're talking about here is a man who killed 19 people delivering up to justice one who whacked five.

The Bull admitted in court that he received $250,000 for a book about his life titled *Underboss*. He is also expected to earn $1 million on a movie deal. The families of those whom the Bull admits to having murdered are unable to get close enough to him to serve him with legal papers in the wrongful death cases they are pursuing against him.

Humiliation

The Borgata is rapidly succumbing to traditional American impulses, primarily the need to be noticed no matter what the cost. We respectfully remind you that your business practices are not, in fact, legal. There is no need for a coronation. Visibility is more dangerous than a band of assassins.

As Michael Corleone said in *The Godfather*, "Try to think as people around you think and on that basis, anything's possible." This wisdom applies in legitimate enterprise, too.

To the thinking of our culture, arrogant displays of power, money, and good fortune are offensive. Even if they are perfectly legal.

In closing, sir, we encourage you to appreciate the power of others. Mr. Gotti baited people with more power, in his case the G. As you know, Mr. Gotti will die in prison. In this life, there is no "boss of bosses." There are *lots* of bosses, including ones that can take you down. This is the essence of *schadenfreude*.

SOME LESSONS OF SCHADENFREUDE

"If anything in this life is certain, if history has taught us anything, it's that you can kill anyone."

Michael Corleone, *The Godfather, Part II*

The public thrives on negative information about celebrated people and things because of their exquisite sensitivity as to where they rank. Most of those who become attackers would like to move up, but if they can't, moving others *down* is the best option.

Schadenfreude allows us to achieve parity with those who pose as our superiors. "If *we* are so weak," we reason, "then why was I able to knock *you* down?"

Attacks rarely succeed on spite alone. There are usually other factors at work. *Schadenfreude* is the beacon that draws attention to a target. What the attackers actually find depends upon what the target has done and how hostile the culture is feeling. This leads to confused emotions such as the hatred for Kathie Lee Gifford and the vocal public support in New York for John Gotti. One would think perkiness and murder were equal crimes.

As the parade of attacks, deserved or not, roll on, look out for the common threads that link who (and what) becomes a target of *schadenfreude*-driven attacks.

The public doesn't like self-appointed monarchs

At the root of many *schadenfreude*-based attacks is a sense of democracy. Americans don't like people—or things—who come out of nowhere and claim to be king. They don't accept the king-as-arriviste because in a democracy, everybody's supposedly equal.

Americans love royalty as long as it is distant and illusory. The nation pines for handsome *assassinated* presidents like John F. Kennedy and adores *tragic* and *deceased* princesses like Diana. The nation fawns over *untouchable* and *mysterious* former first ladies like Jacqueline Onassis. We lionize aloof actresses like Grace Kelly who found her royal blood in a *faraway* country.

True royalty does not pose, dominate ostentatiously, or show ambition. Real kings don't "mastermind" things, they just rule. True royalty just is. Whenever someone gets too close to setting up a throne in America, attacks are set in motion.

The public doesn't differentiate between mystery and malfeasance

In the Culture of Attack, suspense convicts, not guilt. If the public cannot see how something was done, it assumes that act was done illicitly. Americans believe that what they don't know *will* hurt them. Those who evoked *schadenfreude* often sent signals that they might be hiding something. Perceived concealment is distressing.

Americans want to see what's behind the proverbial door number one and reject the concept of privacy as an excuse for not being able to see it. The public wants to see Kathie Lee Gifford's flawed marriage. It wants to see how Archer Daniels Midland's political wizard Dwayne Andreas got Congress to vote his way for decades. They want drug companies to prove that no one who ever took its drug ever showed a side effect.

The public hates contradictions

People want a straight answer and are ruthless about getting one. When recycling is held out as a panacea and then shows signs of failing, consumers are confused. Is recycling an environmental solution or not? Does recycling improve the environment or is it a touchy-feely con-job? "Gray areas" are unacceptable. Americans despise dissonance and want to love something or hate it. In the Culture of Attack, one way to tear something down is to draw attention to its contradictions. Conflict resonates.

Sometimes, miracle people and products provoke conflict by failing. When Hollywood agent Michael Ovitz failed to close a deal for the top job at entertainment giant MCA, folks in show business began questioning whether he was "the most powerful man in Hollywood," as had been repeated in the media for years. The media wanted to report on the most powerful man in Hollywood, not someone who might be.

When someone waffles (or is waffled), it makes the public anxious and justifies resentment. When the truth isn't clear, attackers will exploit a jittery audience.

Don't bullshit people

The public prides itself on being able to ferret out false information. Americans think they're good at it, and like playing the role of the detective who cannot be fooled.

Many Americans felt that Kathie Lee Gifford's portrayal of life was not realistic. The idea of an aging married couple like the Giffords lusting after one another sets off alarm bells. Most lives are imperfect, so Kathie Lee must have a secret down there somewhere. So when the tabloids went out looking for it, they knew their readers would pay for the evidence. Contrast Gifford with the late Erma Bombeck, whose open acknowledgement of the trials of domestic life made her a beloved figure to millions.

When the public is told that the stuff they put out at the curb didn't get recycled because it wasn't cost-effective, they're furious at the broken promise. The idea behind recycling was to purify the masses. Then everyone's told that *cost* plays into it. This wasn't part of the bargain, so recycling was spurned.

When Donald Trump ran into financial difficulties, many people loved seeing a rich man with money trouble. Talk about Trump was peppered with references to the huge head start he was given by his father, a rich developer. It was as if Trump had concealed his father and grizzled journalists unearthed a terrible secret. Trump had never denied his father. His voracious self-promotion, however, implied that he had been dishonest about how he *really* perfected the "art of the deal." "If I had such a father," I heard from more than one friend, "I'd have my name on buildings, too."

Nobody likes a monopoly

Monopolies are always assumed to be sinister. Americans want to hurt anyone or anything that appears to hold undue sway over the marketplace. This is true of businesses such as Microsoft and Archer Daniels Midland; individuals such as Bill Gates and Michael Ovitz; and even outlaws such as John Gotti, who was positioned as towering over New York's multibillion-dollar crime syndicate.

Many of my clients have been attacked because people believe they had too much power. Eli the developer was one of them. Some of them have been grossly overestimated, however, their high public profile provoked suspicions that they were getting away with something.

Resentment-driven attacks work in cycles

All people and things that ride high do so at the pleasure of the culture. Applause is fleeting. Those who enjoy a good run often fail to realize that it's temporary. Fame and fortune say more about the public's state of mind than the objects of adulation. Americans are fickle and when they sense that a target has forgotten who put them on a pedestal, they'll be receptive to attackers who will knock it over. The aggrieved feel that powerful people, popular items, and trendy ideas are the source of their adversity. Attacks against powerful players serve as a catharsis for everyone who ever felt abused by anything or anyone.

A big shot riding high gets in trouble when he believes that the outside world feels the same way about him as he does about himself. People and organizations become accomplices in their own *schadenfreude*-based attacks when they attribute their success solely to themselves and not the wave that carried them.

Fear has its limitations

Targets of *schadenfreude* overestimate their power. They assume they are widely feared and that no one will cross them. Many of my clients have wrongly assumed employees won't leak information, rivals won't sue them, and that there will be some things that the media won't ever find out. They confuse the power they wield in their organizations with power they wield in the universe. Fear is a bad insurance policy. Presidents are voted out of office, dictators are overthrown, gangsters are "ratted out" by underlings, and seasoned prizefighters are knocked out by newcomers.

The flip-side of fear is the anger at feeling helplessness and at those who caused it. Incapacity is dehumanizing, it makes people feel worthless. When helplessness collides with a clean shot at a perceived oppressor, an attacker will emerge.

Guerrillas have nothing to lose

The haves don't possess the control over the country's institutions that they once did. If harassed, a person of means could alert the constable, who would see to it that the offending party was carted off. In the Culture of Attack, the mighty no longer control the courts and they certainly don't control the media and the Internet.

Big shots and businesses ignore the seemingly powerless at their peril. Twenty-two-year-old reporters routinely humiliate sixty-year-old CEOs. A presidency can be put in jeopardy by a bitter functionary with a tape recorder. The Culture of Attack is the perfect democracy where grievances by the weak can be used as weapons against the mighty.

Public "scoreboards" are the kiss of death

When an object's status is easily measured publicly, attackers will regard any non–upward movement as failure. When Mike Ovitz moved from first to second place on the meaningless Power List, this was interpreted as being significant. When the impotence pill Viagra prescriptions dropped slightly a few weeks after its blockbuster introduction, the media characterized the drop along with reports of deadly side effects. Those who live by the scoreboard will die by the scoreboard, especially if they promoted their victory too heavily.

Whether sparked by *schadenfreude* or another catalyst, the motives for attack are age-old; the means, however, are novel. The proliferation of attack vehicles such as the Internet and upstart television networks has occured at such a staggering pace, it is often impossible to identify the originators of a grievance. The growth of the Internet—and the news media's reliance on it—renders the means of attack the most remarkable feature distinguishing our times with past hostile eras.

11. *The Internet/Media Attack Combination*

The Internet and mass media have unleashed an invisible army of attackers.

"Nemo me impune lacessit (No one strikes me with impunity)."
Monstressor family credo in
Edgar Allen Poe's "The Cask of Amontillado."

VIRTUAL MENDACITY

Even crisis managers have vulnerabilities. I'm one of those English major–types who gets near a computer and makes it short circuit. Or maybe it's me who short circuits. With the support of a few smart (and patient) people, I can now get onto the Internet. If I can, anyone can. Therein lies the danger.

There has never been a lack of hostile people with a motive to attack. Aggression is as old as Cain and Abel. Until recently, very few people had the *means* or the *opportunity.* The geometric growth of the Internet has provided attackers with these last two ingredients.

One result of the Internet's growth has been an upsurge of attacks against people, products, and institutions that can be launched anonymously and, therefore, with impunity. Fake names and addresses easily conceal the true identity of the user. The Internet thus allows anyone to make fun of Mike Tyson's lisp from the safety of his own den, something he would never do if he saw Tyson on the street. The Internet caught Americans flatfooted, including the traditional media. Just when I thought I had my clients well versed in how attackers manipulate the press, along comes the Net and a stinging swarm of allegations and agendas. The emergence of the Internet and guerrilla journalism has raised the stakes.

The Internet makes anyone with a modem a reporter, a profession once held in such high esteem that it was Superman's day job. Clark Kent confirmed facts before publishing them. The pursuit of truth was the value-added—and moral—service that made news different from gossip. Global competition and the proliferation of scores of cable networks has made getting information *first* more important than getting information *right.*

In an era when technology is supposed to make our lives better, how can this be?

As with other features of the Culture of Attack, a schism divides American's romantic notions of our morally enhanced lives from the hard truth that advancements haven't made human beings more civilized. The Internet is a Dodge City of information. Because these forums are broadcast using the written word, the worst drivel can look, well, intellectual.

Computers offer us the appearance of journalism without the hard work. Edward Tenner wrote in *Why Things Bite Back: Technology and the Revenge of Unintended Consequences,* "Culturally we use graphics as a proxy for authority." Anyone can set up a web page and make it look like an official publication. Graphics *look* credible. Many Internet users figure that if someone took the time to set up *all this,* it must have been verified, as with traditional media.

The Internet is an attacker's jubilee. It is estimated that 60 million people are "on-line." There are more than 50,000 news groups, where people can discuss issues ranging from useful support groups for medical problems to Elvis sightings at quick service restaurants. The identities, however, are never clear as to who sets up these chat rooms and who contributes to them.

Hundreds of new "home pages" come on-line every day. Home pages are forums that are sponsored by people and institutions that have a message they want to get out. Many home pages identify their sponsors. Others do not. Either way, home pages allow people to traffic in allegation without confirming the source of their information because there is no journalistic imperative to verify computerized information the way there is with the print and broadcast media.

The Internet gives an attack the appearance of momentum because seeing an allegation "in print" makes it seem genuine and can give the illusion of multiple victims. In early 1999, an attack was launched against one of my client's sanitary products when *one* anonymous person e-mailed thousands of media outlets about an adverse reaction. When I asked a television reporter how he could justify running a story critical of my client's product, he pointed to "all of the Internet activity." There had, in fact, been a lot of Internet activity, but it had been launched by one individual whom we could never identify. We suspected the perpetrator was linked to my client's competitor, but could never prove it. The Internet had left us with no one to question or sue for defamation.

THE YENTA QUOTIENT

Allegations move faster than they can be qualified and ricochet among different media. Attackers see the Internet as an access road to the mass media. If they can place their agendas on-line, hostile information can migrate to the networks and prestige newspapers. I call the jump from the Internet to the mass media the "Yenta quotient," after *Fiddler on the Roof*'s matchmaker who always had her nose in everybody's business. Yenta wasn't evil, she just shlepped around the village spreading her version of events. She was a pogrom-era modem who always found other villagers to share gossip with. Similarly, when gossip jumps from the Internet to the mainstream media, it isn't always done out of malice; it's often done because audiences find the information titillating.

Reporters use the Internet as a resource, which has a catalytic effect on the speed and reach of information. Whereas Yenta was limited in the number of people she could gossip with because she was one person, the

Internet and media can reach an unlimited number of villagers. If a network program is doing a story about pretzel hazards, they can type in the words "pretzels + choking" and find numerous sites that deal with the subject. Using this method, they are likely to find potential talk show guests who will be happy to comment on their violent encounters with pretzels.

More and more consumers are getting their news *directly* from the Internet. According to the Pew Research Center for People and the Press, in 1995, 14 percent of Americans retrieved news regularly from the Internet. Today, 36 percent do.

The *Washington Post*'s Joel Achenbach writes that "say-so" is the "weakest form of evidence," but that it can have a powerful effect. He cites Pierre Salinger and the TWA Flight 800 missile rumor (alleging that the U.S. military had accidentally downed the plane with a missile), which began on the Internet but migrated to the mainstream media:

> Salinger was not actually a source of information, but rather a medium for fourth-hand rumor. So here's the information flow: Dan Rather on the *CBS Evening News* reports what Pierre Salinger said in a speech in southern France about a document written by a person in the United States whom Salinger has never met but who, Salinger has been told by an unnamed French intelligent agent, has "strong contacts" with someone, or something, in the Navy. Through this tortuous route travels information so shocking, so horrible—the Navy shooting down a jet-liner!—that you might find it implausible and extremely difficult to believe even if you saw it with your own eyes. Yet there it is on the nightly news.

Around the time of Salinger's folly, the magazine *George* reported a survey showing that 41 percent of the American public believe the government is suppressing the truth about TWA Flight 800. The FBI eventually ruled out terrorism.

Hollywood moguls live in mortal terror of a young Austin, Texas, computer whiz named Harry Knowles who breaks his "AIN'T IT COOL NEWS" about the entertainment business to millions of readers on-line. Using gossip sources throughout Hollywood, Knowles reported on the negative buzz about the movie *Batman and Robin,* including talk of reshoots and internal squabbles among the stars. Other media picked up on Knowles's "coverage," which led some at the studio producing *Batman and Robin* to blame him for the film's box office failure.

NO RECOURSE

Traditional media—newspapers, TV, and radio—live by anonymous sources and leaks: information shared discreetly. The "leaker" hopes he will remain anonymous. Most journalists will either have a good reason to trust the source, or will confirm the source's information using other contacts. If the information turns out to be spurious, the attacker will probably lose his relationship with the reporter. No reporter who signs his name to a story wants to be associated with bad information. As a consequence, the more unscrupulous attackers will avoid going to respectable media in the first place.

This is where the Internet comes in. The Internet provides no filter. An attacker can say what he pleases without being held accountable largely because Internet libel law is still being defined. When a client is attacked, the anonymity of the Internet makes it very difficult to supply cyber gossips with correct information. Where will I send it? Internet attackers rarely leave a return address. With a traditional media attack, I know whom to call. The Internet provides little or no recourse. Even if I can "post" a correction or explanation, the chances are that anyone who received the bogus or hostile information has already made up his mind.

THE DRUDGE REPORT

> "You ought to have at least some standards of decency and some standards of fairness! That's what I object to."
> Jack Nelson of the *Los Angeles Times* to Matt Drudge on CNN

No one is more symbolic of the rise of Internet "news" than Matt Drudge. His "Drudge Report" gets over 200,000 "hits" a day and is growing exponentially each month. Drudge cross-pollinates his media profile by appearing on public affairs shows such as *Meet the Press* along with traditional journalists. At this writing, he is in negotiations to get his own television show on the Fox network.

In the quintessential Yenta quotient attack, Drudge triggered Bill Clinton's Monica Lewinsky scandal by reporting on an impending *Newsweek* story on the subject. In other words, Drudge launched a presidential crisis by announcing that someone else had a hot story, thereby prompting others to report on the scandal before the actual story had been verified.

Commenting on Drudge in the *Washington Post*, Howard Kurtz remarked, "the Internet has turned anyone with a mouth and a modem into global publisher, enabling lone rangers like Drudge to shout their way into the marketplace."

Drudge insulates himself from libel by claiming that his reports are 80 percent accurate. He isn't completely protected, though. When Clinton aide Sidney Blumenthal began his White House job in 1997, Drudge falsely reported that Blumenthal "has a spousal abuse past that has been effectively covered up." There were references to "court records" that supposedly bore this out. There weren't any court records. Drudge swiftly apologized. Blumenthal still sued. The court case is pending. Drudge acknowledged, "This is a case of using me to broadcast dirty laundry. I think I've been had."

The mainstream media's obsession with Drudge wrongly positions him as *the* problem with Internet information. While a flashy personality, he is unique in that he has *some* accountability. His name is on his report. There are thousands of invisible—and unaccountable—Matt Drudges out there propagating attacks that don't appear on talk shows. These are the phantom attackers I fight. Often, the best I can do is broadly characterize my client's position in the mainstream media (through interviews and public statements) that they have been victims of an Internet hoax.

WITNESSES AND DISAPPEARING DRESSES

The scandal broke about President Clinton and Monica Lewinsky on a Monday. On Tuesday morning, Ellen, a reporter friend covering the story for a national newspaper, called me. She had been on-line reading the latest allegations that were supposedly going to be published on the Web sites of major media and was trying to get a perspective on the crisis from independent "spin doctors." I winced at the job description, but offered my handicap anyway.

I told Ellen how, in my cases, I often find initial allegations to be false. I urged her to be careful before trafficking in the chestnuts of gossip.

"Are you insane?" Ellen said. "The guy's toast."

"You're reading the story wrong. People need this scandal too much. That's what's bothering me, not Clinton's innocence. Even my most guilty clients don't do nine-tenths of the things they're accused of."

"Right, but this is Clinton."

"There's a lot of bullshit ping-ponging from the Internet to the media. People are already regarding this stuff as historical fact. Clinton may be guilty in the end, but be careful what you run with."

The *Dallas Morning News*'s Internet site reported on January 25, 1998, that a Secret Service agent was about to come forward as a witness to a Clinton-Lewinsky liaison. The rest of the media, including national wire services, reported the Dallas paper's impending story. The paper then retracted its Internet story on-line saying that its source, "a longtime Washington lawyer familiar with the case, later said the information provided for the report was inaccurate."

Before anyone had time to verify the rumor's validity, major media passed along the witness story as fact, including twin headlines in the *New York Post* and *Daily News* on January 26, 1998, reading "CAUGHT IN THE ACT."

The *New York Times* did not run its story on the rumored witness. Said *Times* Executive Editor Joseph Lelyveld, "We worked very hard on this story and in the end we weren't sure what was true." Today, these acts of restraint are practically extinct.

The *Wall Street Journal*'s Internet site reported that a White House steward told a grand jury that he saw Clinton and Lewinsky together. The *Journal*'s wire service then picked up the story. The steward's lawyer said the report was "absolutely false and irresponsible." It probably was. Said White House spokesman Joe Lockhart, "The normal rules of checking or getting a response to a story seem to have given way to the technology of the Internet and the competitive pressure of getting it first." When asked why it ran so quickly with the steward story, the *Journal* reporter said, "We heard footsteps from at least one other news organization and just didn't think it was going to hold in this crazy cycle we're in." In other words, they had to "break" the story before a competitor did.

"Years ago, people lost their jobs for things like this," Ellen told me later in a phone call.

"Years ago," I said, "this stuff didn't get printed in the first place."

The media self-flagellated about accuracy, and the same Americans who claimed to be "sick and tired" of the scandal increased their use of media Internet sites about 30 percent, according to CNN.

I don't interpret any of these events to mean that Clinton is innocent of the broader allegations—that he had sex (of some kind) with Lewinsky and tried to cover up their relationship. I do, however, believe that the media needed tangible nuggets of information to anchor their story and, at one point, didn't have any. In desperation, they reached down to gossipers on the Internet. In the Clinton case, many of the gossips turned out to be right. With my less-famous clients, however, the gossips are almost always wrong.

Hillary Rodham Clinton, in a powerful series of interviews, attributed the allegations against her husband to a right-wing "conspiracy." I don't buy it. Clinton haters would love to destroy him, but conspiracies don't work. They're too big and require too much precision.

I suspect that the Lewinsky affair was launched by a few Clinton haters aided by the means to communicate and a salivating marketplace. This marketplace included news junkies, Internet hacks, and random folks with dreams of being players "in the know." Some of these people were malicious. Many are not. The attackers gambled that Clinton's reputation was sufficiently bad—and well-deserved—that anything validating his image would be embraced, true or not. The sheer quantity of gossip, ranging from Clinton's alleged liaisons with movie stars to dubious tours of Air Force One, were enough to make the Yenta quotient leap from cyberspace to network television.

Crises aggravated by the Yenta quotient are harder to manage than conspiracies. When I find conspiracies against my clients, I can—and will—expose them because they are concentrated and because the perpetrators are guilty. Reality doesn't hold many cabals. What I usually find are a mix of players who benefit from the same story line—a dress with a presidential stain or a product with a terrible, but unverifiable flaw. All that's needed is:

1. a motivated adversary with an agenda;
2. a public hungry for a nasty scoop;
3. media that want to deliver it; and
4. a fertile Internet and media where the seed can be discreetly—or anonymously—planted.

The Yenta quotient has also converted minor business problems into serious crises. In 1994, a professor reported a calculating flaw in Intel's Pentium chip on an on-line newsgroup. Within days, the flaw—which would have surfaced only in highly complex calculations done by scientists and mathematicians—was positioned as a broad-based consumer crisis because of the sheer volume of unedited on-line discussion. Intel's stock tumbled when the news migrated to the mainstream media. Intel offered to replace the chips of concerned customers. The company's stock swiftly recovered.

In 1993, the Internet was replete with a smear alleging that the national fast food chain Church's Fried Chicken cooked its food in a batter that sterilized black men. (Of course it didn't.) During the same time period, anonymous attackers charged that the hugely successful beverage company Snapple was controlled by the Ku Klux Klan. "Evidence" cited included the appearance of the letter "K" and slave ships on Snapple's label. In reality, the "K" meant "kosher," and the "slave ships" were a rendering of the Boston Tea Party. Both the Church's and the Snapple smears bounced back and forth between the Internet and mass media, forcing the companies to respond formally to these horrible charges.

FLAMING

"Flaming" is the cyberspace term for vicious attacks and unfounded rumors. Some recent Internet flamings include the following:

Attack Summary: Tommy Hilfiger—1997

Victim:	Minorities
Villain:	Tommy Hilfiger
Vindicator:	Unknown
Void:	Concerns about bigotry
Vehicle:	Internet
Value:	Exposing prejudice

- Popular fashion designer Tommy Hilfiger was accused of making racist statements on *Oprah*. He never appeared on the show, and never made those statements. In fact, he markets extensively to minorities and has been one of the most diversity-conscious designers on the scene today. Nevertheless, the attack received widespread mass media coverage.

- A widely posted warning on newsgroups cautioned against using Microsoft's home page and Internet explorer alleging that the "Microsoft home page is possibly infected by a virus." They weren't.

- Database service Lexis-Nexis was accused of marketing the Social Security numbers of private citizens at a profit. It wasn't. The company was forced to respond to numerous angry inquiries and was tarnished with the stigma of being untrustworthy.

- Mrs. Field's Cookies was blasted by anti-domestic violence activists for shipping free products to O. J. Simpson for his acquittal party. A boycott was launched and Mrs. Field's recorded a single-digit drop in sales in a matter of days. The free shipments never happened.

- Nike was hurt shortly before a recent annual meeting by a false rumor that workers died in its Chinese factories due to hazardous conditions.

- Within minutes of Princess Diana's death in an auto accident, Web sites appeared alleging a murder plot and listing the "beneficiaries" of her death. These beneficiaries included the British royal family and American defense contractors concerned about Diana's crusade against land mines.

- McDonald's routinely battles on-line rumors about allegedly unsavory things that wind up in its beef. The company has long contended with similar rumors, but the Internet has aggravated their circulation exponentially.

- CBS's *60 Minutes* was said to have paid the operator of international sex "junkets" tens of thousands of dollars for an interview. They didn't.

No one knows where most of these flamings originated.

FROM "KEYWORD" TO THE KLAN

Getwell Hospital* was controlled by white supremacist "skinheads." All right, not really, but that's what Mrs. Stone saw on-line. Someone claimed to have heard a Getwell executive bragging that the hospital funneled money to hate groups and treated minorities differently from Caucasian patients. Mrs. Stone, who was active in anti-bigotry causes, became concerned. She forwarded the e-mail to her contacts at hate watchdog groups. Little happened until an audiotape emerged of a Texaco executive allegedly making racist remarks. The high-profile Texaco case, which featured protests from Jesse Jackson, sucked Getwell Hospital into its vortex.

The media had become interested in all things hateful. A radio broadcaster came upon the Getwell allegation after typing "racism" in the "Keyword" space on his Internet browser. He repeated it in the context of how bigotry and groups like the Klan had become mainstream. The racism claim was covered on radio and TV. Soon after, churches and civic organizations cited the hospital as a facility to avoid. Protests were held outside of the hospital and business dropped off sharply.

---

*This is a fictitious name.

Getwell had its public relations firm on the case. News releases were written, denials issued, and information posted on the Internet, all appropriate actions. But the onslaught didn't stop.

My firm was retained. Based on existing evidence, we didn't think it was likely that we would find the perpetrators of the flaming and we ruled out a covert operation to find them. We agreed that the best approach was to have a chilling effect on the speed of information shooting around the Internet and media. Our strategy was to gain short-term attention characterizing the smear as a premeditated hoax.

We initiated a private investigation, alerted law enforcement, and publicized both of these things. If we were really interested in learning something, we wouldn't have publicized our investigation because it would have driven the attackers underground. In this case, we wanted the attackers to know they were personally—and criminally—at risk.

At the same time, we put a full-court press on the activist Mrs. Stone, whom we had determined to be a pivotal—but unwitting—mark in the hoax. Mrs. Stone, an intelligent woman, became convinced that Getwell Hospital was not racist or anti-Semitic. She was instrumental in getting hate-watching organizations to repudiate the Getwell rumors.

Our damage control was good but not perfect. We determined that the smear probably originated from a university, but that was all. We could not tie it to a competitor, but suspected either a competitor or a disgruntled former patient. The involvement of law enforcement had a chilling effect on the attackers, but the bad seed had already been planted. The pace of bogus e-mails fell off. Getwell Hospital's revenues are climbing back slowly. They are down about 20 percent from where they were prior to the flaming.

Said Getwell's CEO on a conference call a few months later, "An African American woman who's been going to my church for years looked at me differently after the service. She usually had a big smile when she saw me. Not anymore."

The Internet is, at its worst, a launch pad for attacks. More often, it is a vehicle for trafficking in inaccurate or hostile information where it's hard to distinguish between an attacker and a busybody. Nevertheless, the effect is damaging. The Internet enables attackers to disseminate hostile and inaccurate information without feeling the psychic heat and consequences associated with launching them. Attackers understand this and allow the heartland to be passive consumers, as opposed to active attackers. Audiences can say: *"All I did was turn on the TV. I can't help what they put on,"* or *"All I did was log on. I can't help what they say."*

It took me years to figure it out, but the Internet has taught me one thing for sure: "They" are, in the end, everyone who logs on. Complicating matters is the culture's active desire to believe the allegations that ricochet across media, if only for their amusement value.

12. *Alleging Is Believing*

***An allegation is the Saturday Night Special
of the information-age.***

"For people who like this sort of thing, this is the sort of thing they will like."

Abraham Lincoln

DOG DAYS OF ALLEGATION

Fifteen years before the name "Monica Lewinsky" became front-page news due to her relationship with Bill Clinton, there was another presidential sex scandal involving supposedly taped shenanigans. I got a good sampling of it as a young and bewildered White House aide monitoring media coverage of this breaking news. It forever changed the way I look at allegations.

On July 11, 1983, a Los Angeles lawyer named Robert Steinberg claimed to have a forty-minute videotape of important Reagan administration officials cavorting *in flagrante delicto.* Steinberg told the media about the kinky sex tapes four days after Vicki Morgan, long-time mistress to Reagan friend Alfred Bloomingdale, was beaten to death. Morgan and Bloomingdale were among those who were supposedly on the tapes.

169

I vaguely remember an allegation that somebody on the tape was being made to bark like a dog.

The going theory was that Morgan was killed because she was holding the tapes as blackmail insurance against some heavy hitters, including top Reagan aides. Washington was riveted to the sex tapes story. I was riveted and terrified. I had visions of the administration collapsing and, more importantly, my being out of a prestigious job. Who was on the tape? I speculated aloud. And were any familiar personalities among the barking?

The following day, after being pressed for the tapes, Steinberg had a new announcement: The sex tapes had vanished from his office. Stolen presumably. The thieves must have been awfully cunning. One Reagan-hating friend of mine suggested during a walk through Georgetown that only the CIA's Bill Casey could have pulled something like that off.

Despite the gasps and innuendo, a crisis had been averted probably because there had never been one. Later, Steinberg pleaded "no contest" to a misdemeanor contempt charge for falsely reporting the theft of the sex tapes. Morgan's roommate, Marvin Pancoast, was ultimately convicted of Vicki Morgan's murder (Pancoast, according to his lawyers, had apparently once confessed to the Manson murders).

When all of this came out I felt like an ass. Because of my interoffice speculation at who might have been on the sex tape, one of my bosses took to barking when he saw me. No matter how I try to rationalize it, it came down to this: I was young, gullible, and had been taken in by a sharp lawyer with a flashy allegation. Some of my colleagues and friends were snookered, too.

Some allegations turn out to be true, of course, but more than ever these days, they're not. And people get hurt.

The allegation is to crisis management what the Saturday Night Special handgun is to street crime: cheap, easy to come by, ubiquitous, hard to trace, deadly, and you don't have to be very skilled to use it. The single biggest factor in the growth of my firm's business has been the allegation explosion. The thing about consumers of allegation is that we're not stupid people. We're pretty well educated and rational. This is the problem.

GRIEF AND ANGER AS THE BASIS FOR ALLEGATION

In January 21, 1993, a decade after the Bloomingdale-Morgan sex tapes allegations, I was watching *Larry King Live* in my study. King's guest was a man named David Reynard. I had never heard of him. Reynard's wife, for whom he had bought a cellular—or wireless—telephone several years earlier, had recently died from a brain tumor. The tumor had grown in the area near where she had held the phone next to her ear. Reynard announced his lawsuit against the telephone's manufacturer alleging that its electromagnetic waves had caused his wife's illness.

Attack Summary: Cellular Telephones—Winter/Spring 1993

Victim:	Reynard family, cellular telephone users
Villain:	Cellular telephone manufacturers
Vindicator:	David Reynard
Void:	Explanation for wife's fatal illness
Vehicle:	*Larry King Live*
Value:	Consumer protection

I watched the program from two perspectives. One was that of "The Crisis Guy," the hard-nosed troubleshooter and communications trauma surgeon. The other was that of an inner character I call "The Worrier," a health conscious user of wireless telephones who lost a parent at a young age to cancer. Like others who lived through this misfortune, I was—and remain—conscious of cancer news, especially when the chances of getting sick are associated with a behavior that I practice. In this case, I viewed my behavior—using wireless phones—as a necessity. People in my business get fired for not being reachable anywhere, anytime.

Normally, I look at scare news skeptically. I am inclined to dislike the attacker. David Reynard's appearance was different, though. He shook me. It couldn't have been his evidence that upset me because I can't remember any. Nevertheless, The Worrier was dueling with The Crisis Guy. The Worrier was winning, and thinking about giving up his phone.

Of all people, I should know better than to panic before having the facts, I thought. How could I tell my clients that I planned to stop using my phone and that they wouldn't be able to reach me twenty-four hours a day like I had once promised? The wireless phone people were losing me. How would they get me back?

THE SPRINGBOARD FOR ALLEGATION

Sales of wireless telephones had been growing exponentially at the time of Reynard's allegation. The phones had gone from being an urban status symbol to being an everyday appliance. Immediately following Reynard's appearance on *Larry King Live,* sales dropped sharply. Motorola, the largest manufacturer of wireless telephones, saw its stock drop about 20 percent in a matter of days, reported the *New York Times*. Other manufacturers experienced similar losses.

The major media instantly picked up where Larry King left off, including interviews with people who, like Reynard, *believed* that their use of wireless phones had given them cancer. Allegations about the phones were aggravated by the recent deaths of Republican operative Lee Atwater and tycoon Reginald Lewis of brain cancer. Both had been users of cellular phones.

Within days, the scare had become so bad that entrepreneurs hustled a shield onto the market claiming it protected consumers from electromagnetic waves. Congress held special hearings and, while government responses were measured, a Food and Drug Administration official suggested that consumers "pay attention to their usage." Network TV news doctors such as Dr. Tim Johnson echoed this caution.

The Crisis Guy in me understood one reason why the scare moved so quickly. It was because of where Reynard launched it. Larry King has a huge national following. In an age of gratuitously hostile interviewers, King puts his guests at ease, which is why they come on and speak freely. King would never grill a grieving widower and was unlikely to aggressively block Reynard's allegation. King's forum injected Reynard's claim straight into the heartland with an unqualified message that was guaranteed to scare the hell out of the audience.

In Crisis Guy parlance, Reynard's allegation was of the "top-down" variety because, like the Alar scare of 1989 relating to apples, it moved rapidly from the national media down to the local level. Most allegations are "bottom-up," that is they slowly wend their way up from third-tier local media to the national news.

There was more to the power of Reynard's allegation than just the path it took.

PERSONAL IDENTIFICATION AND FAMILIARITY: WHY THE SCARE PICKED UP MOMENTUM

The morning after Reynard appeared on *Larry King*, I was speaking to a few hundred business people about crisis management at a conference that had been planned for months. By this time, the cancer allegations had migrated to other media and a woman in the rear of the auditorium raised her hand with a question: "I use a wireless phone," she began. "Do you think they're safe?"

I wasn't qualified to answer her from a scientific perspective and told her so, but the wording of her question jogged my thinking.

"*I* use a wireless phone," she had begun. I. Me.

"How many of you have a hand-held phone?" I asked the audience. Almost every hand went up.

At that moment, I understood why The Worrier was beating The Crisis Guy: These allegations about wireless phones were personally relevant. I had felt for David Reynard. So did the people in my audience. We felt for him for different, but deeply personal, reasons. I identified with him because of *my* family medical history and because *I* used a wireless phone. My audience was interested in the subject because they also had wireless phones. More than a few, I'm sure, probably had fears about cancer, too.

Complicating matters, Reynard didn't come off as just another celebrity-seeking agitator or vexatious litigant. He struck me as a good man, a devoted husband and father. I saw myself this way. So did many others. The combination of a ubiquitous product, a scary hazard, a national forum, and a sympathetic attacker caused Reynard's allegation to streak through the culture in minutes. The only thing that was missing were *facts*.

"Truth is incidental; familiarity is fundamental," I told the audience. "The public has a greater desire to see someone punished than find out what happened. They think the punishment will balance out the tragedy and they want somebody to pay *right now*. The facts are boring at best and a nuisance at worst."

My question of the previous evening had expanded: What would the wireless phone people do to get *consumers* back?

WHY CELLULAR PHONES BOUNCED BACK

With health and safety allegations, consumers want to know two things: "Am I going to be okay?" and "What are you doing about it?" After Larry King broke the story, the Cellular Telecommunications Industries Association (CTIA) urgently stepped forward to address the issue of a potential hazard. First, in an exhaustive series of media interviews, CTIA demonstrated an impressive portfolio of scientific evidence showing no links between wireless telephones and brain cancer.* It was hard to turn a channel or pick up a newspaper without seeing a CTIA official talking on a wireless telephone and sharing data highlights.

The industry then launched epidemiological research to further explore any link that might exist between wireless telephones and cancer. The CTIA began working with prestigious, independent bodies such as the National Cancer Institute to get more definitive answers. These were not the actions of a guilty party.

The Crisis Guy was impressed, but The Worrier was relieved. The industry had examined this issue before, but it didn't stop looking. CTIA was willing to invest more in studies. This told The Worrier that he and all the other worriers had power in this situation. The wireless phone people had been listening.

An industry cannot easily challenge a victim like David Reynard, but it can demonstrate contrary evidence and a commitment to resolving the issue, which is what the wireless industry did and continues to do.

---

*Studies were readily available due to the long-standing concerns about electromagnetic frequencies and cancer.

The scare didn't last long. Within days of CTIA's media blitz, the cancer story had been knocked off the front pages of newspapers and top-of-the-hour interviews on the network morning shows. Within months, sales were back up and stocks recovered. By 1997, there were more than 45 million wireless customers, an increase of more than 180 percent from when Larry King's show aired.

Not all of this good news can be attributed to good crisis management. Much of the loyalty to wireless phones was (and is) due to their utility. Plenty of people were thinking just what I was thinking when the scare broke: How am I going to conduct business?

Consumers were looking for permission to keep using cellular phones. That permission was granted in the form of experts' confidence in the safety of the product and the industry's pledge to keep studying the issue. Contrary to the early portrayal of the wireless phone user as a self-satisfied big shot, CTIA reported, "35 percent of wireless customers have used their telephones in emergency situations." This means grandparents driving to the beach and dads taking their kids to Little League, not just smug Hollywood producers. Every day, nearly 60,000 calls are made from cellular telephones to emergency numbers.

The same personally relevant information that terrified wireless phone users at the beginning of the scare made them receptive to the information that ended it. When given the choice between having that phone and hearing about a vague potential hazard that few serious experts believe in, consumers stuck with the phone.

SEX, LIES, AND VIDEOTAPE

Big shots and businesses are distressed by the power of allegation. More than anything else, they can't fathom that baseless claims can travel as far as they do. I usually confront a client's incredulity after our first meeting.

The client takes me aside and asks, "What do you think we should fear most?"

My answer is easy: "The thing you should fear most is an allegation."

"What allegation?"

"Any allegation, any 'assertion without proof.' "

"You're saying the attackers don't need proof?"

"Right. They don't need proof. That's why you should fear it most."

The client looks at me expressionless. His eyes speak, though. I can see the change. For the first few seconds he thinks I'm either psychotic or joking. When I don't break my glance, he realizes something even worse: I'm sane and I'm serious.

My business was built on the backs of two allegations in particular. In the late 1980s, a wire service reported that more than 51 percent of landfills were taken up by plastic fast food waste. The real figure was around 1 percent.

A nationwide panic ensued, including a monologue by actress Andie MacDowell in the film *sex, lies and videotape* about a fear of being buried alive in garbage.

Our researchers tried to trace the source of the dreaded 51 percent figure and weren't successful. We determined that an environmental activist *might* have used that figure in a town meeting that a wire service reporter *might* have been attending. The assault on plastic fast food waste waged for years.

In the second case, activists and the media cited a petition that was signed by tens of thousands of people who said they became sick when they came into contact with a client's product, a popular automotive fluid. Bans, restrictions, and warnings were placed on the product throughout the country. Despite this, nobody ever produced the petition.

By the time we found out that there wasn't a petition, the issue was no longer "hot." The media didn't want to revisit it. The punitive restrictions on the automotive fluid remain in place to this day. The best we could do was halt additional damage by invoking the dubious credentials and motives of the attackers.

Because *anyone* can allege *anything,* allegations are more frightening than evidence. People who introduce evidence usually have credibility. Credible people belong to respected organizations. They publish books and articles so it's not hard to find out where they stand.

I can't monitor every attacker with an allegation any more than the Secret Service knows where to find every would-be assassin like John Hinckley, Sarah Jane Moore, or Squeaky Fromme. The Secret Service is better prepared to fight attackers because there's only one president to guard. I can't do this, because my clients and their products are on TV, supermarket shelves, and in America's driveways.

My clients can't counter-allege. They know they are being watched. If they lie, they'll be sued, so they have lawyers and government agencies approve their actions.

Because the public doesn't like them, the haves take great pains not to confirm suspicions that they are bad. They avoid suing or aggressively fighting attackers' allegations for fear that they will invoke the specter of corporate debacles such as General Motors' 1965 public apology over using private detectives to investigate the personal life of consumer advocate Ralph Nader. Nader had criticized the safety of the company's automobiles.

ATTACKERS HAVE NO RISKS

Attackers with spurious allegations have nothing to lose. An allegation is a guerrilla tool. Guerrillas operate outside of the mainstream. They have no assets to take, no positions to uphold, and if they're sent scurrying back to wherever they came from, they break even.

The haves are paralyzed by attackers' unprecedented freedom. When freedom is combined with an angry culture, the lack of boundaries for public decorum, big possible gains (emotional, political, and financial), and numerous distribution channels like the media and Internet, it's open season. This shocks my clients who confuse their own constraints with the constraints of others: "Because I wouldn't make something up, no one else would." "Because I'd never get away with a scam like that, no one else would." "Because I have to run my ideas 'up the flagpole,' other people must, too."

Years ago, it was much harder to allege something. The culture self-aborted allegations. The media checked its sources because they had more time. With rapid-fire breaking news, journalists often have to go on instinct rather than solid confirmation (editors and producers get fired for getting "scooped" by rivals). Allegations also move faster nowadays because there are more channels for them to travel. There weren't always

Internet "chat rooms" with credible graphics that look like newspapers and thirty-five TV networks with dozens of talk shows to serve as unvetted allegation forums.

In the past, we perceived that there was something wrong, or maybe even illegal, about accusing someone of something. Shame prevented hurt parties from getting on TV to make peace with their adulterous-cross-dressing-dwarf-atheist-skinhead spouse. There were social risks associated with whining and weirdness. The attackers might be thought of as losers, freaks, or liars. Today, provided they get their jab in, attackers don't care how they are seen anymore. They can even be "unnamed sources" and never be seen at all.

Even my most aggressive clients believe in the American ethic of fairness. They are either under the impression that laws exist to prevent allegations or that there are certain things that people just wouldn't do. I once assumed this, too. For all practical purposes, there is no risk associated with making an allegation against a "public person" or institution because public figures or institutions are afforded less privacy under the law. The law basically says, "Life's tough in the spotlight so get used to it."

In order to win disparagement cases, the attack target usually must prove that the allegations were knowingly false and were made *intentionally*. Such a charge can be dodged with the First Amendment or by clever theatrics. When Oprah Winfrey aired a hostile program making allegations about the spread of "Mad Cow" disease, she said that the anti-beef panelists "just stopped me cold from eating another burger." It was a resonant remark, but it didn't constitute an intentional lie. The cattle industry, however, claimed in a lawsuit that Winfrey's remarks had disparaged beef and cost them significant sales. Winfrey was also said to have created a "lynch mob mentality" in the audience against the cattle industry. She may have, but creating hostile environments falls into a soupy area of law that doesn't give most attack targets recourse. Winfrey won the case aginst her.

Allegations are innately slippery because they bypass the checks and balances of journalism, the courts, legislation, and other conventions. Today, nothing can stop anyone from saying they *believe* that Tasty Salad Dressing* causes lupus. The "Icky Feeling Hypothesis" prevails because

---

*This is a fictitious product name. I know of no such product on the market.

if you believe it, you can say it. This is a legitimate and legal expression of personal opinion.

The attackers I worry about most are those who have the demeanor of a concerned citizen. Down-home attackers have unlimited freedom to allege something and are given tremendous credibility by the news media.

The media support attackers for business reasons: No allegation, no story. When I have raised questions about the veracity of allegations against my clients, reporters have quizzed me about my clients' ethics (or my own) for doubting an attacker's claims. When I raised doubts about the activist's petition against my client's automotive fluid, a reporter accused me of "corporate bullying." The reporter did not, however, accuse the activist of having fabricated a petition.

In the wireless phone scare, the media gave David Reynard parity with the wireless industry's scientific might, at least for a while. The broadcast media reward spectacle, which gives attackers a home court advantage against those armed with less photogenic information. Scientific expertise follows a trail of logic that is boring to most people and requires work. Allegations can be received enthusiastically but passively.

THE PATH OF ALLEGATION

Allegations take common routes. It's a formula that includes the following elements of a "bottom-up" path.

1. An attacker makes an allegation: "WitchCream"* lotion gives her lizard skin.
2. The local media cover the allegation sympathetically.
3. The attacker or local media talent pitch national TV programs on the WitchCream story.
4. A network's *Hello USA** morning program runs a hostile piece. They include a WitchCream spokesperson who cites the safety tests that have been done on the product. The split screen shows

---

*This is a fictitious name. I know of no product or show by this name.

an attacker shaking her head no! no! no! and interrupting the WitchCream flack. *Hello USA* host ostensibly sides with the attacker.

5. The activist group BroomWatch, seeing a new franchise, co-opts the attacker and requests a Food and Drug Administration review of all "witch-like" products.

6 A second round of media coverage follows, with "me-too" victims of WitchCream.

7. WitchCream's stock tumbles. WitchCream's competitor, TrollGel,* runs advertisements citing their "lizard-free" compound.

With this formula, one product tanks while another rises. If the attack is noble, the attacker gets justice. Otherwise, he gets fame, revenge, money, or some other form of psychic income. BroomWatch raises money. *Hello USA* gets its story and maybe some new sponsors, while consumers know less about lizard skin than they did before the crisis.

ALLEGATION, TEXAS SIZE

"A gossip's word in Syria kills in Rome."
Middle Eastern Proverb

Allegations are easy to execute against prominent people. Attackers have incentive to attack them, the media have incentive to air their claims, and the public stands ready to believe the allegations. A baseless allegation struck Dallas Cowboys stars Michael Irvin and Erik Williams on December 29, 1996, when Nina Shahravan claimed that they had held a gun to her head and raped her. KXAS-TV in Dallas ran with the rape story. On January 14, 1997, the Dallas police announced that "the allegations were not true and that a sexual assault did not take place." Shahravan was ultimately charged with perjury.

In between the time of the accusation and the vindication, millions of

---

*This is a fictitious product name.

people were told via national and regional print and broadcast media that these two men were alleged rapists. A March 1997 poll by the Pew Research Center for the People and the Press showed that 37 percent of those surveyed thought that Irvin and Williams had committed the crime.

In another Texas smear, disgruntled employees and jealous competitors engineered an attack by San Antonio–based KENS-TV on a local cardiologist. The four-part series in February 1985 alleged that Dr. Sudhir Srivastava knowingly performed dangerous surgeries, sometimes killing people. The station piqued resentment against the doctor by using footage of him driving around in his Rolls Royce. His lucrative practice was destroyed immediately following the story and he had to leave town in an attempt to begin anew.

News coverage did not mention that Srivastava had fired the boyfriend of one of KNES's confidential sources. Nor did it share with viewers the business and personal agendas behind the story.

Srivastava sued the station. At trial the jury heard outtakes, which included the reporter telling sources that the doctor should not be told that a story was in the works so that he could not be prepared for an ambush. According to a report by watchdog group Accuracy in Media, "The Texas State Board of Medical Examiners reviewed each of the patient deaths and found no misconduct by Srivastava. . . . Other doctors had told KENS-TV that two of the patients who died were hopeless cases when Srivastava tried desperately to save them; none of these favorable comments got on the air."

Dr. Srivastava prevailed and won damages in court, which is not the norm. On leaving the court, Dr. Srivastava concluded, "Had the television reporter been decent enough to give me the chance to respond to these charges before putting them on the air, this suit would not have been necessary." And he would not have been forced to rebuild his life and medical practice under the false shadow of butchery and immorality.

LACK OF EVIDENCE AS PROOF

The most devastating proof of an allegation is a *lack* of evidence. In vengeful times, if they *can't* prove it, the attackers reason, the telltale heart must be buried out there somewhere underneath the floorboards. That the evidence cannot be found is certification that the plotters must have been diabolical indeed. The culture's imaginations, neuroses, and fears weigh the evidence based upon what the public is already inclined to believe. A typical case of mine features activists linking devastating health effects to a client's product. The attackers especially like chemicals with complicated names, the logic being that if it's hard to pronounce and the research isn't complete, it's a carcinogen or endocrine disrupter. Examples of how lack of evidence "proves" allegations abound in our culture:

- Kennedy assassination buffs support their notions of conspiracy by connecting a string of opaque but sexy concepts like "puffs of smoke," "three tramps," and "umbrella men." That no one knows what these things mean signifies a plot.

- The animal rights movement assures us that there are ways, such as computer models, to conduct medical research without involving animals. No one can find these models, which begs an assumption that the computer software industry is holding back its miracle programs so people can torture more bunnies.

- The "reasonable doubt" principle of law, as best evidenced by the O. J. Simpson case, has been vulcanized to mean "any conceivable doubt." That the defense team could not prove that racist cops planted evidence became proof that the police must have done a flawless job of framing Simpson. (These were the same officers who the defense accused of having left a "cesspool of contamination" at the crime scene.)

- When Audi 5000 owners alleged that their cars were bewitched, suddenly accelerating like rockets, activists and the media validated this with *X Files*–type assertions that "something" was happening within the engine, although no one could demonstrate what.

- An author alleged that J. Edgar Hoover was a transvestite based on a photograph that no credible person has seen. A gangster, who is long dead, of course, was supposedly holding it as blackmail.

Americans have long enjoyed allegations, especially those backed by vague conspiracy theories. In the early 1800s, a book was circulating through the young nation that a sinister German cabal known as the "Illuminati Order" was engineering Thomas Jefferson's presidency. Whether it's the Illuminati Order, the Jews, the Mafia, witches, the Tri-Lateral Commission, aliens, the Vatican, or the man in the moon of Procter & Gamble's logo, our society believes that, as sociologist Daniel Bell wrote, "There is . . . in the American temper a feeling that 'somewhere,' 'somebody' is pulling all the complicated strings to which this jumbled world dances."

Add to this mindset a sophisticated media for leveling and spreading allegations and Americans haven't traveled far from Salem. At the millennium, however, the accusers are not religious leaders, but a loose affiliation of tradespeople with pulpits that reach a broader population than Salem's Reverend Parris could have ever imagined.

13. *The Accused Face the Press*

**Fear of the press gives them their power,
but attack targets are getting braver.**

"Among journalists and reporters, the sense that something has gone
wrong with the American media can create a defensiveness that touches
the fringe of paranoia. When it comes to accusations of rough play, we
have settled on what might be called the modified Menendez Defense*:
Hey, they were *asking* for it."

Adam Gopnick, *The New Yorker*, December 12, 1994

THE "NAILING PREROGATIVE"

I left about twenty voice messages for Olson, a reporter at the nationally
respected *Daily Bugle* newspaper. He never called me back and my client
was upset. Olson's coverage of her product had been devastating and was
based in "scientific" research that supposedly proved the product was
hazardous. My staff had traced the research back to a foreign scientist
who had been funded by my client's archrival. Throughout Olson's story,

---

*This name is derived from the case of Eric and Lyle Menendez, who were convicted in
1996 of murdering their parents. The brothers claimed they were driven to murder because they
feared their parents would kill them in the culmination of years of mental and sexual abuse.

he had unwittingly positioned the research as being independent. The research had been "laundered" overseas. Laundering research is done by finding a seemingly independent expert, often from overseas, to disparage a target. Such "experts" often use research that would not hold up to U.S. peer review. The expert is usually paid.

A month went by with no response from Olson. I asked one of my colleagues to write to his editor requesting a fresh examination of the issue. Olson finally called back, furious that his coverage was being questioned. He said he would investigate *me*. He said I would regret tangling with him and the powerful *Daily Bugle*.

At this stage, diplomacy would not have helped, so I fired back. I told Olson that he was doing precisely what the corporations he criticized did: threatening the whistleblower; trying to cover up an original mistake that could have been easily corrected; and using the might of his institution to quash debate.

The discussion ended with another promise that I would regret having placed my first call to him. He would be providing a larger service by exposing me. I thought of Russell Baker's quotation: "Usually, terrible things that are done with the excuse that progress requires them are not really progress at all, but just terrible things."

Olson had no self-doubt about his capacity—his right—to hang his witch and anyone who stood in the way of the gallows. He viewed my investigation of his story as a presumptuous attack on his territory. He characterized my efforts as being unethical. This is a common trick: When in doubt, attackers characterize their target's defense as malfeasance.

Olson was operating with a "nailing prerogative," the unrestrained option reporters have to nail somebody, to annihilate them. Reporting becomes incidental; destruction of the target becomes the goal. Implicit is the belief that the target deserves to be destroyed.

I feared Olson's wrath, not because of anything he "had" on me but because of his position as a reporter. He didn't need evidence linking me to something bad to make trouble for me and he knew it. He possessed the triple threat of being a *vindicator* claiming to be on a mission to expose wicked corporate interests; having a *vehicle* through which to share his story with millions of readers; and having the *value* of protecting his readers from "bad guys" like me.

To date, Olson and the *Daily Bugle* have not retaliated. I suspect it's either because the paper lost interest or the editors found my evidence to be credible. But Olson is out there and I never pick up the *Daily Bugle* without checking his by-line to see if my number has come up.

Olson's behavior isn't the norm, but it has become the defining obstacle between my clients and the press. Seasoned journalists know it, too. Dorothy Rabinowitz of the *Wall Street Journal* writes, "The facts remain—among them the truth that many journalists continue to believe that they are involved in a calling so high as to entitle them to rights not given to ordinary citizens, among them the right to deceive without consequences."

The media didn't capture its nailing prerogative violently. The public gave it to them.

LUNCH MONEY

> "I'd rather have him inside the tent pissing out than outside the tent pissing in."
>
> Lyndon Johnson on J. Edgar Hoover

In 1993, ABC's *PrimeTime Live*, anchored by Sam Donaldson, aired an aggressive report on how members of Congress traveled to a Florida resort to play golf on electronics industry money. Donaldson, it turned out, had accepted a speaking fee from the same association that sponsored the junket. Later, ABC pursued a similar story. This time, the insurance industry was targeted. Donaldson had accepted a $30,000 speaking fee from the insurance industry a year earlier plus first-class air travel, a limousine, and deluxe accommodations at New York's Waldorf-Astoria Hotel. Said Donaldson, when confronted about the apparent speaking fee conflict, "I was not beholden to them and they were not beholden to me."

The subject of reporter compensation has provoked a flurry of critical media coverage implying that the media may go easy on those who pay them. On the other hand, corporate clients ask, "Why do we keep paying big money to reporters who attack us?"

The issue of journalists being paid to speak at industry functions fascinates the public because it tugs at a fundamental question: Which cultural villain has more power, the media or big business? When attacks are at issue, there is no question who has more power: the media.

The reason why businesspeople consistently pay big money to reporters who attack them is because they are scared to death of the press. The nailing prerogative is the source of this fear. Panic in the face of a media attack is an appropriate Darwinian response because being ruined is a possibility. Business interests reason that by staying close to reporters, they can better control them.

The "lunch money game" works this way. Corporations and trade associations need to show their constituents—members, customers, shareholders—that they are on top of current affairs, that they know the game. One way to do this is to invite exciting and famous people to speak at their functions. Some of the most exciting and famous people around are big-name reporters. By having reporters speak at functions, it gives sponsors the narcotic fix that they have some control over an institution that they believe could have them for lunch. When Sam Donaldson speaks at an industry luncheon, the sponsor gets to stick his head in the mouth of the lion and say, "Behold, my constituents, we're all friends here." The logic is that if high-powered Donaldson speaks at our function, he won't attack.

Corporate communicators and industry coalitions peddle the line that there is a "symbiotic relationship" between business and the news media. Having the press "inside the tent pissing out" is portrayed as a value-added service. On traditional public relations matters, this is true. A good communicator can keep the media apprised of events and trends that impact business, which is one essential function of public relations firms and trade groups.

When attacks happen, though, all bets are off. An attack target's relationship with the media only begins to be symbiotic when the target has something of value in its quiver (e.g., critical information) to offer that impacts the direction of the story.

The power in any relationship belongs to whoever doesn't really need it. In the "symbiosis" between the media and the corporate community, business leaders know that they need the press more than the press needs them. *Paying* reporters makes businesses feel better, as if they are *doing* something. It's just like brown-nosing a state trooper who pulls you over for speeding. It's all you can do, really, to decrease your chances of getting a ticket.

In attacks, the relationship between the news media and business is abusive. I have yet to detect any correlation between journalists accepting money from industry and calling off or mitigating an attack. On this score, Sam Donaldson is being absolutely honest: He was *not* beholden to his sponsors. In fact, speaking fees have gotten progressively higher during the same time period when attack journalism has become meaner. If an attack is either merited or is otherwise resonant, it will occur regardless of how much kissyface has taken place.

The incorruptibility of the media has less to do with ethics than it does raw power. Big media don't have to compromise. They can have both speaking fees *and* their hosts for lunch because business keeps paying them and viewers keep tuning in.

PLAYING THE ADVERTISING "CARD"

A popular theory among business bashers is that corporations control the media through advertising. In other words, if a company didn't like an *Oprah* episode, they would retaliate by not buying advertising on the show. This makes intuitive sense, but assumes that the corporations are *willing* to use this leverage. They are not.

Pulling—or threatening to pull—advertising is rarely done and for good reason. It is disruptive to business, which relies upon steady exposure for sales. Executives believe that a disruption in advertising will lead to lost sales. My experiences bear this out.

Pulling advertising is also considered heavy-handed by those who have the power to make life hard for corporations. Those with power include consumers, regulators, legislators, and other media. Any of these audiences can make trouble by drawing attention to the fascist signals that using advertising leverage sends. Businesses fear that the strategy itself will become a news item that will aggravate whatever problems the attack has already caused. Then, the corporation will have three big problems on its hands: the controversy that started the mess in the first place, no air-time for its products, and the wrath of the republic.

Pulling ads is only done in cases of unequivocal media abuse such as when General Motors sued NBC when *Dateline* blew up a GM truck to demonstrate its flammability upon certain angles of impact.

As a practical matter, industry does *not* unite to help an individual company with its media problems. The notion that the chiefs of Coke and Pepsi are going to help each other out in battles against the press is absurd. Companies either compete with each other and are enjoying their competitor's adversity or are too busy running their own businesses to care about another company's problems.

Political commentator David Gergen argues that speaking to business groups encourages a more insidious form of co-opting: a gradual sensitivity to business life that "tends to encourage a pro-establishment viewpoint." Media critics say that editors and producers may be deterred from targeting a big sponsor in the first place due to a fear of retaliation. These are disturbing arguments that are difficult to prove or disprove. I can only register my own experiences, which are unequivocal: My corporate clients who are major advertisers avoid using their advertising leverage to impact the media's editorial content at all costs. Businesses shun confrontation with the media because it is disruptive to their marketing efforts and because they are afraid that the news departments will retaliate by positioning the company as being heavy-handed. If a client's advertising leverage has had any prophylactic benefit, I have yet to see it.

UNREALISTIC EXPECTATIONS OF THE MEDIA

Big shots and businesses deserve much of the blame for their bad relations with the press. Many have ridiculous expectations of the media that fuel animosity and paranoia. When the media don't defend them, it's seen as evidence of bias. The real explanation is more banal: *Not everybody loves you or your widget as much as you do.*

In an interview with me, Gordon Platt, former producer of ABC's *Nightline*, said, "I don't have time to deal with the guy who called me just as the Gulf War was breaking out to see if Ted Koppel would do a show on his client's new battery." It's easy to see why few reporters answer their own phones anymore and let voice mail do the job: to avoid public relations people whose clients have said, "I don't care if they blow up Baghdad, where's the story on my battery?"

The *Wall Street Journal* reported that immediately following the death of Princess Diana, numerous commercial interests sent out press releases trying to inject themselves into the news. These included several Hollywood psychologists sharing thoughts about what Diana's children would be experiencing; a statement by the American Medical Association; urgent news from flower companies; and a press release from a concerned Hollywood publicist weighing in on the perils of the paparazzi.

The *Journal* should know about being besieged by public relations paparazzi: The paper once estimated that it receives 600 pounds of faxed press releases from public relations people every day. Given this, publicity seekers should not be surprised if their press releases go right into the garbage can. To the extent that journalists find flacks to be obnoxious and disruptive, many of those who relentlessly seek publicity have brought voice mail and other media blockades on themselves.

GO ASK MALICE: WHY LIBEL LAW OFFERS LITTLE RECOURSE

> "Who steals my purse steals trash—'tis something, nothing;
> 'Twas mine, 'tis his, and has been slave to thousands;
> But he that filches from me my good name
> Robs me of that which not enriches him
> And makes me poor indeed."
>> William Shakespeare, *Othello,* Act III, scene iii

Celebrities' and businesses' fear of the media is deepened by the difficulty of winning libel suits. Most of my new clients have a very poor understanding of defamation law, believing that false information is grounds for winning a suit. Not so. Others believe that consistent hostility toward a target is somehow actionable in court. This isn't true either.

The media are within their legal rights to show prejudice. Under the

U.S. Supreme Court's landmark 1964 ruling in *New York Times* v. *Sullivan* (and in many subsequent decisions), to win a libel suit, any plaintiff who is a government official, well-known personality, or even a relatively unknown person involved in matters of public interest must prove that the media defamation was made with knowing falsity or reckless disregard for the truth. Complicating matters, the net of who is a "public figure" has been extended very broadly in some states, including all business entities. This introduces a formidable hurdle to winning a media defamation case.

To prove that the media acted with malice, the plaintiff must have evidence that essentially captures the mental state of the reporter. This means that the plaintiff must prove that the reporter *intended* to defame the target. It's hard to prove that a reporter told a friend, "You know, Bob, I really want to hurt Whoopi Goldberg." Because of the malice imperative, few defamation cases get very far.

In their white paper, *Legal Restraints and Crisis Management,* attorneys Seymour Mansfield and Marshall Tanick note that most defamation cases don't reach a jury verdict because of pretrial dismissals, settlements, or plaintiffs who are unable to persevere to the trial stage. "About 70 percent" of all defamation claims reaching juries are won by the claimants. However, "about 70 percent of the parties who won, and then faced an appeal by the losing party, had their rewards reversed or their damages significantly reduced."

Complicating matters is the ease with which attack targets can be identified as "public figures." The public figure characterization is bad for targets because it gives attackers more opportunity to go after them under the rubric of "free speech." Write Mansfield and Tanick, "corporations engaged in heavily regulated activities which are subject to public scrutiny or involved in aggressive advertising can become public figures." In a climate where attack venues such as the Internet are multiplying, it's much easier to argue that a celebrity or a company has become a public figure.

The media approach libel suits the way insurance companies approach car accidents—they calculate that only a small percentage of those who could cause trouble, will. The bet is that most targets will not sue because it's not worth the trouble. This is a good gamble; very few targets sue for precisely this reason.

In recent years, attack targets have gotten braver. Some of this bravery can be attributed to the new ruthlessness of attacks. Targets have more to lose in a savage assault than they did from a balanced, but critical, story. This newfound confidence is also fueled by media arrogance and carelessness that have been backfiring at a staggering clip.

In the early summer months of 1998 alone, embarrassments have included the resignation of reporters at the *New Republic,* the *Cincinnati Enquirer,* and the *Boston Globe* for fabricating stories. The *New Republic* believes that Stephen Glass made up all or part of the twenty-seven out of forty-one stories he wrote for the magazine during his tenure. The *Cincinnati Enquirer* apologized because a reporter was "involved in the theft" of voice mail messages from Chiquita Brands. It also conceded that its negative representations about Chiquita were untrue. The reporter was fired. During the same time period, CNN apologized to viewers and retracted a story alleging that the U.S. military attacked American defectors in Laos in 1970 using nerve gas. An executive producer quit over the controversy and two other producers were fired.

Outright fabrications are comparatively rare, but embellishments, hearsay, and ignoring evidence that contradicts the "news peg" or story angle is common. Some of these behaviors can be addressed by defamation law. Media leaders are squirming because they have limited control over the line that divides aggressive reporters from attackers. Though that line is debatable, one thing many journalists and crisis managers agree on is the watershed event that sparked the media's identity crisis and the newfound bravery of attack targets: *Dateline*'s attack on General Motors.

A ROCKET IN DATELINE'S POCKET PROVOKES GENERAL MOTORS TO FIGHT NBC

> "For the great majority of mankind are satisfied with appearances, as though they were realities, and are often more influenced by the things that seem than those that are."
>
> Niccolo Machiavelli, *Discourses on Livy*

The only antidotes to fear of the media are outrage and proof that they got the story wrong. General Motors' handling of its conflict with *Date-*

line NBC is the gold standard for this unusual—and dangerous—type of confrontation.

General Motors got tough on November 17, 1992, when *Dateline NBC* broadcast a segment to 17 million viewers about GM's C/K pickup trucks. During the segment, which was apocalyptically entitled "Waiting to Explode," NBC featured the parents of Shannon Moseley, a Georgia teen who died in his GM pickup; consumer advocates who referred to the pickup trucks as "rolling fire bombs"; a mother who spoke about the death of her two children; footage showing the remains of a little girl who was killed in a GM pickup truck; and, most critically, side impact tests that supposedly portrayed what could happen when the trucks were hit.

Attack Summary: GM C/K Trucks—November 1992–February 1993

Victim:	GM C/K pickup truck drivers
Villain:	General Motors
Vindicator:	The Institute for Auto Safety, *Dateline NBC*
Void:	Explanation for deaths, distrust of big business
Vehicle:	*Dateline NBC*
Value:	Consumer protection

"It just didn't look right," Ed Lechtzin, then General Motors' director of legal and safety issues, told me. Lechtzin, and a dozen or so of his colleagues, who were watching the *Dateline* broadcast, agreed that given the way the vehicles were hitting, fires "couldn't happen this way." The GM team reviewed the videotape slowly and concluded that there were sparks flying *before* the actual collision.

GM immediately assigned a small internal "SWAT team" to set the record straight. The team requested an inspection of the trucks that had been used in *Dateline*'s tests, but was told the vehicles had been discarded. As GM wrestled with the fate of the test trucks and other unknown factors, the SWAT team reviewed what it did know. For one thing, GM knew all about the consultant who had conducted the crash "test." It was an outfit called The Institute for Safety Analysis (TISA), which provides support for plaintiffs in litigation against auto companies.

TISA was, in fact, affiliated with a group called the Institute for Injury Reduction (IIR), which was founded in 1988 by trial attorneys. Wrote *AutoWeek* of IIR co-founder Benjamin Kelly's approach: "Get your message broadcast into hundreds of thousands of households today and you've got the eyes and ears of tomorrow's product liability jury pool." There was big money to be made in auto liability: A jury nearly three months after the broadcast awarded Moseley's family more than $100 million in damages, a verdict GM appealed and which was subsequently overturned.

A FIREMAN SPARKS AN INVESTIGATION

In the weeks following the *Dateline* report, one of the firemen who had been at the scene of NBC's crash "test" near Indianapolis as a precaution was becoming increasingly disturbed about the segment. He was surprised that the procedure used during the "test" had not been disclosed (although such disclosure is not routine, *Dateline* had informed test participants that the procedure would be revealed). The fireman was aware that the procedure had included the use of an incendiary device that triggered the explosion. He had also read a column about the NBC segment written by Pete Pesterre, editor of *Popular Hot Rodding*. Pesterre had owned GM pickups and gone through a crash in one of them and did not believe what NBC reported.

The fireman called Pesterre and told him how the tests had been rigged; Pesterre called GM and, in due course, GM lawyer William Kemp Jr. scoured Indianapolis-area junkyards, found the four test vehicles and purchased them for $400. NBC had claimed the vehicles had been scrapped. Among the things they discovered was a rocket motor that remained fastened to one of the truck doors. GM's attorneys then secured the firefighters' videotape of the staged crash tests. While all this was happening, IIR's Kelly, however, was going at full-throttle making the most of *Dateline*'s anti-GM program. Toward the end of January, Kelly sent out a mass mailing seeking funding for more crash tests to be used in litigation against General Motors.

"OUTRAGEOUS MISREPRESENTATION AND CONSCIOUS DECEPTION"

On February 2, 1993, GM privately approached NBC with its new evidence and requested a retraction. NBC examined the proposal and declined. On February 8, GM responded with a brilliantly staged spectacle of its own, a heavily attended two-hour news conference where General Counsel Harry Pearce produced the "scrapped" trucks that had been used in the rigged test and showed what GM had found. He also announced that GM was suing NBC for defamation, citing "outrageous misrepresentation and conscious deception."

NBC News boss Michael Gartner issued a statement in response to GM's news conference again defending its broadcast: "We at NBC watched the General Motors press conference today very carefully. . . . We remain convinced that taken in its entirety and in its detail, the segment that was broadcast on *Dateline NBC* was fair and accurate." In addition to this statement, Gartner was preparing a script to be used by *Dateline*'s anchors to underscore this point on its program the following evening. It was never used.

Prior to the airing of the program, NBC's parent company, General Electric, in the face of devastating evidence, agreed to a public apology. On February 9, 1993, anchors Jane Pauley and Stone Phillips read the complete retraction on the air, which included an admission that the footage "was not representative of an actual side-impact collision. . . . We deeply regret we included the inappropriate demonstration in our *Dateline* report. We apologize to our viewers and to General Motors. We have also concluded that unscientific demonstrations should have no place in hard news stories at NBC. That's our new policy."

FALLOUT

Not long after the *Dateline* segment, NBC News Chief Michael Gartner resigned. There was no reason to believe that Gartner had played a role in the use of incendiary devices, but he had vigorously defended the program afterward. Gartner had also had a history of making controversial decisions, including NBC's identification of Patricia Bowman, who had accused William Kennedy Smith of rape several years earlier.* The segment's producer and anchor were also fired and several other producers resigned.

Media bashers rallied round the Hollywood-style "gotcha" ending to the GM/*Dateline* affair. GM had beaten *the media*. There was an undercurrent of industry's moral superiority (or, at least, equivalency) to the Fourth Estate.

Traditional manufacturers and the news media are actually very much alike. In addition to getting careless with its production line the way other big companies do, NBC's employees, when confronted by a crisis, acted like their industrial counterparts: Management tensed up, stonewalled, obfuscated, and avoided confronting its mistakes. In NBC's sober internal report on the crash tests, attorneys for the company concluded

> As GM stepped up its protests and made more persistent requests for the test material, the *Dateline* producer mistakenly thought the complaints were abating. Without consulting either the reviewing attorney or anyone else, the producer told GM the trucks had been junked and were unavailable. That was misleading. Second, when GM learned about the igniters and threatened to bring suit for defamation, NBC personnel failed to mount a sufficient investigation into the facts and thus made the initial decision to defend the whole story without having an adequate understanding of the facts concerning the demonstrations.

NBC's internal report also concluded that *Dateline* never resolved the extent to which it was portraying a test of truck safety or a dramatic re-enactment of a side-impact crash; the re-enactment wrongly associated NBC News "with an event of questionable safety and professionalism"; *Dateline* failed to report the results and circumstances surrounding the crash "fairly and accurately" and wrongly used multiple camera angles to portray "a larger and more threatening fire"; *Dateline* failed to disclose its use of explosive devices in its simulation, after having indicated to crash test participants that it would be disclosed; the traditional "checks and

---

*Bowman had previously been identified by a supermarket tabloid.

balances" within NBC did not work, especially with regard to accepting the concept of "unscientific crash demonstrations" without adequately defining that term and the conditions of the tests; the poor professional judgment exhibited during the *Dateline* affair was not intented to misrepresent the truth.

INCENDIARY SYMBOLISM

The GM/*Dateline* debacle served as a symbolic turning point in the Culture of Attack. A respected media outlet brazenly pursued its own interests at the expense of consumer interest and crossed into pure entertainment territory where factual information is no match for good visuals. It was the most quantifiable instance in recent memory of the media not protecting us against Big Brother, but of the media *becoming* Big Brother—a juggernaut of propaganda and one-dimensional advocacy. Whatever NBC's intentions were, the GM episode validated the subtext of a ratings-obsessed, out-of-control media that warranted the fear it inspired.

Since the *Dateline* incident, it has gotten easier to demonstrate malice in libel cases because, well, there's a lot more malice. It's also easier to show reckless disregard due to the mindset of juries who are children of the Culture of Attack primed to seek a pound of flesh from anybody, including the press. Juries are not always rational, nor do they necessarily understand the subtleties of the law. If they don't trust the press, they sometimes *infer* malice.

In 1996, Alan Levan, chairman of BankAtlantic, was awarded $10 million for a story ABC's *20/20* did on his purportedly shady business affairs. Also in 1996, a Texas mayoral candidate was awarded $5.5 million for a story KTRK-TV in Houston did assailing his qualifications as a mayoral candidate. In 1997, a jury gave Food Lion $5.5 million deciding that *PrimeTime Live* trespassed and committed fraud against the supermarket chain when it aired a segment on hazardous food.

Other cases have been settled in order to avoid a jury trial, including Philip Morris's $17 million award for legal fees and a public apology against Capital Cities/ABC for charging that the company "spiked" its cigarettes with nicotine order to addict them; and General Motors' undisclosed award and public apology for *Dateline*'s rigging of the pick-up truck explosion.

Hoping for the media's remorse is useless. Only a weapon like GM's evidence could have stopped this attack. Only outrage can overwhelm whatever reticence corporations like GM might have to fight the press. Only a mortifying debacle—or the threat of one—can send powerful media like NBC on a search for its soul.

In the end, sales of GM's pickups were not impacted by the *Dateline* broadcast; the resale value of the trucks actually increased afterward.

Despite the rejoicing over how the media "got theirs," the joke may be on the media bashers in the end. The summer following the "Waiting to Explode" segment, *Dateline*'s ratings were 43 percent *higher* than they had been the summer prior to the GM segment and the show expanded from one show per week to three shows.

To be sure, the media "get it" right far more than they get it wrong. Nevertheless, targets that are unnecessarily hurt are hurt badly. More than ever, potential targets are searching for approaches that can be used to reduce the chances of being attacked, whether it's by the press, the Internet, or by some other means. Fortunately, there is an approach that can provide relief.

14. *Dissuasion*

**Unconventional approaches
are required to defuse attacks.**

"If it be not now, yet it will come: The readiness is all."
William Shakespeare, *Hamlet,* Act V, scene ii

Attack targets are having second thoughts about surrendering to their assailants. Slowly, targets have become aware that they are facing fundamental
threats to their way of life, as opposed to annoying jabs from the disaffiliated.

At the millennium, new approaches for defusing attacks are beginning to surface because the old ways have failed. Public debates have
gotten meaner because the haves are hitting back. Bill Clinton has no
intention of shuffling into the Rose Garden and commiting political suicide by resigning. Clinton may be guilty of many of the things he's been
accused of, but he has chutzpah and that's what the public notices and, I
think, respects.

Americans liked it when General Motors dispatched private investigators to the scene of a pickup truck explosion and determined that an
ambitious producer rigged the explosion. They liked it because the
attackers had crossed an ethical line and had, in fact, attempted to hood-
wink the public.

Americans applaud when ABC's John Stossel has the temerity to unmask self-described victims and expose them for what they really are: attackers, or just con artists who have failed at their scam.

What follows is the thinking behind the new jihad, the holy war to stop the attackers.

A COMMUNICATIONS PROBLEM?

Imagine this: Two people are walking down the street side by side. One is a crisis manager. The other is in public relations. A sinister-looking character in a trenchcoat emerges from an alley, draws a knife and asks for their wallets. They both say no, the attacker cannot have their wallets. The attacker becomes angry and demands the wallets.

The PR person's interpretation of this encounter is that there are poor communications. He begins to explain to the attacker why the wallets are not forthcoming. "We need our money." "You're breaking the law." Apparently, the PR person believes the attacker needs to be better informed. Perhaps if there is an *exchange of views*, a dialogue, or if the request is enunciated more clearly, the attacker will understand why the wallets are not changing hands.

The crisis manager does not believe there is a communications problem. The crisis manager believes there is a *conflict*. He explains this to the attacker: "You want my wallet and I want my wallet, too. You can have the PR person's wallet, after all, you only have a communications problem with him. He is welcome to communicate his money into your pocket. With me you have a conflict and a new problem."

The crisis manager reaches slowly into an inner pocket. Now it's time for the attacker to ponder several trenchant questions: "How badly do I want this guy's wallet? Is this crisis management guy psychotic? What the hell does he have in his jacket?"

WHAT IS DISSUASION?

Dissuasion is what's inside the crisis manager's pocket. *Dissuasion is an expanded mindset for convincing attackers to stop attacking or not to attack at all.* It means GO AWAY. Dissuasion is a stance, rather than a bag of tricks, an unconventional approach of limited tolerance and righteous indignation. Dissuasion asks not why you were targeted but why *shouldn't* you be? It rejects the core belief that all grievances are equal; that all attacks are noble; and that attackers and their surrogates have a rights to your demise. You may not have started your crisis but dissuasion demands that you end it.

Dissuasion consists of three major elements:

- introducing *risk* to the attackers—offering a down-side to their aggression;
- transferring the subtext of malice from the target to the attacker;
- inoculating against future attacks in the long-term by making known the deleterious consequences of unwarranted aggression.

Dissuasion is different from *per*suasion, which means to get someone *to* do something (and be happy about it), the traditional role of public relations. It focuses on what is done to *defuse* the threat at its origin. Conventional communications theory assumes that someone needs to be educated, that facts are needed. In order for a message to be communicated, however, it has to be received. Attackers are not receiving, they are attacking. An attacker doesn't want information, an attacker wants to destroy his target.

Dissuasion is a stance of conflict. Its mission is survival. Dissuasion eschews political correctness and "happy" talk in favor of a hard-nosed approach for making problems go away. Dissuasion rejects the belief that if one communicates the benefits of a product or service—the "good news"—people will forget about the hazards being alleged. While benefits play a role in crisis management, they cannot necessarily play the leading role. An allegation is rarely about the target's benefits. During the Tylenol cyanide crisis, nobody was asking, "Do these capsules cure headaches?" Rather, people were saying, "Will my central nervous system implode if I take one of these?" These are very different questions. Accordingly, Johnson & Johnson didn't respond to the crisis by saying, "Hey, four out of five doctors say that our pills cure headaches." Nobody cares about headaches if instantaneous death is at issue.

Dissuasion is not a ticket for spiteful attacks on one's enemies, a diversionary tactic for despicable behavior, a replacement for responsible actions, or an appropriate approach for managing all attacks. Dissuasion is a response technique for unusually hostile times. Anyone who interprets it as a license to pillage loses the privilege of righteous indignation that justifies aggressive responses to attacks. If the attackers have been genuine victims of the target's malice or carelessness, repentance is the answer, not hardball tactics. Nevertheless, the extent to which a threat justifies a dissuasive response must be determined by the target. If the attack lacks merit or otherwise jeopardizes the target's survival, it's time to consider unconventional means.

The decision making process in which dissuasive strategies are entertained tends to be very painful. Contrary to cinematic portrayals of powerful people and business, in reality, society's leaders avoid playing hardball with their public at all costs. What it ultimately comes down to is how grievously the target believes he has been wronged. There is a direct correlation between a target's anger and his willingness to take dissuasive measures. A target that does not feel truly wronged—or suspects his attacker may have a good point—will inevitably retreat to conventional handling, which often consists of weak apologies, soft hints of repentance, and a big helping of avoidance.

THE PRINCIPLES OF DISSUASION

"Wherever possible go outside the experience of the enemy."
Saul Alinsky, *Rules for Radicals*

Dissuasive Principle #1:
Attacks are defused on emotion, not analysis

A fact is to an attack what a tire is to a car—a good thing to have but not the fundamental mechanism in the vehicle's movement. What the car really needs to move is an engine. What an attack really needs to move is emotion: basic fears and impulses, resentments, and gut instincts that ultimately connect to our values.

In the same way that emotions overpower facts, spectacles over-whelm science, which is why attackers rely on spectacle. Attack targets, in their discomfort, embrace facts—science and reason—because these concepts are trusted and familiar. This is noble but not helpful. The facts may help but they cannot be the cornerstone of a defense, especially when terrible things are being alleged. The only weapon against spectacle is sometimes . . . a better spectacle.

A better spectacle is rooted in personally relevant images that hit close to home. Assaults against automobiles and cellular phones have failed because consumers cannot do without them and were outraged by punitive or restrictive measures. The spectacle of deprivation won the day because the purported hazards did not override the benefits. In these cases, we asked ourselves, "How will this impact me?"

The attacks on Bill Clinton for adultery and pot smoking have not caught on because most Americans would rather not be asked about their own sex and drug histories. The attacks on food and alcohol products have failed largely because consumers like these things and remain unconvinced that the dangers outweigh the pleasures. What's more, many see neo-Prohibition efforts as a plot by a sanctimonious elite to dictate how we should live, and they don't like it.

Personally Relevant Appeals

When fighting tough issues, empirical facts are incidental, as evidenced by Bill Clinton's notorious testimony that he "didn't inhale" his marijuana joint. Inhaling is a fact, a clinical description. When it comes to defusing the "character issue," Clinton's *"What do you want from me?"* tilt of his head has served him better than the facts because if somebody nailed us with a personal question, most of us would want to shrug it off, too.

Similarly, the activists known as the "food police" can weigh and mea-sure grams of fat all they want and it doesn't move the public. This isn't because they are always factually wrong, it is because they treat the public like uninformed fools. Consumers respond *emotionally* to this treatment. Besides, many people know the facts and if, occasionally, consumers want to scarf down a bag of potato chips, smoke a cigar, or sunbathe on vaca-tion, they're going to. (It may even be a right.) The public *considers* facts and figures but *resents* being analyzed and patronized. The former is intellectual, the latter is emotional.

Far more effective at reducing abusive consumption have been appeals to vanity and personally relevant experiences. There's nothing like the massive heart attack of someone with one's own genes to get people eating right. Similarly, the community only becomes outraged by media and law enforcement tactics when the people getting nailed could be one of us (e.g., vindicated Olympic bombing suspect Richard Jewell, beaten Los Angeles motorist Rodney King). This is why juries these days are being won over not with evidence but with emotional appeals to put oneself in the plaintiff or defendant's position.

Emotions and personally relevant appeals dissuade attackers because it forces them to fight human nature, namely the drives toward well-being and self-preservation. An attack on a product's safety or integrity must be fought with demonstrations that prove it.

This was a lesson the plastics industry learned when it was under attack by environmental and consumer groups in the late 1980s and early 1990s. Jean Statler, who presided over the industry's communications program during these difficult times, shared her assessment of how and why the American Plastics Council was able to turn the tide against environmental and competitive assaults against plastics in an interview with me:

> It became clear to us that criticism of plastics was being driven by an elite that was benefiting too much from the attacks to stop. This included competitive interests. Once the industry had begun to make environmental progress, especially in the area of recycling, it launched an advertising campaign to directly remind consumers how plastics had improved their lives. People had forgotten what life was like before shatterproof bottles. They had forgotten the days before plastic wrap when people handled meat and poultry with their bare hands. The advertising campaign went directly to the American consumer, bypassing the environmentalists who had previously positioned themselves as the plastics industry's translators to the public. The results speak for themselves: Americans understand that the benefits of plastics far outweigh the environmental risks.

In time, the solid waste issue dissipated and the public became more resistant to anti-plastics propaganda.

Another example of emotion-driven dissuasion came in a battle between retail establishments and the music industry. The American Society of Composers and Publishers (ASCAP) was aggressively demanding that retail establishments pay licensing fees for playing music in stores and restaurants. If chefs in a restaurant were playing a radio, musicians could request royalties from the restaurant in the same way that they could from a radio station playing the song. Understandably, many proprietors were upset by this heavy-handed practice.

The issue of the music industry's *modus operandi* came to light when the media reported in 1996 that ASCAP had also been muscling in on the Girl Scouts, who were asked to pony up money for singing songs like "Happy Birthday" around the campfire. The public was outraged and the music industry changed its practices. The emotional spectacle of shaking down Girl Scouts effectively drew attention to a larger issue that was also hurting a less sympathetic audience: businesses.

Dissuasive Principle #2: Noncommunications methods can be the best defenses

Most targets under attack believe the "smart bomb" that will defuse an attack lies somewhere in the communications process—a well-worded statement, a glib spokesperson, or a special event designed to reinforce a perception. Communications approaches are too limiting. Targets must evaluate noncommunications options—legal action, investigations, innovative business policy options—which may be leveraged in communications to defuse an attack. What follows are noncommunications approaches that have successfully helped defuse attacks.

Legal Dissuasion

Litigation is the only language that some attackers speak. Legal options may include actions for slander, libel, tortious interference, and even antitrust. It is much easier to defend against an attack if a defense is anchored in legal action because litigation supports the pretext that the attack was unwarranted. Suing an attacker can also be an effective *communications* tool with a variety of target audiences (e.g., media or business relationships) because it provides a defense forum for the target. It introduces risk to attackers and gives them something to lose.

Suing one's attacker is not a first course of action. It is a last resort assuming that peaceful measures (e.g., negotiations or ignoring it) have failed and that there is an actionable claim.

More and more attacks are baseless at worst and unmerited at best. When an attack isn't merited, the attackers must be stripped of their halos, and should be treated like any other dangerous adversary—a rival corporation, a political opponent, or a stalker. Legal action is fair game but must be anchored in legitimate legal recourse, as opposed to nuisance suits or investigations, which are dangerous as attack defenses. Pepsi-Cola benefited greatly from the prosecution of the people who inserted syringes into the soft-drink cans during the scare of 1993. Johnson & Johnson was well-served by the prosecution of an extortionist who attempted to profit from the 1982 Tylenol cyanide tamperings. On the other hand, a consortium of energy companies was embarassed when its investigation into the personal lives of environmental activists in Alaska was publicized in the news media.

"Tempest in a C Cup." A lesson in legal dissuasion can be learned from the pages of the Victoria's Secret catalogue. A New York woman sued the company on the grounds that it was discriminating against women. Denise Katzman claimed that an "adult male with a higher income level" received a Victoria's Secret catalogue with a better discount offer. The company fought the suit hard, especially because it contained ugly allegations including fraud, racketeering, and discriminatory practices.

The "adult male," who was allegedly benefiting from this scheme, according to a *Wall Street Journal* exposé (entitled "Tempest in a C Cup"), turned out to be Katzman's attorney, who had a history of suing companies "often to compensate for seemingly small humiliations of daily life." A U.S. district court judge threw out the suit against Victoria's Secret for its "flagrant lack of merit" and fined the plaintiffs because the suit was filed for "improper purposes." Fines and ostracism temper vexatious litigants and are being pursued more and more.*

---

*Similarly, a U.S. Supreme Court ruling on the inadmissibility of unproven scientific data has repulsed litigation on vague ailments such as "enviromental illness" and has led, in some cases, to fines against plaintiffs.

Another example of legal dissuasion occurred when grocery giant Food Lion sued ABC for a *PrimeTime Live* report alleging that the store deliberately sold spoiled food. Food Lion sued ABC for violations of a law in North Carolina (where the segment was filmed in 1992) involving trespass, fraud, and breach of duty. A jury decided that ABC's story had been fraudulently obtained. (ABC had used undercover operatives linked to a labor union at odds with Food Lion.) The jury awarded the grocery chain punitive damages in excess of $5 million and also ordered two of the show's producers to pay fines.*

These high-profile losses have made media outlets more careful about running with a story before verifying the facts. While throwing dissuasive measures at a journalist may not stop a hostile story (especially if the target is guilty), it may have a chilling effect on the intensity of negative coverage.

Attack targets have been reluctant to take legal action against attackers because corporations are not considered to be sympathetic by the public and juries. Those worried about this positioning are beginning to realize that those who are inclined to dislike them probably already do. By the time the litigation begins, the sides may be so well established that image building may be useless. A little audacity may only help matters.

As terrible as many targets are at playing defense, attackers are even worse because they have so little experience with dodging the kinds of stones they throw. The media and courts are gradually becoming aware of how badly allegationists have abused them in recent years and are more receptive than at any time in recent memory to arguments against them.

The reluctance of targets to fight attackers, especially activists, in court and in the media is slowly changing because wanton attacks are doing damage as opposed to falling under the relatively harmless category of "public relations problems." When the potential for business damage outweighs short-term public relations concerns, the risks of suing diminish because the target has little to lose by striking back.

If litigation is the only route remaining, targets must remember the real objective: stopping the attackers while doing the least amount of

---

*Food Lion lost $1.5 billion in stock market value around the time of the *PrimeTime Live* broadcast and its sales dropped $4.6 billion after the program aired. Several thousand workers were laid off.

damage to oneself. Humiliation is not the objective of crisis management; getting back to business-as-usual is.

Inoculating Practices

> "The fox feels safe as long as the leopard has others to prey upon."
> Greek Proverb

Uncommunication. One of the shrewdest ways potential targets can avoid being attacked is to keep a low—or better controlled—profile. An attacker can't shoot at a target it cannot see. Those whose businesses or lifestyles do not require exposure should avoid the limelight. At some point, strategic publicity can cross over into malignant narcissism. One wonders just how many cover stories were needed to validate Newt Gingrich's rise to power. In 1994, it was hard to pass a magazine stand without seeing a pensive looking Newt photographed pointing America in some grand direction. Looking off into the distance may imply vision but it can also suggest daydreaming. Gingrich's platform suffered because his publicity machine was more aggressive than his political muscle.

There is an intangible correlation between a very high profile and a noteworthy failure. Michael Ovitz's and Newt Gingrich's troubles came following an endless barrage of publicity promising grandiose things. Madonna's and Michael Jackson's careers plummeted after the press deified them. Jennifer Capriati's tennis career flamed out after she was hailed as "the next Chris Evert" long before she ever really returned a serve at Wimbledon.*

Biodegradable garbage bags, telephones with screens, recycling, the DeLorean, the IBM PC Junior, solar power, a paperless workplace, and many other things received publicity promising great things that never happened. There were many factors involved in the demise of these people, ideas, and products, but they all had two things in common: stronger promotion than performance and profiles so high that they invited more detractors than supporters.

---

*As a general rule of thumb, anyone or anything branded "The Next So and So" will invite self-destruction. One annoints himself king at his peril.

A Visionary Offense. Establishing socially progressive business practices that make a potential target difficult to hate is an ideal dissuasion strategy. The aluminum industry skirted the garbage crisis of the late 1980s because it had established a recycling infrastructure decades before solid waste ever became an issue. It did this because aluminum had inherent value and recycling was a viable business. The industry accelerated its recycling efforts as a result of the anti-litter movement of the early 1970s. In addition to its commodity value, recycling also provided tremendous public relations leverage when the industry inoculated itself against attacks during the garbage controversy.

Fashion designer Tommy Hilfiger's longstanding support of ethnically diverse music acts such as Snoop Doggy Dogg and Sean "Puffy" Combs cut short the lifespan of false allegations that he made bigoted remarks. When, in 1997, unidentifiable Internet dirty tricksters leveled the charges, his most important audiences recognized the sheer absurdity of these claims due to Hilfiger's pattern of supporting many different audiences. Both Hilfiger's sterling record in minority affairs and the falseness of the allegations quickly shut down the attacks.

Food companies have inoculated themselves against attacks by offering consumers choices that deprive attackers of targets. When quick-service restaurants came under fire for serving fattening foods, they introduced salad bars and other heart-healthy options. These were fundamental *business* moves that had public relations value as opposed to being public relations maneuvers alone.

Dissuasive Principle #3:
Attackers are unoriginal and, therefore, predictable

There is rarely anything unique about an attacker. Attackers share motives, behavior patterns, and even sponsors. This is good news because these common denominators often make attackers easy to predict. The challenge then becomes *how* to predict attackers' behavior. The answer lies in collecting, maintaining, and analyzing available—and sometimes unavailable—information.

Investigative Dissuasion

The proper type of investigation should be thought of as news reporting; gathering information that will be shared in a court of law or public forum with an audience that may impact a cessation in hostilities. The opportunities for independent reporting have multiplied because traditional media have become more focused on entertainment, as opposed to breaking stories. As mainstream media are being distracted by competitive pressures, more hard news stories are originating not with news outlets but from watchdog groups and other vested interests.

The Clinton White House-as-hotel fundraising scandal and "The Buying of the President" study on buying influence in presidential politics, among others, were "broken" by the Center for Public Integrity, a nonprofit group. The traditional news media picked up on these stories after the center released its information. Businesses themselves are conducting investigations and breaking stories because they cannot rely on traditional media to ferret out the truth for them.

Dissuasive investigative options have nothing to do with dirty tricks or digging up personal dirt on an adversary. This kind of activity tends to backfire badly, as it did when tobacco giant Brown & Williamson allegedly leaked information about whistleblower Jeffrey Wigand in an attempt to discredit him. Wigand had accused Brown & Williamson of allowing dangerous substances to be used in tobacco and the company's chief executive of lying to Congress about nicotine being addictive. The allegations about Wigand involved alleged shoplifting and spousal abuse, which had nothing to do with the health controversies being raised over tobacco. The resulting news coverage, such as a May 1996 *Vanity Fair* exposé, ultimately focused on the ethics of Brown & Williamson and all tobacco companies, who failed to stop a whistleblower but succeeded in creating a martyr when the media found the industry's alleged crimes to be worse than those alleged against Wigand.

What Investigations Should Look For. Investigations should locate evidence of misrepresentation, fraud, or premeditated efforts to damage a target's reputation. Factors that may not be germane in a court of law may be in a communications battle. Investigators have uncovered information about attackers including criminal records, capacities for violence, competitive sponsors of an assault, medical experts short-selling stock in companies whose product they were attacking, patterns of vexatious litigation, and false information that had been embraced as fact by pivotal audiences.

Sometimes a "smoking gun" emerges in an investigation. Other times, nothing turns up at all. Often, new information surfaces that may not neutralize an attack, but may shed valuable light on the situation. In several of our firm's cases, the attackers turned out to be parties with legitimate grievances. Had we accused the initial suspects of hostile behavior, we would have looked foolish—or worse.

The media don't always check all the facts surrounding an attack. In one of our firm's cases, a couple, the Hendersons,* claimed that a hotel's staff had "peeped" on them during intimate moments. My client, the hotel chain, learned this when a national television magazine show contacted them and asked for their comments about the lawsuit the Hendersons were filing. The couple had cited a hole in the hotel room wall as evidence of peeping.

My surprised client questioned its staff, which vehemently denied the charges. The employees also expressed their willingness to take lie detector tests. We asked the magazine show to delay broadcast until we had the chance to examine the hotel room in question. The show agreed, but gave us very little time.

Upon investigation, we found two things. First, the plywood in the hotel wall was perfectly intact and was stamped with an installation date from the 1960s. Had the staff been peeping on the Hendersons, the hole would have had to have punctured the plywood so the workers could watch from the next room. At the same time, our investigators determined that the Hendersons had a record of perpetrating cons. As the television show was editing its story, we simultaneously alerted both law enforcement and the show's producers about the notorious couple.

The segment was killed. Had the media run with the story, it would have done irreparable harm to our client and also made the TV program vulnerable to a libel suit. In a case like this, the media were not the adversaries—they had been potential victims, too.

---

*A fictitious name.

Had we not produced something of value, this program would have run with its hostile story. What had initially been a story about corporate malfeasance was transformed into a criminal matter. This shifted the pretense of malice away from the client and onto the con artists, where it belonged.

Neutralizing Zealots and Showboats. Most attacks lie somewhere on the continuum between legitimate claims and selfish conflicts of interest. In these cases, investigators usually learn that the attackers are zealots or garden-variety attention seekers.

Zealots are true believers who may be raising issues that merit attention. Attention seekers don't care about the issue at hand. Their motives are selfish (e.g., fame, money, revenge). I call attention-seekers "Elvises" because of their need for the limelight and their vaguely pathetic quality. Zealotry and showboating are not exactly grounds for arrest; however, understanding an attacker's motives is useful because attackers have patterns of exploitable weaknesses.

Zealot-driven attacks have limited lifespans even if they are legitimate concerns. A good risk manager may even be able to assess where an attack is in its lifespan by judging the degree of media interest in it. This is critical because a target needs to determine what resources will be needed to combat the attack. If the attack is young, it is likely to take more time and money to defuse than if it is on its last legs.

The key with zealot-driven attacks is for the target to plan its response in accordance with the potential lifespan of the attack. This can be done with the assistance of tools such as public opinion research that can help gauge the depth of the public's concern about the issue.

It is usually only a matter of time before the public moves onto another scare *du jour* and the zealot is diminished from hero to gadfly and, eventually, to nuisance status. In the case of the environmental scares of the late 1980s, the public's depth of commitment was tied largely to feelings of economic security. When the recession of 1991 hit, environmental protests evaporated because people were more worried about their survival than they were about the global environment, although environmental problems alleged to be in their own back yard could attract considerable attention.

Attacks that are driven by attention-seekers present very different challenges. The information age has wrought more lonely, isolated people who are driven to attack in order to feel a stronger sense of identity and self-worth. Their issues tend to be more subjective and less legitimate than those fanned by zealots.

The greatest vulnerability of attention-seeking Elvises is that they tend to wear out their welcomes quickly. Those who suddenly find themselves at the center of attention tend to misinterpret their fame, seeing their newfound status as destiny—the long-deserved reward for their suffering. Elvises don't understand that media glory is fleeting. They raise their profile to the point where it provokes attacks on *them* or just saturates people until they stop listening.

Given the Elvises' need for publicity, they lose the capacity to differentiate between strategic attention-getting and narcissism. They run into someone who doesn't buy their act. In one of our cases, an Elvis was setting up so many media appearances for himself that he had a publicist coordinating his interviews. One smart reporter began wondering how he got himself a publicist. It turned out that the publicist was employed by marketing people being paid to attack the same product as the Elvis. They had been connected all along. While there was nothing illegal about this activity, this Elvis's need for the limelight overwhelmed his judgment and he discredited himself altogether.

DISSUASION AND MORAL POSTURING

"He who fights with monsters must take care lest he become a monster."
Friedrich Nietzsche

The aggressive undertones of dissuasion inevitably provoke debates about ethics. Because many attackers claim to be victims of something, targets are reticent to fight back in a heavy-handed manner. My clients have confronted adversaries that have included organized crime and the Unabomber and, in a perverse way, I would rather go up against criminals and terrorists than the predators of meekness. With the former, at least it's clear where they stand; they blow stuff up. It doesn't take too long for anybody to figure out where their actions intersect with morality, so somebody calls the authorities. The bunko artists of the victims' movement, however, can hide gangland tactics (usually extortion) behind the values that decent people cherish: compassion, charity, freedom, justice, and security.

Targets often ask themselves questions like "Shouldn't I hear these people out?" In some cases, there *is* a peaceful solution because attackers may have a point. It's when attackers *don't* have a point—or their point is not commensurate with the price being exacted—that it's time to tee up dissuasive techniques. Targets are under no touchy-feely obligation to "hear out" their attackers when they already know what the attackers believe (e.g., you = bad; me = good).

The concern then becomes not so much one of true morality but one of the *appearance* of immorality. How does fighting back *look?* If the attacker seeks your destruction, how things look should immediately move down your list of priorities because you're not going to look very good bankrupt.

One way to address the appearance issue is to have surrogates fight back on your behalf. Independent parties often exist who share views and values with an attack target. There is also merit in framing the attack in the context of broader societal issues such as the backlash against scare-mongering. So many high-profile accusations have turned out to be false recently that people don't want to be used. Many believe they were conned by attackers.

Key media have expressed regret, for example, in how the scare over "gender bending" chemicals was managed. Diane Katz of the *Detroit News* writes

> The endocrine apocalypse has been canceled, but word in the press is harder to find than a humbled green activist. A Nexis search turned up only two newspapers that carried timely reports on the retraction of some alarming estrogen research published in *Science* magazine: the *News and Observer* of Raleigh, N.C., and the *Times-Picayune* in New Orleans, home to Tulane University, where the original study was done.
>
> Not a word in the paper of record, the *New York Times,* which had characterized *Our Stolen Future,* a book touting the endocrine disrupter theory as "ingenious." Nor in the *Philadelphia Inquirer,* which had

termed the book "momentous," the *San Francisco Chronicle,* which called it "frightening," or the *Los Angeles Times,* which declared it "meticulous." . . . Whatever the reason, the endocrine scare now joins a long line of other highly publicized environmental threats—Alar, asbestos in schools, cyclamates, dioxin, electromagnetic fields—that turned out to be not so threatening.

The media, in particular, are well aware of how they have been used in recent scares. Invoke these broader hustles if it looks like you may be the next victim of something similar.

15. *Likability and Attack*

*Averting and defusing attacks
often comes down to basic likability.*

"[He is akin to] the enviably attractive nephew who sings an Irish ballad for the company and then winsomely disappears before the table clearing and dishwashing begin."

Lyndon Johnson on John F. Kennedy

THE CHIEF DEFINES CHILDREN

At seven o'clock in the morning in a cold studio on Eye Street in Washington, I cue up the videotape for my clients. One of them shivers, as he sits in a folding chair set up in a semi-circle with several others around the TV screen. I press "play" and a magazine program featuring an interview with the CEO of one of the nation's most famous companies begins. The subject is the company's alleged use of child labor overseas. I thought my clients would benefit from seeing the tape because they were confronting a similar problem.

The CEO on the screen seems like a nice enough guy. His interrogator does not. The interrogator is angry, with thin lips that appear to be holding back a torrent of bile or very, very hot soup.

216

My clients are squirming as they watch the interview. The shivering man averts his head when the TV interrogator shows the CEO photos of dead children. Their bodies were lined up after a fire in a plant that the famous company allegedly used to make some of its products. The CEO is visibly uncomfortable. Even though he is being accused of something awful, it's hard to square the image of this normal-looking guy with that of a demon who supposedly contributed to a tragedy. Watching the interview, you feel terrible about the dead kids, but you don't believe that this man is responsible. My clients' hands are tugging at their chins, playing with their glasses or doing other things that keep their hands near their faces. It is as if they, themselves, are preparing to be attacked.

After a series of rapid-fire questions, the interrogator asks the big one about whether or not children should be working in factories like this. The CEO responds: "You and I might perhaps define 'children' differently."

My client's hands now fall down toward their laps or their sides. The tension is relieved in the same manner that it is when Columbo trips up the murderous socialite in a lie. We are safe.

I push "pause" and ask my clients what they think. One woman lets out a deep breath. She points to the frozen image of the CEO and says, "I don't like him."

SOMEBODY TO ROOT FOR

Sophisticated ways of measuring the popularity of people, messages, and institutions obscure a basic tenet of good crisis management: Most of it comes down to whether or not folks fundamentally like and believe the target. Likability is an emotional, not a rational, response. Likability is impacted—for better or worse—more by style than substance.

Likability is at the core of the American character. Hollywood producers, when evaluating scripts, have been known to ask, "Who do we like here?" They are attempting to determine whether or not the audience will find the main characters appealing enough to identify with, to believe in, and to root for. If people don't "like" the character, the movie won't fly. It probably won't even get made.

Likability can mean different things. Does the character fulfill our fantasies in some way? Is the character someone like us? Is the character believable? Likability doesn't have to correlate with virtue. If movie and book sales have taught us anything, it's that we "like" scoundrels, too. A scoundrel is likable, however, only if he is doing something that strikes a chord—exacting vengeance, showing a soft side, standing up for a principle, or getting away with something naughty.

In an entertainment-driven culture, the Hollywood principles of likability are transferrable to business and public affairs. Whether or not a target survives an assault is determined largely by who the good guys and bad guys are believed to be. In the same way people make decisions about liking a Jodie Foster character or believing a David Mamet plot, we ask ourselves whether or not we believe someone's story or her spokesperson.

When the parents of JonBenet Ramsey, who decked out their little girl like a vamp, are implicated in the press in her murder, do Americans empathize with them? When then-Virginia governor Chuck Robb admitted that he and beauty queen Tai Collins were together, naked, in a hotel room, but that it was only a massage, were voters awestruck by Robb's self-restraint or did they think he was lying? When an American business executive has trouble defining what a child is, are we okay with this?

No, we are not. The public doesn't define children differently, not in our culture anyway. Basic values are not in the eye of the beholder. When it comes to who is liked, there are few complexities, just visceral instincts.

Somewhere along the line, public relations people got the notion that cute word-turns and invented definitions could fool people. This puzzles me because it doesn't work. It's hard to imagine that the shareholders of an airline had their spirits lifted by an annual report that referred to a plane crash as an "involuntary conversion of a 727." Perhaps the flacks would have fooled more people if they just called the disaster a "layover in Cleveland."

Voters balked when Speaker of the House Jim Wright and Richard Nixon responded to charges of malfeasance by "welcoming" the investigation. Who would *welcome* such an investigation?

Activists are rightly enraged when the government calls ugly wars "conflicts" and inner city problems "benign neglect." Most workers now know that "early retirement" usually means that Ted in Accounts Receivable got fired; "rightsizing" means that Ted's whole department got fired; and "restructuring" means that the entire population of a small town got fired. Sure, the public can be fooled, but it's not just words that do it.

APPEARANCE COUNTS

One of the reasons many people were susceptible to conspiracy theories about the Nicole Brown Simpson and Ronald Goldman murders was that O. J. Simpson didn't *look* like a killer. Simpson is handsome, affable, and charming. None of these things are surface traits associated with killers. Never mind that many long-term abusers and sociopaths are appealing on the outside, which is why they get away with vicious acts for so long. Simpson sent mixed signals and dissonance hurts. Some weren't fooled by his charm, but others, including the jury, found it implausible that appealing social skills could coexist with murder.

When it came to boxer Mike Tyson very few people had any trouble believing he was a rapist. Tyson has always conducted himself in ways that are outside the boundaries of cultural values. It's plausible that a man who smashes up luxury cars, gets in barroom fights, and sends his first wife hiding in closets for cover, would rape someone.

Few public figures better understand the perils of coarse packaging than radio personality Howard Stern. On the subject of censorship, Howard Kurtz quotes Stern as once saying, "'Penis' out of my mouth is bad. But 'penis' out of Donahue's mouth is good. Donahue can say he's talking about penis because he wants to help people and I'm talking about penis because I want ratings. Bullshit. Donahue talks about penis in November because he wants big sweeps."

Donahue, Stern is saying, is more likable because he has packaged his product—titillation—in the higher principle of "helping people." This packaging inoculated the bourgeois *Donahue Show* against scrutiny from the Federal Communications Commission, Stern believes. It also gives Donahue's audience a socially acceptable excuse for doing the same thing that the abrasive Stern's audience does with pride—listen to taboo discussions that feature naughty words and subjects such as "vanilla lesbians."

A QUALITY OF ETERNAL REASSURANCE

My five-year-old daughter was sitting on my lap as we watched the dual coverage of Princess Diana's and Mother Teresa's deaths. She was mesmerized, her mouth and eyes wide open and her head tilted dreamily to the side, as she watched news footage showing Diana sparkling as she entered various galas. In the footage, light bulbs were flashing, making the princess look like a willowy strobe light. When the file footage turned to Mother Teresa, however, my daughter physically recoiled when the camera focused on the elderly nun. "She looks disgusting," I was told.

I share this story not out of any agreement with my daughter's assessment of these two women but to point out how an unbiased human being reacts on a visceral level to how people present themselves.* In the case of Princess Diana and Mother Teresa, my daughter's reaction was based on looks and looks alone. Enough social psychology studies have been done indicating that attractive people are better liked than unattractive people that they need not be re-hashed here. However, who is liked is about more than beauty, it is about human signals. These signals are sent not only by human beings in a contest of some kind but by institutions that find themselves in the public eye.

One of the things the public *thinks* it likes most in people is honesty. "If I value honesty," I reason, "I am a good person." If Bill Clinton's survival has taught us anything, it is that honesty is not cherished. What Americans are comforted by is consistency. Americans found none of the revelations about Clinton as president to be alarming because they had heard them all when he was first running for office. Nor were Americans alarmed by Ronald Reagan's creative use of facts. The public was not expecting an expert statistician when he ran for office; why would things change when he became president?

The American public does not assess honesty on a letter-of-the-law basis. It seems to go with a spirit-of-the-law interpretation. The question

---

*I had a similar experience with my son several years earlier when we were paging through a book about the presidents. At about four years of age, he found a cartoon of Richard Nixon to be "scary." A photo of John F. Kennedy smoking a cigar on a sailboat, however, was deemed "cool."

with politicians like Bill Clinton, therefore, isn't, "Is he telling the truth?" but rather, "Is what he said consistent with his persona?" Clinton's persona on the issue of philandering, for example, doesn't lie. The man has never claimed to be virginal and his nonverbal gestures and "aw shucks" head tilt say, "Gennifer Flowers? Okay, I did—what do you want from me?"

Clinton is everything that fraternity boy undergraduates said they hated in college—the rogue who consistently won the affections of the prettiest girls on campus, who claimed to hate him but tended to misplace apparel in his dorm room. "Why?" we nice guys ask bitterly. Because what masquerades as contempt is really a perverted form of admiration. Clinton's persona does not lie about who he is. He's a guy who gets away with stuff and his nonverbal cues don't deny it. You can be liar without being a poser. Lying is forgivable, posing is not.

The Republicans would never get that kind of break on a philandering issue. They send both verbal and nonverbal signals of purity. Philandering is at odds with these cues. A philandering Republican, voters reason, is a liar and voters don't think they like liars, because it is personally insulting. *"You're trying to fool us because you think we're stupid, don't you?!"* Morality is less the issue than how the message relates to what the attack target thinks about his audience. It always comes back to our personal relationship with the target.

Bill Clinton "gets away" with more than other leaders would for the same reason beautiful women don't get speeding tickets: Because that's how the world works. The little crisis management chestnut about confessing right away does not apply to the extraordinarily charming: smooth-but-dishonest presidents; affable-but-murderous football players; and stunning women who drive too fast.

Like Bill Clinton, Ronald Reagan didn't put us through cognitive misery either. Reagan was quintessentially American in this regard. F. Scott Fitzgerald's description of Jay Gatsby could have easily applied to Reagan:

> It was one of those rare smiles with a quality of eternal reassurance in it, that you may come across four or five times in life. It faced—or seemed to face—the whole external world for an instant, and then concentrated on *you* with an irresistible prejudice in your favor. It understood you just as far as you wanted to be understood, believed in you as

you would like to believe in yourself, and assured you that it had precisely the impression of you that, at your best, you hoped to convey.

One of the reasons why Reagan could usually overpower a news
media that hated him was that he *out-liked* his attackers. Reagan liked
Americans more than the media did, that is. There were the party-pooping
media seeing through the electorate by catering to its love of spectacle,
and Reagan was delighted to see everyone's patriotic little faces.

Reagan didn't see through his constituents one bit. He loved the
voters, which overwhelmed everything, including Orwellian notions that
his "handlers" had coordinated his good image independent of the man.
The media always beat up on a president that voters like. "Screw 'em,"
the country decided, and elected Reagan with two landslides.

DISPLAY BEHAVIOR

"It is better to look good than to feel good."
Comedian Billy Crystal impersonating Fernando Lamas

Ronald Reagan was called the Teflon president because nothing bad stuck
to him. Bill Clinton has been similarly wily in the face of continued
scrutiny. Reagan's slickness was attributed to the cunning of his staff;
Clinton's has been attributed to a sympathetic media. There are better,
more gut-level explanations for the political success of both men: Clinton
and Reagan both tap into dual essentials in the American spirit. Reagan
was America as we like to see ourselves: strong, uncomplicated, honest,
and above reproach. Like adolescent love, our projections are ideal and
pure. Clinton, on the other hand, is the America we are: glib, glossy, lovable, lustful, winning, and wily. Voters are okay with that, too, provided
that a politician doesn't go too heavily on the "wily." No one wants to
think they admire cunning.

Personality traits are conveyed now, more than ever, through visual
media. With the shift in debate from newsprint to video cues, information
bypasses reason and goes straight for the heartstrings. One of the most
promising areas of research that has been done to measure the impact of

visual cues was conducted by professors Roger Masters and Baldwin Way of the department of government at Dartmouth College. Their experiments "explore the interaction of emotion and cognition in viewers' responses to televised imaged of politicians." Masters and Way refer to the use of facial expressions and nonverbal signals as "display behavior."

"Broadly speaking," the research concludes, "happiness/reassurance elicits positive feelings (and can reduce negative ones), whereas fear/evasion is most likely to produce negative feelings in viewers." The research also concludes that the "resulting pattern of emotions observed in our studies was parallel to that found to predict voting behavior in national public opinion polls."

Masters and Way cite the Iran-Contra scandal as an important case study in display behavior. The scandal arguably marked the downturn in the Reagan presidency. They studied two key communications opportunities when President Reagan addressed the issue with the American public. One was a November 13, 1986, speech from the Oval Office. The other was a live news conference where Reagan answered questions from the press on November 19, 1986.

According to the study, "Immediately after the speech, an ABC poll found that voters who had watched the speech (approximately half the sample of 1,000) were more likely to believe the President than those who did not." On November 19, Reagan reiterated the same message points he had made in his speech—that only defensive weapons had been sent to Iran, that no arms-for-hostages trade had taken place, that Iran had been encouraged to "use its influence" in the Middle East to free hostages in Lebanon.

The results of Reagan's performance in the Oval Office and in his direct give-and-take with the press showed markedly different results. It is no secret that Reagan was a better script performer (Oval Office speeches) than an improvisational performer (news conferences). Masters and Way suggest one reason why:

> When answering the journalists . . . Reagan's nonverbal behavior was sharply at odds with his usual reassuring manner. He exhibited facial displays of anger (especially when listening to hostile questions) and fear (notably when trying to answer on several points). Another ABC poll immediately after the press conference found that those who had watched television were now *less* likely to believe Reagan than those who had watched no television.

Masters had conducted similar research with Dartmouth professor Denis Sullivan on the 1980 Carter-Reagan presidential debates. Their conclusions suggested that Carter demonstrated "threat" facial reactions when contrasted to Reagan's reassuring demeanor. This was one of the reasons the "warmonger" label didn't stick to Reagan in 1980: It was *Carter* who displayed hostility.

Display Behavior in Attack Management

While there is no known research that correlates the Dartmouth studies with how businesses and institutions project themselves in the spotlight, the basic principles are transferrable. Sophisticated pollsters such as Richard Wirthlin have been shifting away from just measuring opinions and are measuring "core values" that probe what we like, what we don't, and why. Dick Wirthlin has counseled, "Persuade by reason; motivate through emotion."

The "display behavior" principles that resonate in attacks include the following:

- decisions to support and/or attack a target may depend heavily on visceral, emotional reactions as opposed to analysis;

- those under attack convey nonverbal signals that reinforce perceptions of guilt and/or innocence;

- "the facts" only matter with an elite tier of gatekeepers who maintain a quaint interest in empirical truth—the rest of us think with our enzymes;

- understanding beliefs may be more important than understanding opinions when managing an attack: opinions change, beliefs tend not to.

A commentator observed after the O. J. Simpson murder trial that the prosecution was communicating on the AM frequency and the defense was communicating on FM. The jury was listening to FM, said the commentator. If "AM" represents evidence and reason, "FM" represents emotion, primitive impulses, personal experiences—id-based communications. If the public is receiving on this frequency, attackers and shrewd communicators will fight back on the id level. Remember how a TV advertisement featuring furloughed convict Willie Horton helped defeat Michael Dukakis in the 1988 presidential election? What the public thinks is irrelevant. What the public *feels* is everything.

GOODWILL

An elevated form of likability is what businesspeople call "goodwill." It can apply to attackers and activist groups just like it applies to corporations and celebrities. In the same way that, say, Campbell's goodwill equates with good soup, the Center for Science in the Public Interest's goodwill equates with reliable information. Quality—goodness—is simply assumed.

Goodwill can be used and abused. A good leader or corporation can be exempted from attacks based upon past good deeds. Bogus attacks can also be deemed credible if trusted parties launch them. Either way, goodwill does not originate in the ether. Good deeds must have been done at some point to inspire a link between the country's most cherished values and those who boldly exhibit them. McDonald's is a case in point.

A Case Study in Goodwill: Why McDonald's Got a Break During the Los Angeles Riots

"If you are going to take money out of a community, give something back."

McDonald's founder, Ray Kroc,
in John Love, *McDonald's: Behind the Arches*

On April 29, 1992, a Los Angeles jury acquitted four police officers who had been videotaped beating African-American motorist Rodney King. The verdict set off riots throughout Los Angeles. More than 2,000 people were arrested and 53 were killed. Looting ravaged the city. Over $1 billion in damage was done and Police Chief Daryl Gates lost his job. Particularly hard hit were black neighborhoods themselves. Several hundred businesses were ruined, including many owned and operated by African-American proprietors. *In the citywide melee, not one McDonald's restaurant was damaged.*

Soon after the police-enforced curfew in South Central Los Angeles had been lifted, every McDonald's in the region was operating again. Members of the National Guard, Los Angeles Police Department, ambulance squads, and fire fighters, not to mention residents of the community, could be seen patronizing McDonald's as neighboring businesses smoldered. Reported *Time* magazine, "The St. Thomas Aquinas Elementary School, with 300 hungry students and no utilities, called for lunches and got them free—with delivery to boot."

The Dividends of Vision

> "There is no such thing as a bad community. You just have to concentrate on bringing the good out."
> Herman Petty, McDonald's first African-American franchisee, in
> *McDonald's: Behind the Arches*

McDonald's longstanding commitment to the communities where it does business and to minority affairs accounted for its exemption from attack. Said McDonald's USA president and CEO, Ed Rensi, shortly after the riots, "Our businesses there are owned by African-American entrepreneurs who hired African-American managers who hired African-American employees who served everybody in the community, whether they be Korean, African-American, or Caucasian."

Company and franchise managers alike play leadership roles in community organizations. McDonald's constitutes one of the largest volunteer campaigns in the country. About 25 percent of McDonald's executives and a staggering 70 percent of its restaurant managers are made up of women and minorities.

Despite the company's impressive showing during the Los Angeles riots, McDonald's learned about crisis management the best way, the hard way. Profound adversities deepened McDonald's commitment to its outreach programs.

In 1968, McDonald's came under fire in Cleveland from a group of African-American activists led by a militant figure named David Hill, who objected to the low number of black franchisees in the McDonald's system. McDonald's had initiated a search for black franchisees but the effort was moving slowly, with only four African-American franchisees in the nation.

Hill called for a boycott. According to John F. Love, author of *McDonald's: Behind the Arches,* "hundreds of black demonstrators were picketing the six white-owned McDonald's on the town's predominantly black East Side." To make matters worse, there were racial tensions far beyond McDonald's purview. Wrote Love:

> It was the worst time and the worst place for McDonald's to become involved in a racial controversy. Martin Luther King Jr. had just been assassinated, and Cleveland was one of the most racially divided cities in the country. It had elected its first big city black mayor, Carl Stokes, but rather than ease racial tensions, Stokes' mayoralty aroused them. Stokes had courted the support of the Black Panthers and other militant groups and in so doing had fanned the fires of prejudice that burned in the hearts of thousands of politically active residents on the town's mostly white West Side.

The protesters grew violent, shattering windows and intimidating patrons. Hill demanded that McDonald's oust the white franchisees from the African-American neighborhoods. McDonald's was forced to import help from other regions to run the stores. The Cleveland police did not exactly ease tensions. When a seasoned African-American McDonald's manager came to town to help reopen the stores, a police officer gave him a gun and advised him, "If you have to use this, shoot to kill."

McDonald's began an aggressive political outreach and negotiating effort with the militants and city officials. Hill demanded that he be appointed an agent to help select black franchisees. He also requested that he and fellow agents receive a "commission." While McDonald's agreed to install African-American franchisees in Cleveland, the company rejected the "commission" proposal. After the meeting, the McDonald's negotiator was told that "one of the coalition representatives sitting across from him was holding a gun under the table."

Finally, a prominent African-American doctor named Kenneth Clement, who had once been an ally of Mayor Stokes, came forward and dubbed the boycott a "shakedown." Other black leaders agreed that the militants had ceased to represent the rest of the community, after all, McDonald's had agreed to install black franchisees in the six restaurants in question.* The activists had become attackers.

While McDonald's minority licensing efforts had begun well before the Cleveland troubles surfaced, Cleveland was the catalyst for more rapid change. "Cleveland made people in the regions aware of the danger and sensitized them to the need to move a lot faster on minority licensing," said Bob Beavers, McDonald's director of community action and development in 1968, and an African-American. The number of black franchisees soared from four in 1969 to fifty by 1972, nearly 10 percent of all outlets in the United States.

Business Incentives

The increase in black franchisees stemmed from McDonald's progressive approach to minorities who did not have access to the amount of capital needed to open a restaurant. The company worked with organizations including the Office of Minority Business Enterprise and the Small Business Administration to help African-Americans secure the loans needed to open a McDonald's franchise. The company, according to Love, "granted minorities exceptions on its 50 percent limit on borrowed capital, allowing black candidates to purchase their franchise and equipment with as little as $30,000 in up-front cash, or about 20 percent of the total investment."

The case of Herman Petty, McDonald's first black franchisee, provides a good illustration of how the company's impact on the community benefited from its approach to minority franchisees. Petty had been a Chicago-area bus driver and barber who had industriously saved his money in order to open a McDonald's restaurant. When he finally did, he "carried the McDonald's message to all the churches in the area—and even provided free hamburgers at church socials," wrote Love, "because he knew the churches were the community's centers of social activity."

---

*David Hill was later convicted of blackmail in this affair and fled the country.

Petty expanded his operations throughout Chicago, also buying other businesses that had deteriorated and investing in their improvement. Among Petty's more visionary ideas, he pledged to build a new McDonald's in a particularly run-down area if the local alderman made a commitment to better lighting, roads, and landscaping. A gas station owner who was about to shut down his business and move elsewhere was sufficiently impressed with the improvements that he expanded his station instead of shutting it down.

By the early 1980s, Petty, who opened his first McDonald's in the late 1960s, employed 500 African-Americans, many of them young people who would have otherwise been jobless. Said Petty, "There is no such thing as a bad community. You just have to concentrate on bringing the good out."

McDonald's also brought the good out by holding affirmative action seminars for its managers, employees, and franchisees well before it became fashionable to do so. Reported *Time*, "Each year 3,000 employees complete affirmative action programs that last one and a half to three days. Ideas originated at headquarters and by individual franchisees have led to programs such as McJobs, which takes on mentally and physically impaired employees, and McPride, which keeps students in school and rewards them for academic achievement while they work."

In its McMasters program, McDonald's hires retirees to work with young staff members; thousands of handicapped individuals work as full-time employees; and academic associations and institutions have publicly praised the company for its devotion to the education of its employees. Today, in the United States, minorities account for nearly 20 percent of McDonald's approved franchisees and more than half of those being trained to become franchisees.

All of these things contributed to the creation of a company with a "trustbank" that nobody wanted to loot. By the time of the riots in Los Angeles, the Golden Arches had become more than a sign denoting a place to eat; McDonald's meant opportunities for African-Americans and others. Corny as it may seem, the Golden Arches represented the American Dream—status even—and there are anecdotal reports of people chasing potential looters away from McDonald's outlets during the riots. If rage over the Rodney King verdict stemmed from a sense of *losing* ground for African-Americans, the community protected McDonald's because it had become a symbol of *gaining* ground.

McDonald's inoculated against attacks during the Los Angeles riots because of a crisis management program it had begun implementing decades before Rodney King ever encountered the L.A.P.D. Its good fortune resulted from decades of tangible action and investment. The company did not respond to racial unrest with relativism. Instead, McDonald's became likable because it took a clear position that an important community believed was right. Through its actions, McDonald's inspired respect and protection. Despite their anger, people in Los Angeles wanted good things to happen to McDonald's because what was good for McDonald's was good for them.

Racial prejudice has justifiably provoked high-profile scrutiny of people and institutions throughout American history. While not all individual accusations and acts of protest have merited the attention they have received, the overall cause of social justice has been well worth the elevated level of attention that bigotry—and the war against it—has yielded in recent decades. The Information Age, however, has wrought less noble causes of conflict and attack. The motive that I am confronting more and more is the rabid desire on an attacker's part to be famous, no matter the cause. The thirst for fame does not warrant the collateral damage it often wreaks.

16. *No Fame, No Gain: The Desperate Lunge for Visibility*

Attackers will do anything to be famous.

"And here's the ultimate insanity. Two star-struck parents of a preadolescent proudly pack their son off for long weekend at the Neverland Ranch, even though the only thing they know about their child's thirty-five-year-old confirmed bachelor host is that when he's not having elective facial surgery, he's grabbing his crotch more frequently than Lenny Dykstra in mid-August. What were they thinking? Well, I'll tell ya what they were thinking. They were thinking, 'The most famous person in the world is on the other side of that door, and if my child is the skeleton key that unlocks that door, well then, so be it.' "

Dennis Miller, *The Rants,*
on children sleeping over at singer Michael Jackson's estate

JESSICA'S CHANCE TO SOAR

On April 11, 1996, I was skimming the channels in search of a story that was supposed to air about a client when I was sidelined by CNN's Breaking News. Seven-year-old airplane pilot Jessica Dubroff was killed as she took off in bad weather in a heavily publicized attempt to set a record flying across the continent.

"Did you find the story?" a colleague asked, popping her head in my office door.

"This little girl was my son's age," I said, ignoring her question.

I pointed to the TV as the anchor recapped the news about Jessica. We both watched in horror as cameras panned the smashed airplane in a Wyoming street, as if the audience needed to see precisely where Jessica's body shattered. "She's my son's age," I said again, trying to imagine his face obscured beneath giant goggles and his little hands on the plane's controls.

The segment cut to an aviation expert who said that the important thing was the experience, not the age, of the pilot. He said this with a straight face. There's always a relativist principle to justify the absurd, I thought.

I flipped off the television and asked my associate to try to find our client's story on another TV. I had had enough news for one day.

I stopped seeing media whoredom as a benign quirk long before Jessica was killed. Said *Nightline*'s Ted Koppel on the tragedy, "We need to begin by acknowledging our own contribution. . . . We feed one another: those of you looking for publicity and those of us looking for stories."

Playing for the cameras was important enough that Jessica and her flight party failed to remove the wheel blocks before attempting to taxi down the runway. Her fame was that urgent.

Many *want* fame but attackers *need* it. Whenever I see someone going after someone else on TV and don't know what their point is, the chances are their appearance on TV *is* the point. In the past ten years, I have seen a dramatic upswing in attacks that are rooted in someone's maniacal desire to be noticed. The need to be a celebrity used to play a role in a minority of my cases. It was an aberration. Today, about a third of them contain somebody looking for attention. As media have proliferated, malignant camera lust has gotten worse, and fame-seeking attackers have seen their opportunities expand.

Attackers pursue fame even if the price tag is the destruction of someone else. In the process, they do not differentiate between being famous for their own achievements, because of some serendipitous incident, or due to an association with a famous person. They'll take a public identity however they can get it. Attackers draw no distinction between celebrity, which implies achievement, and being exposed.

THE ENDS AND MEANS OF FAME

"In my stars I am above thee, but be not afraid of greatness. Some are born great, some achieve greatness, and some have greatness thrust upon 'em."

William Shakespeare, *Twelfth Night,* Act II, scene v

There are three kinds of fame-seeking attackers. I divide them into *Elvises, opportunists,* and *serendipitous fame-seekers.*

Elvises

Elvises, which, as I mentioned in chapter 14, derive their name from their obsession with the limelight, attack primarily because they want attention or notoriety. For these rare birds, fame is an end, not a means. The classic Elvis is the Reverend Al Sharpton who, in 1987, alleged that a fifteen-year-old girl, Tawana Brawley, was raped, beaten, smeared with feces, and had racial epithets scrawled on her body in charcoal. Sharpton and his aides declared that a young Caucasian district attorney from Dutchess County, New York, named Steven Pagones was one of the suspects. Pagones was repeatedly referred to as a rapist on national television. The previously unknown Sharpton found himself at the center of a media firestorm and became a featured guest on television shows like *Nightline, Geraldo,* and *Donahue.*

In time, the Brawley affair was determined to be a hoax. Among other evidence, forensic tests could not find DNA support linking Pagones to the crime. The feces were traced to a neighborhood collie. Pagones sued Sharpton, Brawley, and others for hundreds of millions of dollars. After ten long years, Pagones won his suit; Sharpton and aides Alton Maddox and C. Vernon Mason were found liable for defamation. Pagones is not expected to collect much money, if anything. Said Pagones's wife, Niki, after the victory, "You'd think I'd be elated, but I'm saddened. . . . This whole episode has encompassed our marriage . . . It's been a long ten years."

Like most Elvises who have been unmasked, Sharpton has hidden behind the "larger truths" about racism that he supposedly exposed. He has spoken of conspiracies against brave souls who dare to speak the truth.

Attack Summary: Tawana Brawley Hoax—1987–1988

Victim:	Tawana Brawley, African Americans
Villain:	Steven Pagones
Vindicator:	Reverend Al Sharpton
Void:	Explanation for Brawley's defilement, rage against racism
Vehicle:	Public rallies, media appearances
Value:	Exposing racism

These canards and delusions are a key personality trait of attackers and their supporters. The late activist/lawyer William Kunstler remarked in the *Wall Street Journal*, "It makes no difference whether the attack really happened. . . . The black community knows that there are a lot of Tawanas out there."

While racism exists and is evil, the degree of chutzpah and deception Sharpton employed in the Brawley hoax was so incredible as to cast serious doubt on the depth of his commitment to civil rights. This is especially true considering how many other controversial civil rights leaders have not resorted to attacks like this to make their points.

Few Elvises become as notorious as Sharpton because the issues they promote are less volatile than racism. They also tend to be less audacious. Nevertheless, garden-variety Elvises sprout up in my practice every day with spurious allegations ranging from sexual harassment to runaway cars.

The one good thing about most Elvis-driven attacks is that they tend to collapse quickly because there is little to support them. Handlers like me find this out very quickly. Those with the power to create or prevent attacks —primarily the media—won't support someone's personal agenda unless there is something in it for them, such as a good news story. In an Elvis-driven attack, only the attacker benefits. When the facts don't bear out the allegation or the subject matter turns out to be of limited interest, Elvis dies.

Opportunistic Fame-Seekers

Most of my clients' fame-seeking attackers fall into the second category: opportunists. For opportunists, celebrity is currency—fame is a means to an end. Opportunists use fame as leverage to get something else: money, book sales, influence in a legal case, or furthering an agenda. Their grab at the limelight often causes more trouble than the injustice being alleged. Opportunistic attacks can do a lot of damage because there is often something "in" the attack for a variety of parties, including a hard, if tiny, kernel of truth.

The worst opportunists threaten to "go public" with a terrible allegation unless their demands are met. Washington and Hollywood are the breeding grounds for opportunistic attackers because of the premium placed on being "in the know." In these industry towns, everybody yearns to be a "player." One way to be a player is to be perceived to know something bad about someone that no one else knows, from a president having sex with interns in the Oval Office to a macho movie star who people "know for a fact" is gay.

Autumn Jackson, who claimed to have been the illegitimate daughter of comedian Bill Cosby, was an opportunistic attacker. In early 1997, Jackson attempted to cash in on Cosby's fame by alleging that the wealthy comedian was her father. While she wasn't Cosby's daughter, the media found it plausible that she might have been. Cosby conceded having an affair with Jackson's mother and admitted sending $100,000 to Autumn's mother over a twenty-year period in exchange for her silence about their affair.

According to press accounts, Autumn had threatened to disclose that the popular father figure was *her* father unless he forked over $40 million. Autumn wouldn't have had a shot at this money without publicity. Negative publicity, she reasoned, would embarrass Cosby into paying her off. If Cosby paid, she would stay *out* of the news. If Cosby did not pay, she could hold his lovable image hostage by staying *in* the news until he paid up. In July 1997, a court found Autumn guilty of attempted extortion.

On the Washington front, Paula Jones and her supporting cast of handlers have become opportunists. Jones initially had a legitimate reason for making headlines: suing President Bill Clinton for sexual harassment. Her charges were especially plausible considering Clinton's reputation for philandering. Even if Jones enjoyed being followed by reporters—attention she most certainly would not have gotten unless she had gone after Clinton—she did, in fact, have a legal case pending.

I didn't put Paula Jones in the category of opportunistic fame-seeker until she turned up at the 1998 White House correspondent's dinner where President Clinton was also in attendance. This was a gratuitous stunt, irrelevant to her case. While Jones may very well have been harassed, she became an opportunistic attacker by exploiting current events to needlessly extend the life of hostile coverage of Clinton.

Those who sought publicity by claiming to find syringes in cans of Pepsi were opportunistic fame-seekers. What they really wanted was money, a goal that could not be achieved without visibility—the real threat to a consumer product company like Pepsi.

Radical 1960s activist Jerry Rubin pathetically became an opportunistic fame-seeker in the summer of 1998 by claiming that Nestle's "Nuclear" chocolate bar made light of atomic warfare. The candy bar was a tie-in with Disney's film *Armageddon*. Rubin opposed the candy through his "Alliance for Survival." Despite miniscule public support, Rubin succeeded in positioning his campaign as a "boycott" in the national media. The "boycott" was a bigger media success than it was a true boycott. "Nuclear" chocolate sold its entire stock in weeks.

Other opportunistic attackers exploit trendy scares to grab headlines. Jeremy Rifkin of the Foundation for Economic Trends is a genius at injecting himself into the headlines whenever the public has an anxiety attack over a specific subject. When fears of biotechnology were making headlines, Rifkin attacked the scourge of genetically altered fruits, sending biotech companies running for cover. When fears of hormone-injected beef captured the media's fancy, Rifkin attacked the cattle industry. When the gene-spliced tomatoes and mad cows headed for the greener pastures of unsupported scares, Rifkin re-emerged as an information/workplace guru.

In addition to loving the limelight, Rifkin is intelligent and sincere. He also focuses on important issue topics, so he cannot be passed off as a vapid Elvis. The real harm lies in the media's knee-jerk support for a colorful, fame-seeking, pop-culture–exploiting allegationist. The fundamental difference between an Elvis and an opportunist is the extent to which the issue at hand has merit. Tawana Brawley was almost certainly not raped. Raising questions about food and public safety, on the other hand, is a legitimate pursuit, however misguided some of its advocates turn out to be. Industry spokespersons usually lose in the public's latest scares *du jour* because, in defending their products, they are limited to facts, which are boring.

Serendipitous Fame-Seekers

Serendipitous fame-seekers do not necessarily set out to attack or even to become famous. Because they are thrust into the limelight, however, they make the best of it and became *de facto* attackers by virtue of staying in the press. Serendipitous fame-seekers tend to be passive and without malice. Serendipitous fame-seekers, nevertheless, learn to enjoy their fame.

Monica Lewinsky, for example, did not want to become an attacker. However, by becoming a fixture on the Washington social scene and posing for glamour shots in *Vanity Fair*'s July 1998 edition, she kept the Clinton sex scandal in the news, which, in turn became fodder for Clinton's critics. Everybody got a little benefit from the attack. Monica got air time and, perhaps, some sympathy for her case, *Vanity Fair* got its pictures, the media got more fodder, and the political right kept the attacks on Clinton alive.

My favorite serendipitous attacker of the Clinton scandals was Paula Jones's Fabio-esque hairdresser, Daniel DiCriscio, who came to Washington to help with her "case" by styling Jones's hair. I nearly missed a flight out of Washington because the media throng around DiCriscio blocked my departure gate. He became a serendipitous attacker by getting publicity that, as a byproduct, extended the life of hostile coverage of Clinton. O. J. Simpson houseguest Kato Kaelin falls into the same category: Every time he appeared on TV, he reminded viewers of Simpson's weak alibi.

THE MAGGOTS OF FAME

The story I was looking for when Jessica Dubroff's plane crashed was about maggots. A consumer, Gil Grief,* said that he opened a client's product and found maggots inside. He called my client, Useful Stuff Corporation,* a major consumer goods manufacturer, to complain. Grief also approached his local TV consumer reporter with his tale of maggotry. The

---

*These names are fictitious.

reporter did the story and displayed the original maggot-infested product, sparking additional consumer concern in the region.

Useful Stuff sent representatives out to talk to Gil Grief and invited him to tour their plant. They wanted him to see how hard it would be for maggots to get into their product, although they acknowledge that, in a small number of cases, it could happen. Grief seemed satisfied after seeing how Useful Stuff's product was packaged and quietly retreated. For a week.

Useful Stuff then got word that Grief had approached one of the national network news programs with his maggot story. I suggested a psychological profiling of Grief. Had he been satisfied with Useful Stuff's initial—and appropriate—response, a "psych profile" would not have entered the picture. But all this media attention over something so trivial made me wonder about what Grief really wanted. Why did he return? What would it take to make him go away?

Information about Grief came in. His successful wife worked and provided the family's income. He stayed at home with a young child. He had no criminal record. Grief did have a recent history of hypochondriacal behavior, an important clue. Attackers are notorious for being hypochondriacs and malingerers. I also noticed that after Useful Stuff gave him attention of some kind, he backed away for a short while.

In the absence of evidence of a specific motive, I concluded Gil Grief was a garden-variety malcontent, a classic Elvis who probably felt overpowered by his successful wife, was bored with hanging out with the baby all day, and wanted attention. I doubted that Grief had even found maggots and counseled Useful Stuff to exploit Grief's greatest vulnerability: his vanity.

The company discreetly opened its doors to a core group of media interested in the subject to demonstrate how maggot infestation was unlikely. Grief was not invited. Useful Stuff acknowledged that packages could be—but probably weren't—damaged during the course of shipping tens of millions of them over a year. Useful Stuff also detailed the chronology of its relationship with Gil Grief and how it had responded to him at every turn.

When the press went to Grief for his comments, he was angry. I suspected he would be. The focus of his rage was not the maggots: He was angry that he hadn't been contacted for the plant walk-through. A show had

Attack Summary: Useful Stuff and Maggots (composite)	
Victim:	Gil Grief, consumers
Villain:	Useful Stuff Corporation
Vindicator:	Local investigative reporter
Void:	Need for attention
Vehicle:	Media coverage
Value:	Consumer protection

taken place and he hadn't been at center stage. The media were appalled by Grief's behavior. No further stories ever ran. I encouraged Useful Stuff not to rejoice. The success we enjoyed in this instance was not the norm and Grief had proven his capacity to get media attention. Characters like Grief don't burn out, they just find maggots in some other package.

BECOMING MEDIA

"Watching news or sports interviews on TV, you doubtless have seen people, not all of them adolescents, who carefully position themselves just in the background and jump up and down and wave frantically while wearing theatrically broad smiles. Hoping to be distinguished if only for a moment by being caught by 'a media' and recognized—glory!—by family and friends. . . ."

Paul Fussell, *Class*

To understand why fame-seekers become attackers, it's important to look at the premium placed on celebrity in the broader population. Fame-seekers, after all, are overzealous members of the culture, not aberrant invaders from outer space. Most who seek celebrity do so harmlessly. Many Americans have *become* media themselves—communications vehicles—as opposed to the "target audiences" they once were in the eyes of advertising agencies. Consumers don't just wear clothing crafted by famous designers anymore, they wear clothes with the *designers' names* emblazoned in bold letters on them. The size of the designers' names on sportswear has gotten progressively larger over the past twenty years. Originally, they appeared inside the garment on a tag. Slowly, they moved to the exterior of clothing or with a small emblem. Designer emblems have also expanded and look remarkably like a coat of arms for an English royal dynasty, which hints at a link between someone else's recognizable name and a higher state-of-being.

The hugeness of designer's names are creeping into higher fashion items as well, with names like Ralph Lauren and Kenneth Cole appearing noticeably on cuff links, eyeglasses, and watches.

The culture is also finding more vehicles for displaying itself. In 1983, according to the Photo Marketing Association, Americans bought 4.5 million cameras. By 1995, that number jumped to 10.8 million cameras. In 1988, the year figures were first recorded for disposable cameras, Americans bought 3 million units. In 1995, 54.1 million one-time use cameras were sold. In 1995, consumers spent $5.4 billion developing 710 million rolls of film up from $3.5 billion to develop 482 million rolls in 1984. According to the Photo Marketing Association, 55 percent of American households actively took photographs in 1996.

Camcorder sales hit an all-time high in 1996 with 3.6 million units selling at a cost of at least $500 each. In 1987, 1.6 million sold. The home-video recording industry is brutally competitive with manufacturers reducing costs by thousands of percents to make this equipment more affordable. In addition, the size of camcorders has been dramatically reduced and their ease of use has been improved to facilitate celebrity-dialysis so consumers can hook video cameras into their television sets to see themselves on the same tube as their favorite television programs.

Today, if I were so inclined, I could put a little camera above my computer and watch myself compose e-mail. One of the great draws of electronics stores is a camera at the entrance that allows me to step before it and see myself on the TV screen above me.

It's not enough to get attention, more and more fame-seekers want to get attention naked. Frank Sinatra's daughter, Nancy, recently posed nude in *Playboy* (May 1995), as did Drew Barrymore's mother, Jaid (September 1995, not to mention Drew herself, January 1995), dismissed O. J. Simpson juror Tracy Hampton (March 1996), and Nicole Simpson's friend Faye Resnick (March 1997). Suzen Johnson, Frank Gifford's regrettable conquest, posed for *Playboy* in the November 1997 issue. Patti Davis Reagan posed in *Playboy* in July 1994. Actress Demi Moore's mother, Virginia Guynes, posed nude for *High Society* in 1993.

Whether you've got it or not, flaunt it. Of course, the pose is never marketed as a raw grab at, forgive me, exposure. The "copy" accompanying the "layouts" inevitably hints at artistic or social values. Said Farrah Fawcett in her *Playboy* body-painting layout, "I wanted to use my body as a brush, to actually paint with parts of my body. . . . Historically, Americans have been known to have a problem with both art and nudity."

REALER THAN REAL

Television is replete with programs designed to bring fame to more and more people. There is *America's Funniest Home Videos, America's Funniest Kids,* and, of course, *America's Most Incredible Animal Rescues,* so even pets can get a little applause. In these programs, participants can get noticed by demonstrating a talent like singing or dancing or by filming somebody throwing a schnauzer on Grandpa's head as he naps. One key to higher visibility is shamelessness. Writes Robert Hughes in *Culture of Complaint,*

> Television has contributed hugely to this. To be on TV, if you *believe* in TV, is to break through the ceiling, to become realer [*sic*] than real. Many think that vulgarity is the opposite of snobbery; but snobbery is only a form of the vulgar. The real opposite of vulgarity is dignity. But this hardly matters on TV, which prefers emotion to dignity and positively loathes reserve. . . . All one needs, then, to reconcile the dreams of celebrity with the loss of dignity is a belief that self-exposure confers distinction.

As Islamic fundamentalists drive explosive-laden trucks into military barracks to get into heaven, Americans heap mortification upon themselves to get on TV. *The Jerry Springer Show* receives 2,000 calls each day from people vying to attack—and be attacked—before tens of millions. Daytime programs are filled with folks who learn for the first time that their spouses have cheated on them by watching a private investigator's surveillance tape. The betrayed spouse inevitably breaks down and cries in front of millions of people. Howard Stern regularly has women come onto his show to be questioned—and spanked—by him and to share their lesbian encounters.

Few are more willing to embarrass their targets than the near-famous. Actress Jodie Foster's brother released a book, *Foster Child,* exposing private dish about his clan. LaToya Jackson made headlines by taking shots at her musical family in *LaToya: Growing Up in the Jackson Family.* Ronald and Nancy Reagan's daughter, Patti Davis, has leveraged her genes by posing nude and publishing thinly veiled accounts of her unhappy family life. The marketplace eagerly snaps up the unauthorized biographies of famous people written by the angry ex-lovers of celebrities such as Saul Bellow, Johnnie Cochran, Clint Eastwood, Dennis Rodman, and Philip Roth.

I'LL HAVE THE MAGGOTS WITH MY CEREAL

> "When well-meaning crusaders see hysterical syndromes in the context of social crises and then publicize their views through modern communications networks, these misconceptions can give rise to epidemics and witch hunts."
>
> Elaine Showalter, *Hystories*

People who use hazards as leverage for visibility do not abandon them in the face of contrary evidence. An attention-seeker will just lower the bar and redefine the issue to keep the attention focused on him and his witch. The allegation keeps changing form so that it can creep into more places. Attackers habitually use hazards as leverage for visibility. The following scenario, as exemplified by my maggot adventure, is becoming more common:

1. Customer complains about maggots in cereal to Useful Stuff.
2. Useful Stuff engages customer.
3. Useful Stuff implements program to reduce incidents of maggots.
4. Useful Stuff is pleased with itself that it's defused the situation.
5. Customer voices second complaint about lizards in pastries.
6. *Action News'* Consumer Watchdog Report interviews customer, and baffled/angry Useful Stuff spokesperson.

As soon as the target solves the problem, the attacker takes a narcissistic hit and starts looking for other bad things even if he has to make them up. He often invokes the democratic necessity of activism to justify his behavior. This is not activism, it is what my psychiatrist friends call "acting out," narcissism masquerading as a social issue.

In a grab for visibility the actual hazard is irrelevant. Both the hazard (the maggots) and the motive (visibility) must be addressed. Had Useful Stuff based its response to Gil Grief on a vast Maggot Reduction Program, Grief would not have been satisfied. Why? No maggots, no forum. Nothing could keep Grief away from the camera. In a few short weeks, he had gone from frustrated Mr. Mom to a celebrity with camera crews on his front lawn—and he liked it.

Like mythical Narcissus, who fell in love with his own image in a fountain and turned into a flower, the culture loses its way when angling for fame melts into obsession, provokes attack, or makes us lose sight of more pressing matters. It is in this desperate spirit that in Richard Linklater's critically acclaimed film *Slacker*, one Generation X character attempts to sell her friends Madonna's pap smear test sample, claiming it came from a Hollywood gynecologist. Disgusting? Sure, but it says something about what is now exalted.

Eventually, a crash like Jessica Dubroff's is inevitable when the malignant aspects of fame-seeking become undeniable when once-normal people come to see celebrity as their birthright. Robert O'Donnell learned this when he saved another little girl named Jessica, Jessica McClure, the baby who fell into a Texas well in 1987. O'Donnell committed suicide in 1995. By most accounts, the suicide was tied to the evaporation of his fame. His suicide note read, "No help from nobody but family."

When celebrity is a byproduct of a legitimate crusade, no harm is done in letting the new star revel in his fame. The desire to be noticed, however, has become malignant in recent years because fame is being pursued at the expense of society's best interest and, in some cases, the attacker's as well. Sadly, I have become handy at spotting star-seeking attackers and have experienced the havoc they wreak. It is often in both my clients' best interests—and the culture's—to facilitate attackers' return to a richly deserved obscurity.

17. *Usual Suspects: Crisis Cast of Characters and Dissuasive Facts of Life*

Knowing who's who and how to deal with them offers a dissuasive head start.

> "Now I'm hiding in Honduras
> I'm a desperate man
> Send lawyers, guns and money
> The shit has hit the fan."
> Warren Zevon, "Lawyers, Guns and Money"

My partner, Nick Nichols, and I were greeting people as they arrived at a party commemorating our firm's tenth anniversary. One of our clients asked what the attacks we've worked on have in common.

Almost simultaneously, we remarked, "Usual suspects."

What we meant was that the same cast of characters keep showing up to attacks. Over the years, I have kept track of these players, by type. While the composites that follow are involved in many types of attacks, they are especially active in corporate attacks. I have included profiles of the attackers and descriptions of those who often find themselves under siege to offer insight into the people and motivations that comprise attacks.

What follows is a list of personality types, what makes them tick, and practical rules of thumb for approaching and assessing them and defusing attacks. Keep an eye out for them.

244

CAST OF CHARACTERS

Offense: The Attackers

The Zealot: True-believing child of the 1960s or wants to be. Highly educated, intelligent. Persuaded that the nemesis *du jour* is the Anti-Christ. Easily switches Anti-Christs. Nothing is a little bit harmful: IT WILL KILL YOU. Fondness for hyperbole. Keeps enemies list longer than Nixon's but believes *your* enemies list is immoral. Tends to confuse those having opposing views with Nazi Waffen SS and may, in fact, be liberal with Third Reich references. The Zealot has a distinct advantage in attack situations due to symbiotic relationship with the media and his absolute believability. Tends to fumble big issues due to lack of institutional infrastructure. *Watch for a Smart Target to* fear and respect the Zealot; avoid giving the Zealot a forum but challenge him when he's wrong. Never debate him on television. Characterize him as out-of-touch with mainstream values and priorities.

The Opportunist: Single-issue attacker who gets a big charge out of celebrity. Were it not for the serendipitous attack, the Opportunist would be nowhere, which is probably where he's going when the attack is over. Believes one looks right at camera during media interview and overuses host's name to feign familiarity with Hollywood. May be independently wealthy or utterly desperate. May also disappear and re-emerge upon discovery of new issue. *Watch for a Smart Target to* let the Opportunist self-destruct.

The Progressive: Mainstream activist organization leader who may look "crunchy" but is a shrewd capitalist and political operative. The Progressive denies this. Works well with business interests. Tends to pick up issues that were fumbled by the Zealot such as the attacks in the late 1980s on plastic food service items. Views attack topics as fundraising franchises and guards them jealously. *Watch for a Smart Target to* appeal exclusively to political, strategic instincts. *Words* should imply you believe the Progressive is a crusader. *Actions* should assume Progressive is in business. Attack may be defused if the Progressive knows how a truce benefits him.

The Weeping Extortionist: Victim for the purpose of getting money. Very likely a sociopath, but highly sympathetic. Chronically aggrieved. Thief. Intelligent but doesn't always cover tracks due to years of getting away with extortion, both emotional and financial. Maintains enablers who truly believe in the Weeping Extortionist. Has financial problems. May be avid church-goer or could maintain some other moral cover. Cries easily, especially when caught. *Your Approach:* Use all legal means necessary to stop and make an example of the Weeping Extortionist. Target will feel guilty about doing this. That's the point.

Mrs. Kravitz: Busybody, pseudovictim of grievance-chic, named for the Stevens' neighbor on the TV series *Bewitched.* Very difficult personality. Claims to have relative (e.g., politician, brilliant attorney son) who will bury the target. Main thing afflicting Mrs. Kravitz is too much time on her hands. She could care less if problem is solved; she needs there to be a problem due to huge narcissistic investment in heartache. *Watch for a Smart Target to* listen, buy time, suck up, feign fear. In time, Mrs. Kravitz usually finds a new villain.

The Barrister: Plaintiff's lawyer. Postures as one of the little people, but may have personal aircraft. Well connected with media, especially consumer reporters and magazine programs. He's the single most powerful force in Culture of Attack because of media access and fear factor. *Watch for a Smart Target to* characterize issue as tort-driven and make sure the media know who's behind their "consumer report."

The Victim's Network: Collection of mean-spirited people united in the belief that there is a single cause for their misfortunes: the target. Not to be confused with legitimate support groups for life's misfortunes (e.g., AIDS, alcoholism, family tragedy). Tends to be manipulated, if not organized, by plaintiff's lawyer. Never satisfied. *Watch for a Smart Target to* divide them by pitting one egomaniacal faction leader against another by giving media attention to the number two player in the Network. Hear them out because it will release tension, not because anything will be learned. Designate one (very patient) point-person to politely manage them.

Chicken Little: Activist/scientist who certifies danger. Quasi-scientific credentials. May like wearing lab coats or reading glasses during interviews. Close to the Zealot. Only formulates conclusions using mostly negative research. Dismisses contrary evidence as being flawed by virtue of its having been done by someone else. Demands that attack target prove an outrageous negative (e.g., that certain chemicals didn't create lesbian seagulls). *Watch for a Smart Target to* get good science and appeal to top-notch experts for the purpose of comforting the public, not educating them.

The Victim: One who *genuinely* suffers through no fault of his or her own. If the target contributed to the Victim's problem, the target had better contribute to the Victim's recovery. Targets should have no illusions about good behavior paying dividends. Focus on doing the right thing because it's right, not because there's a payoff. In a public relations war, the Victim always wins. The Victim reminds a spoiled culture about true suffering and why the Culture of Attack is so dangerous. The Victim also presents us all with a chance to repent. *Watch for a Smart Target to* repent.

The Child Prop: Kid being used by special interests. Bright, glib, and attractive. Ambitious parents. May have school science project validating basis of attack. *Your approach:* Never debate the Child Prop; consider funding Child Prop's future projects. Best to fight the Child Prop by propping up one's own Child Prop and let 'em slug it out, or just let Child Prop have his fifteen minutes of fame.

The Vampire: Expert in discretionary warfare often hired by corporate or political interests to smear a target. The Vampire is never honest about his sponsors. Works out of home office, operates under cover of darkness, and usually seeks to link target with a hazard. The Vampire is often a semi-retired "consultant" who assembles a team including Internet whiz kids, mass mailing houses, counterfeit activists, PR people, and "expert testimony" hucksters. He probably reports to the attacking organization's general counsel to keep his work privileged. *Watch for a Smart Target to* expose the covert role of the Vampire. Vampires hate sunlight. Make the Vampire the issue by educating the media about how they were duped.

Defense: Those Who Are Attacked

The following cast of characters assumes that a team has been established to fight the attack. These folks turn up most frequently at corporations under siege.

The Chosen: Person on whom fate smiled too broadly for the mob's liking. Thin-skinned. Besieged. Had parent who instilled in him a colossal sense of destiny. The Chosen maintains this sense throughout life. Dreadfully concerned about invincible public opinion, which hampers defense. Will only survive if he appreciates that destiny is siezed, not bestowed.

Thatcher: Official in charge of crisis, named after the audacious British prime minister (Thatcher can, of course, be male). Thatcher is not necessarily a CEO. Women are somewhat better at being crisis team leaders because after years of exclusion from institutional power they have taken more risks, suffered greater adversities, and are, therefore, less preoccupied with job security than male counterparts. Thatcher has solid moral rudder and superb instincts. Decisive, brave, wholesome, charismatic, however, she tends to be ornery. Understands that "crisis" means danger *and* opportunity. Crisis becomes her.

Denialasaurus Rex: Disengaged chief executive who delegates the crisis, delegation being perceived as a good thing. Angles for delegatee to get nailed, not him. Not in control of operation. Obsessed with appearances. Makes statements like: "We gotta get back to making widgets," implication being that the crisis shouldn't be happening to him. Short-term thinker who makes expedient decisions in order to avoid confrontation.

The Top Flack: Top communicator in organization under siege. Highly vulnerable employment-wise when under attack. Knows this. Very media savvy. Rightly accepts NASA's dictum: "When things are going well, tell the media everything they want to know; when things are going badly, tell them even more."

The Runway Model: Outside public relations consultant; immaculately dressed salesperson often with advertising agency experience. Believes good manners are key to attack resolution. Will rule out any course of action that offends anyone. Tends to offer chestnuts of wisdom such as "Speak with one voice" and "Don't wear white shirts on TV." Trades heavily on long-standing relationship with Top Flack. Has equally attractive aide de camp. One can tell that the Runway Model's counsel was influential if the attack response consists of vapid, but highly publicized stunts, whereby the target demonstrates affection for children.

The Flower Child: Believes if the target "just sits down and talks" to the attackers, everything will work out fine. May come to meetings taking detailed notes on laptop, which will be used against the target in court. Favors the words "inappropriate" and "boundaries." The Flower Child is an attacker's greatest unwitting ally because he preaches surrender.

The Oracle: Grizzled veteran of a thousand attacks, nearing retirement. Has served in numerous capacities throughout the organization. Unassuming and able to sublimate ego. Title may not be impressive but top management cherishes the Oracle.

The Jackal: Operative who takes attack too personally. Wants attacker eliminated, and means it. May engage in dirty tricks to this end. Jackals have been dying off since Watergate.

The Esquire: General counsel. Anxious. Risk averse. Despite profession, does not want to litigate. Opposes all forms of communication. Very close to Thatcher. You know the Esquire is running things when the target accepts no responsibility and denies all culpability (witness tobacco industry executives' appearances before Congress).

The Man with No Name: The outside crisis management consultant who's only objective is to make the problem go away. The Man with No Name is impatient, doesn't schmooze, doesn't want to be anybody's friend. Work is labor of love. The public rarely sees the Man with No Name, if ever. Motto: "It doesn't do to leave a live dragon out of your calculations if you happen to live near one" (from J. R. R. Tolkien's *The Hobbit*).

The Psychic: Person who says he saw the attack coming. May be harmless internal personality or whistleblower, depending upon personal finances. The Psychic believes self to be morally superior to everyone else. If the Psychic just claims to have made a prediction, target will be faced with nuisance. If the Psychic told other people, target has a problem. If the Psychic has evidence of his prediction (e.g., memorandum), target has a crisis. If the Psychic is correct, target must heed his warning and remediate. If Psychic is incorrect, Psychic must be removed from the team. Target must make no hostile moves on the Psychic if there is a smoking gun, publicly or privately—audiences will empathize with the Psychic. Target must demonstrate in excruciating detail how and why it did not heed the Psychic's warning.

The Independents

Following are profiles of attack players who, technically, aren't supposed to be on any one side but will end up siding with attackers.

The Producer: Broadcast honcho covering attack, perhaps for newsmagazine. Obligated for business reasons to side with party that appears helpless. Nothing personal. Thinks visually, as if reality is a TV show. May say that target will be pleasantly surprised with segment. Target won't be. Vindictive as hell. *Watch for a Smart Target to* return all calls for the purpose of listening, not sharing. Think visually like the Producer. Negotiate interview ground rules; confirm everything in writing; keep detailed logs. Go above Producer's head only in extreme situations.

Lois Lane: Print reporter covering attack for major publication. Has a sense of mission. Obsessive; may know more about target than target. Possibly very young, but not to be underestimated. Lois cannot be fooled, so don't stonewall. Fairer than broadcast counterpart but will turn on target if lied to or if betrayal is the better career move. *Watch for a Smart Target to* give Lois an excellent scoop. Maintain qualitative, long-term approach to Lois by providing her with consistently good information.

The Politician: Political figure who takes on attack, usually as hostile party. May be in cahoots with the Producer. Motivated by votes and is, therefore, media obsessed. Shameless. *Watch for a Smart Target to* introduce political risk as soon as possible. Concentrate on voters. Find Politicians or constituents sympathetic to target and have them fight with hostile Politician so target doesn't have to.

DISSUASIVE FACTS OF LIFE

> "An old Oregon rancher once told me, 'There are three types of men in the world. One type learns from books. One type learns from observations. And one type just has to urinate on the electric fence himself.' "
>
> Listener to radio psychiatrist Dr. Laura Schlessinger, 1996

What follows are points of counsel about what works—and what doesn't—in managing attacks. Targets should factor in this advice.

The truth will out. The emergence of the real story should be the moral and strategic objective of most defenses. In the Culture of Attack, everyone expects a coverup, so the target must make plans to reveal the truth or a hostile party will reveal it for them. Said comedian Bill Maher in *Playboy*, "Whenever you bury the truth, it comes back to haunt you. It's like telling a lie on the first date. Somewhere down the line she's going to find out it isn't a loaner, that the piece of shit you drive is really the only car you own."

If guilty, repent; if innocent, attack. Innocent targets should initiate a savage defense, which must include efforts to expose the attacker's facts and motives. Make the issue the attacker's unholy agenda. The public expects innocent targets to defend themselves passionately and doesn't trust passive victims of hostility. Silicone breast implant manufacturers insisted upon the safety of their products and were ultimately vindicated by scientific panels, albeit at great cost.

A target should "break" his own defense to the media. The one with the most to lose should drive the defense. Targets must engineer a defense as if they were reporters on the trail of a "hot," counterintuitive, man-bites-dog story. Targets may find allies but remain essentially alone and must fight ruthlessly and audaciously for vindication. My firm once counseled a client to announce that it would discontinue broadcasting a controversial advertisement rather than wait for the media to notice that the ad had stopped running. By making the announcement, we deprived the ad's critics of an opportunity to "uncover" a controversy.

Determine if the attack has "legs" before firing back. Some attacks don't catch on, so targets mustn't start a fight if there doesn't need to be one. Hypersensitive people take such offense at criticism that they risk extending the life of negative exposure by fighting back needlessly. This frequently happens when a target becomes obsessed with one inaccuracy in a news story that no one, other than the target, really cares about. In a scare-a-minute age, the public has a limited attention span. This attack might just be the one that no one cares about. More and more, the day after intensive coverage of a given attack . . . nothing happens. A clothing manufacturer I know once insisted on writing an angry "letter to the editor" denying a litany of charges he felt he had been accused of. After the letter had been printed, investigators—having been unaware of some of the accusations—proceeded to expand their inquiry into the manufacturer's activities.

If the attack has "legs," targets must fire back right away. When an attack catches on, not responding is an endorsement of the attacker's position. Time is the second most important variable in attack resolution after basic guilt or innocence. Targets forfeit their right to equal time if they wait too long before responding because audiences find delays suspicious even if there is a reasonable explanation for the delay. *In an attack, suspense convicts, not guilt.* The public gravitates toward loudmouths, so targets should yell as loudly as their attackers. The notion that challenging an attacker only gives him credibility is nonsense. The chances are that a target under attack has no credibility in the first place. The chairman of Exxon was intensely —and rightly—criticized when it took him two weeks to visit Prince William Sound after the 1989 *Valdez* oil spill. His delay made the company appear to be unfeeling about the disaster.

Defuse attacks on visceral emotion, not reason. Targets must know and communicate the facts of their case but not rely on them. The public responds better to emotional cues than it does to facts. Targets must communicate on the frequency their audience receives, a frequency that easily processes basic instincts such as believability, likability, and empathy. To do this, targets must stand in the audience's shoes. Would they believe their argument if they were in the audience? How would one expect an attack target to behave in this situation? If innocent, targets should show distress, but if guilty, they should share the plan for repentance. Ronald Reagan neutralized public perceptions that he was insensitive to human struggles by peppering his speeches with references to extraordinary achievements by ordinary Americans. He often saluted these people who were in the audience during his State of the Union addresses.

Differentiate between strategic and narcissistic publicity. If a target is selling something, he can promote it, but should keep focused on his target audience. If there's no direct business objective, targets should avoid the press. Drawing broad attention to oneself, one's product, one's idea or service is too dangerous in this climate. Narcissistic publicity is a key factor in *schadenfreude*-driven attacks. A handful of high-powered Washington lobbyists have gotten into trouble by publicizing their plush offices, hefty fees, and client lists. The appearance of profiting from political influence has outraged lawmakers, journalists, and clients alike.

Driving up positives alone—image building—won't reduce the negatives being alleged. Audiences don't appreciate benefits unless they are convinced that the risks aren't serious. Image-building campaigns assume that everybody likes a target's goodies as much as they do. It's a dangerous assumption. Targets can't hide from the fundamental allegation-at-hand and must be prepared to drive down the negatives with a defense that includes contrary evidence, a roadmap for improvement, or discrediting their attacker.

The "benefits" approach is a public relations gimmick that was used by financier Michael Milken's handlers when he was under indictment for securities fraud. Milken was photographed taking kids to baseball games. But Milken wasn't indicted for being mean to kids. This publicity stunt didn't neutralize the root accusation: stealing.

Good crisis management teams are not democracies. A number of people on a crisis defense team should have *influence* but only one should have *authority.* Not everybody gets an equal vote. Targets must designate a leader with whom the buck stops and keep the team as small as possible. Good chief executives under fire for product safety allegations will seek the input of their scientific advisors, but rarely will let them govern the crisis management process. This is because scientists usually speak in statistical terms and are often bad at addressing the emotional concerns of consumers.

Bypass attackers. In responding to an attack, the target audience should be limited to those who can impact a resolution. Hostile parties are hostile for a reason: They don't like the target. They should be written off. Targets are under no obligation to educate their attackers. Ronald Reagan knew that the press hated him so he avoided press conferences and spoke directly to the people when he wanted to get something done.

Embrace the "Anti-Story." Contrary assessments often follow an attack. If attackers get something wrong in Round 1, targets should exploit their mistakes in Round 2. Sometimes it pays to wait for the avalanche to pass before unleashing the best response strategy. The public expects targets to fight back and won't respect those who don't. Targets must create and exploit opportunities to communicate a counterintuitive message. Manufacturers of disposable food service items were not fully able to communicate the sanitary benefits of their products until the land-fill shortage "crisis" was exposed as being baseless. The debunking of the scare made the media and consumers alike more willing to reexamine the benefits of disposables.

Operate with brutal self-knowledge. Targets should know and cherish their deepest weaknesses and should not attempt to execute a macho dissuasion strategy if they are incapable of seeing it through. Anyone under siege should be true to their flawed nature. Pose and perish.

The rules aren't the same for everyone. Beautiful, charming people; manufacturers of wildly popular products; and messengers of fashionable thinking can get away with things that most cannot. Though this is mad-dening, targets must work within the objective laws of the cosmos, not ideal notions of the way things should be. President Jimmy Carter's efforts to take a "hard line" on foreign policy issues almost always back-fired. Carter has been far more successful in his post–White House career as a peacemaker and healer, which he truly is.

Targets must make their defense about something other than themselves. Nobody cares about a target's problems. In a fight, targets must stand behind a principal or a personally relevant experience. Bill Clinton deflected many of the serious legal questions about his conduct by emphasizing the sexual nature of the inquiries. Clinton and his aides understood full well that no one wants to have his or her sex life investi-gated and, therefore, the public would be sympathetic to his position.

Targets must not show support for those who attack them. Doing so is not shrewd. It is stupid. The notion that concessions to hostile par-ties might be an investment for future purposes is absurd. Corporations under attack by Greenpeace have been giving them money for years on this premise and Greenpeace keeps attacking them anyway.

If a target is ethical, it should be ethical and be quiet. Nobody believes public displays of morality anymore. The most upstanding people are discreetly upstanding; they don't campaign on it. Advertising campaigns and sermons about ethics are regarded as jokes. Quiet morality is respected. Hypocrisy is always big news.

Not everybody who disagrees with a target is an attacker. Paranoia is not pretty. Targets must be sparing with the attacker label because attackers can be right. When they are, the problem-at-hand must be addressed. When the attackers are wrong, they must be challenged, but targets must not characterize the hostilities as a plot to get them, even if it is. These things make targets look insane, unless the public shares your view that there already *is* a conspiracy.

Attacks on corporate interests and high-profile people are viewed as victimless crimes. Attackers are outraged when targets defend themselves. Targets must demonstrate humanity and vulnerability. Corporations should, whenever possible, show the *effects* of attacks that people can personally relate to, such as the deprivation of a popular product or service or a real-live employee impacted by an attack. Statistics are useless. Fifty thousand people getting laid off is acceptable. One crying kid is not. When an activist group has planted spies within corporations, the public tends to view this as being gutsy. When my corporate clients have employed covert methods to catch infiltrators, the press tends to characterize their tactics as being sleazy—despite the damage the infiltrators have done to their businesses.

Differentiate between strategic and therapeutic responses. There are times when striking back at attackers would feel good but won't accomplish anything. The objective of dissuasion is to make the attack go away, not teach someone a lesson.

If a target doesn't win the fight, it wasn't necessarily mishandled. Modern culture has lost sight of the world's great outside forces: gravity, disease, human nature. Failure is a part of rather than an exception to life. Not all victories were engineered by geniuses and not all losses were botched by fools. Audi's flawed handling of accusations during the mid-1980s that its luxury model spontaneously accelerated certainly didn't help the company resolve its crisis. Media and activist attacks, however, were so vicious that there was little the company could do to reverse the momentum of negative publicity.

What targets don't know may destroy them. Investigations, be they cursory Lexis-Nexis checks, or in-depth intelligence-gathering efforts, can help determine the potential cause of an attack and how much may—or may not—be needed to defuse it. An analysis of the opposition may reveal an adversary's true intentions, his "Achilles heel," and his *modus operandi.* Had General Motors' investigators not located the rocket motor used by *Dateline NBC* to detonate one of its pick-up trucks, the company product would have been forever labeled a hazard.

The goal is to defuse the attack, not get a valentine. When targets defuse an attack, their attackers won't like them. No one should be shocked by this. People hate losing even if they deserved to lose. If being loved is the target's true objective, let the attacker win right away and get it over with. A lawsuit by cattlemen against Oprah Winfrey for making anti-beef remarks may not have garnered much sympathy from the public, but reckless media coverage of "Mad Cow" disease dropped off precipitously after the suit was filed.

The greatest attack weapon in our climate is the pretense of weakness. Never confuse histrionics with suffering. Not everybody's grievance is on par with genocide, so targets must not accept their attacker's victim status too quickly. On several occasions in my career, purported victims of client negligence have turned out to be convicted extortionists.

Ignore all pundits. Those outside of the attack are operating with limited perspective and selfish agendas. Pundits often know more about personal publicity than they do the subjects about which they comment. Pundits are not a target's relevant audience. They're salespeople, not experts.

The media aren't always the enemy. Targets must respect the media because destruction is their prerogative, but one should not assume that destruction is the media's *objective.* News is just another consumer product, and the media are its manufacturers and merchants. A target can either help the press make its product or distract them from the assembly line. Targets must either bring reporters a commodity of value—like hard facts—or not expect any help. A good reporter has been at the core of every unwarranted attack that I have ever helped defuse. Hard-nosed journalists can be an attack target's best friend.

Targets must question their attackers' "rights." Unless attackers carry with them the force of law, targets should feel no pressure to surrender under the pretense of democratic principles. Targets should ask their attacker to cite the amendment to the Constitution where they are granted the *right* to destroy them.

18. *The Anti–Nail 'Em!*

To survive the Culture of Attack, worry about it.

"Real culture lives by sympathies and admirations, not by dislikes and disdains; under all misleading wrappings it pounces unerringly upon the human core."

William James

When a client in trouble hires me, bravado closes the deal. People who aren't used to firefights like the idea of being in a foxhole with someone who has spent his career in combat. "You love it—and it doesn't get to you," Big Dave, a chief executive told me admiringly. "That's why I went with you."

Confession time. Down deep, I know my aggressive rap has helped build my business. It's a benign narcotic that gives me a charge. But Big Dave is wrong about my nature. I love my business *because* it gets to me.

I see my clients as decent people trying to make a living. In the Culture of Attack, however, they are not seen as people. They are pop-up "bad guys" like the characters who get killed on *NYPD Blue* one week and turn up on *Homicide* the next. Only once my clients are hanged, they don't just pop up elsewhere in our electronic Vaudeville. They're gone—fired, bankrupt, ridiculed, shamed. And because they have been deprived of their humanness, their attackers and the public don't let such personal or corporate destruction get to them.

The noncrimes of Richard Jewell, Admiral Boorda, and Cardinal Bernardin are on the record forever. We've heard of their cases, which makes them unique: The public has been informed that what happened to them was wrong. Americans were informed because these targets found themselves in the nation's headlines and the media self-flagellated after their attacks.

We only get a few media self-flagellations a year and that's enough for me. I have an aversion to public displays of reflection, whether they are put on by reporters, executives, activists, or politicians. These vigils allow theater to replace penitence. The culture should be equally bothered by supercilious corporations that drone on about "good citizenship"; activist groups that invoke hazards whenever they need cash; and reporters who soul search on the air to score points with their audience. Genuine penitence is painful and doesn't get ratings because the same public that may find it amusing doesn't find it sincere.

The real casualties of the Culture of Attack are the ones no one ever hears about because they happen all the time and blend in to the crushing throng of allegation. Sometimes the casualties even work for big companies.

Not all of my clients get rescued. Not all of them deserve to be. It's a lot more fun to expose an extortionist than it is to try to make people feel better about the recall of a damaged product.

The thrill of working for someone who is wrongly under siege is that I can help affect the outcome. I will win or I will lose. If I win, I will love the win. If I lose, I will hate the loss. If my client deserved to get hit, I will enjoy helping him mend his ways. If he refuses to redress a wrong, I will curse my limitations. But no matter what happens, the fight will "get" to me.

The hardest part of writing about the Culture of Attack has been to avoid positioning all aggressive discourse, the backbone of a free society, as being somehow illegitimate. There is no test to differentiate where spirited debate ends and spiteful attacks begin. What worries me is that America's attack-fest makes communities lose sight of the things that really need attacking. I can't mandate what our biggest worry should be—cancer, poverty, or asteroids. All I know is that Americans should be able to judge a crisis when one comes along and I don't think this is easy to do anymore.

The prescription for stopping attacks is to first be bothered by them. Indifference is acceptance. The next step is to discard the delusions that we occupy a gentler planet than that of our forebears. Modern attackers just use different gadgets and ideologies of congratulation that weren't in vogue before. Attackers are often cavemen with collegiate polish.

The country is a lot jumpier these days because of its anticipation of the third millennium. The great changeover has been a recurring theme in everything from marketing campaigns to religious predictions. Only now, the big moment is here and no one is sure what it means, or if it means anything at all.

The millennium is a milestone for symbolic reasons. It's either associated with scary things or opportunities for renewal. The year 2000 is getting to us and I'm happy to see it. "Worrying works," wrote Philip Roth in *American Pastoral.* Worry builds businesses, protects our children, and keeps our genes moving into the next generation. In turn-of-the-century Salem, the people became distressed by the hangings. So they corralled Reverend Parris and got back to the business of building a nation.

Attacks are getting to a lot of people, including presidents, journalists, and people like my clients. Targets are hitting back in a crusade that I'll call the "Anti–Nail 'Em!" Sometimes I agree with those who are under attack, sometimes I don't. Either way, I love the sound made by the new resistance: General Motors going after *Dateline NBC*; Bill and Hillary Clinton swinging back at their critics; Richard Jewell taking on the FBI; my clients who let me expose their faux-victim attackers as extortionists. I like seeing an accused witch of any stripe enumerate for her attackers the rights they *don't* have.

Targets are hitting back because they have begun to recognize attacks for what they are: threats, pure and simple. Their struggles are part of a broader campaign for survival. As the millennium turns, expect to see even more resistance. I'll be out there somewhere on the range, disabusing attackers of their conviction that "nailing" a target is their constitutional right. Rest assured that the fight will get to me.

19. *Icon Power!*

The personality and character of the leader trumps "strategic planning."

"The first responsibility of a leader is to define reality."

Max DePree

Ah, "strategy." The very use of the word implies both steely intelligence and a comprehensive plan that can, at the flick of a switch, put the most insidious crisis safely in the past. In two decades in the damage control business, I never cease to be amazed by the sense of relief that executives feel when they are told that a "strategic crisis management plan" has been prepared. When I raise the issue, however, of the "personality" and "character" of the chief executive, expressions go blank, as if I were talking about something trivial such as whether the CEO wears briefs or boxers. Truth is, when a crisis hits, the personality and character of the chief executive matter far more than strategic planning.

In ugly times, strategic plans are at best marginally useful. This is because the devil (the creator of all crises), by nature, has already read your plan. He has a list of your strengths, your resources, and the scenarios for which you have planned. He also has a list of your weaknesses, your liabilities, and the scenarios for which you have not planned. Guess which list he's going to use?

Contrary to what is increasingly being taught in business schools, crises are crises because they usually cannot be anticipated. If they could, corporations would not hire crisis management advisors, but rather purchase crisis management versions of the magic 8-balls sold at novelty stores. Crises generally arrive as unannounced guests, and that fact of life sends professors and public relations people into paroxysms of denial. Why? Central to conventional crisis planning is disdain for uncertainty and celebration of a cozy belief in fixed variables and tidy solutions. Every question has a clear answer, every problem has an unfailing solution, and every business functions in a risk-free utopia.

But a risk-free environment does not exist.

We live in a world of fluid change that all but precludes the utility of anything presuming to be an all-encompassing "plan." Your best friend one minute is your worst enemy the next. An organization you've never heard of suddenly shows up at your corporate headquarters demanding to know why your product is causing cancer. *60 Minutes* decides that you, not Lee Harvey Oswald, killed JFK. The last example may seem extreme (though based on my experience, not entirely unfathomable), but the central point remains: crises are predators that do not discriminate among their prey.

For that reason, when my firm is retained to help defuse an attack, we tend to focus more on the executives in charge than we do strategic plans. Put another way, we prefer having the stances, actions, and, on occasion, gut feelings of those in charge determine the strategy; not the other way around. Why? Because we have found that the executives embody the strategy. In fact, there is a direct relationship between the leadership of the chief executive (not always the corporate CEO) and the successful resolution of a crisis. I have never found such a correlation to exist between crisis plans and happy endings.

INSTANT ICONS

Attack Summary: Terrorist Attacks on America—2001–present

Victim: Citizens of the United States
Villain: Osama bin Laden; al-Qaeda
Vindicator: United States government
Void: Leadership
Vehicle: Media statements; military action
Value: Freedom

After the September 11 terrorist attacks on the United States, the focus of the American public and news media shifted drastically. Gone from the front pages were harrowing tales of sharks attacking without cause and warnings of their unprecedented numbers (although later reports revealed that the number of incidents actually decreased from the previous year and, for the century, remained statistically flat). Gone from broadcast monitors were images of Congressman Gary Condit walking to his car, leaving the Capitol grounds, and mum-lippedly performing other banal tasks.

Now, Americans had to face real events, true terror, and a stream of disquieting hard news. And from the accompanying narrative sprung several new faces, largely unknown outside the Beltway, whose words and actions would determine the course of our now-changed lives.

The American public bore witness as the news media scrambled to find and instantly disseminate information on the new players, both domestic and global. And in the end, the images and stories that rolled off the presses and bounced off satellites into our homes gave us three instant icons.

But before examining in greater detail how George W. Bush, Donald Rumsfeld, and Rudy Giuliani emerged as unlikely heroes, consider the mechanics of what exactly took place.

There's some truth to the saying "You can only make a first impression once," and based on the public's overwhelmingly positive opinion of Bush, Rumsfeld, and Giuliani during the first hours and days after the tragic event, it's clear that they made good ones. Furthermore, that opinion endured with incredibly little deviation throughout the weeks and months that followed the crisis.

And there's that word again. Crisis. It begs the question of how effective Bush, Rumsfeld, and Giuliani were at crisis management.

The answer? Very successful. But why? And how much of it was genius?

At least initially, their successes were more a function of style—of branding—than they were about effective strategies to respond to the worst episode in modern U.S. history. Facing an unknown, unthinkable situation, the fundamental characteristic shared by those three was strong leadership. They said and did things that, by nature of their clarity, shaped and drove later strategy. They didn't turn to contingency plans (and for these events, there weren't any), and they certainly didn't run and hide. They simply and unequivocally did what leaders do: they led.

FROM "STRATEGERY" TO "WE WILL NOT FALTER"

"The future has a way of arriving unannounced."

George Will

On September 11, George W. Bush found his "brand."

Prior to September 11, one of my friends who was bewildered by my vote for Bush summed him up as a "shit-kicking Texan," a present-day Yosemite Sam. While he didn't elaborate, it was clear that this had been no compliment.

One of Bush's greatest assets, however, was his gross underestimation by the news media and, for that matter, much of the American public. Prior to September 11, Bush had been widely portrayed as an idiot at worst, a nonentity at best, and a one-lining shoot 'em up caricature of the Wild West in between, as typified by my friend's remark. Thought not at all flattering, this seemingly disadvantageous characterization became, in fact, an opportunity. Because of the situation created by external factors (Bush's lack of foreign relations experience and the clear need for foreign relations), any Bush decision or action perceived to be anywhere north of mediocre would elicit a positive public response. And that is precisely what happened.

In the early hours of the crisis, some in the news media attempted to position Bush as having fled responsibility by jetting off to a nebulous sequence of "secure locations" rather than go to Washington and take command. This charge didn't stick, nor should it have. As later recounted in a *Washington Post* series on the day of and days following 9/11, Bush's repeated declarations that he wanted to "go back home" to the White House took backseat to security protocol. And more importantly, most Americans intuitively understood that the United States was under attack and that the nation's leaders were attempting to determine the extent to which the president was being threatened. As a result, the media appeared to sense that Bush-bashing was not an option, and coverage became heartily patriotic.

It's no secret that in times of crisis Americans rally behind their leader—any leader—but President Bush proved himself to be uniquely deserving of support. He used clear and direct rhetoric, and repeated simple themes such as "resolve," "justice," and, of course, "evil." He was emotional, tears visible in his eyes as he spoke of devastating casualties. He was vocal and spontaneous as he descended upon New York City with confidence to rally firefighters and other rescue workers. A once aimless Bush, in fact, had found his specialty, that of a concerned but strong big brother who didn't need perfect board scores to govern effectively.

As it turned out, a "shit-kicking Texan" was precisely what we needed.

Prior to 9/11, President Bush was widely portrayed in the news media as a childlike preppy who achieved the presidency only as a result of his obscene good fortune to have been born George H. W. Bush's son and Prescott Bush's grandson. His public image, at worst, was personified by *Saturday Night Live* comedian Will Ferrell, who played Bush as an overgrown prep school smart aleck who could be driven into hysterics by the mention of the word "underwear" or the first name of his vice president, Dick. The European media corps dubbed him a "toxic Texan" and questioned his ability to navigate the sea of international diplomacy. And at best, Bush was widely thought of as the aloof company founder's son, who has the smarts to hire a professional chief executive officer in Vice President Cheney. Bush hadn't achieved anything great since being elected, the reasoning went, but he hadn't done anything bad, so who cared?

When Bush got word of the attacks—he was reading to second-graders at an elementary school in Sarasota, Florida—he appeared to be stricken. Of course, he was distressed by the loss of life, but he also recognized that History had come looking for him, and the planet was watching. Neither his family connections nor his fabled sense of humor would gain him much now. Complicating matters was that the United States wasn't up against a clear-cut enemy that the nation could retaliate against. In the hours after the attack, Americans weren't sure who the enemy was let alone had tangible plans to retaliate or secure our borders. Existing plans and past experience did not account for the crisis that actually walked through the door, as often is the case.

In the absence of an obvious action, what Bush would need to dampen our rightful sense of terror was to realize that leaders and leadership, not pieces of paper, often carry the day. And to demonstrate that mindset and instill confidence in the American public, he would have to come forth with a certain personality, a character that sent a simple message: I am the right leader for this terrible time.

ELEVATION TO ICON

What Bush did that worked, and why.

In horrible times the American public wants to like its leader—at least for a while. It is a major premise of this book, supported by countless hours spent in corporate boardrooms, that the proverbial benefit of the doubt is quite a reality. America is a country built on giving people a chance. But as a pampered beast accustomed to starkly high standards, the American public also demands results in exchange for that chance. People will not be forgiving if a leader does not deliver, either by demonstrably solving the problem at hand or by providing reassurance that we're on the road to recovery.

To do so, Bush needed to define himself and his mission to the American, and global, public. Put another way, he needed to create his brand.

For perspective, corporations often pump millions of dollars into building a product's brand. They spend countless hours analyzing market research to determine what consumers want. Then they tweak their product's composition, packaging color, or a host of other attributes to try to meet that demand. And then they retest. And retest ad infinitum. It's a painstaking process that involves measured steps, careful evaluation, and, above all, time.

Bush, however, didn't have that luxury. He needed to project an image—the right image—and he needed to project it now.

So how did he succeed?

Clarity: Bush spoke in understandable terms

From the onset, Bush used clear, decisive rhetoric to help establish his brand. When crafting an image, he could not afford to be misunderstood. He had to let the American public know that he would protect them, and he had to let his country's enemies know that he would come after them. In other words—in his words—he had to communicate that he would "make no distinction between the terrorists who committed these acts and those who harbor them."

Emotion: Bush connected with his audience

In a photo opportunity in the Oval Office several days after the attacks, Bush answered a few questions from the press. As he described himself as "a loving guy," his eyes reddened and welled up. It was a visceral reaction. Bush caught himself, and his expression turned to anger, but his words remained measured.

This and other poignant emotional displays are what helped the American public understand the Bush brand. And ironically, the clearest way of understanding this emotional connection is through cold, hard numbers.

Disagree with him personally or politically as they may, the citizens of the United States connected with Bush's agenda emotionally. His approval rating soared upwards of 90 percent immediately following the attacks. It remained near 80 percent in January. And in April, six months removed from September, it hovered at an inordinately high 74 percent, despite the return of domestic issues to the public's mind.

Specialty: Bush defined his role

Upon taking office, Bush very wisely recognized his own limitations and surrounded himself with very smart people. That is not to say Bush himself lacks intelligence; I would argue the exact opposite. By delegating authority over matters outside his core area of expertise, Bush freed himself to focus on matters falling inside his core area of expertise—management.

As the quintessential CEO, Bush's primary responsibility was to dictate the country's strategic path and sell. It was up to his lieutenants to craft actionable plans with measurable outcomes. After deciding that al-Qaeda was the foremost problem, ousting al-Qaeda became the solution. Bush obtained the information he needed, made the tough call, and left it to the experts to determine how to do it.

Results: Bush showed us the money

The Bush brand became associated with actions that lead to results. Within months of the attacks on New York and Washington, the United States had driven the Taliban from Afghanistan and won several battles with al-Qaeda forces. The United States had gathered intelligence materials from caves and captured ranking members of Osama bin Laden's network of terror.

Clear rhetoric? Check. Connection with audience? Check. Definition of roles and responsibilities? Check. And now, results? Check.

Recognition: Bush became associated with greatness

As a result, George W. Bush, the man-child who favored impersonations of Austin Powers over studying the writings of Thomas Jefferson, started to be compared to America's—and the West's in general—greatest leaders in broadcast after broadcast and article after article.

William Kristol of the *Weekly Standard* likened him to Ronald Reagan and Harry Truman. Editors at the *New Republic* compared Bush's State of the Union speech to the one Franklin Delano Roosevelt delivered in 1942, directly following the bombing of Pearl Harbor. And scores of pundits, including Mark Crispin Miller, author of *The Bush Dyslexicon: Observations on a National Disorder*, chimed in that "at that moment of catastrophe, there was so fierce a hunger for a national father-figure that the audience saw one in [Bush], who therefore came across like Churchill, or like FDR, despite his lack of stature." Winston. Franklin. And now, George.

Bush's fortunes, of course, may very well change in the wake of another terrorist attack or prolonged war. Americans will rally behind a leader but will not hesitate to turn on him if conditions worsen. Already the public has expressed frustration with vague terror warnings, the failure to capture bin Laden, and the government's ham-handed handling of threat intelligence. In the absence of another terrorist event, Bush's best efforts must be to fight terror behind the scenes. If another tragedy occurs, it'll be all about tangible, decisive actions.

Demonstrable battlefield victories backed by a straight-talking John Wayne style made Don Rumsfeld a crisis management winner.

WHY RUMMY RULED

Nobody ever confused Don Rumsfeld with Mick Jagger, but you would never know it attending one of his news conferences in late 2001 and early 2002.

Despite receiving rightful plaudits for his deft communication, serious students of Rumsfeld's performance cannot ignore two external factors Rumsfeld had going for him. The first was moral authority. The 9/11 attacks were wicked beyond the continuum of anything that most Americans had experienced in our lifetimes. Many news reports and editorials opened with the sentiment that "everything changed" on September 11, and no one accused the media of sensationalizing the way they might have in happier times when such melodramatic sentiments were ascribed to the death of Elvis or the *Challenger* explosion. No, it was a fact that everything had changed because of the depth of the horrors, which also implied an understanding that extraordinary measures were called for.

Prior to September 11, had a secretary of defense casually said it was the intention of the United States to "kill" those who perpetrated attacks on our country, it may have ignited a New Age debate about compassion and perhaps a call from Hollywood celebrities for an examination of how America's enemies were victims of imperialism. Outside of a few moronic poses by the likes of author Susan Sontag and TV personality Phil Donahue, the cultural left by and large shared America's outrage. In the fractious post-Lewinsky era, there were no liberals or conservatives, just Americans.

The other external factor that helped Rumsfeld was this: The United States was winning the war big-time. People don't rally around losers and, despite our nation's overuse of the metaphor of "spin," success is the greatest spin. In the early weeks of the war, when the United States was bombing Afghanistan with no dividend in sight, the media were not, in fact, supportive, and the public, while supportive of the war, was by no means enthusiastic. There is a direct correlation between when the Taliban began to fall and Rumsfeld's popularity crystallized.

But even then, Rumsfeld followed one of the many golden rules of crisis management: He did not pretend to know things he did not know. When questioned about Osama bin Laden's status, he consistently responded that absent absolute confirmation, he did not wish to speculate. When questioned about when the United States and allies would win the war on terrorism, he held fast to the party line—that this was a sustained effort that would require time. In other words, he took the John Wayne approach of gruff talk that doesn't overpromise.

And within the media, it caught on.

Suddenly, Rumsfeld was a household name and the secretary of defense was run up against questions and characterizations normally reserved for celebrities stalked by paparazzi. During a live C-SPAN interview, Rumsfeld acknowledged that he was wearing "Taos, N.M., hiking shoes," though he refused to allow cameras to capture them on film (per-haps out of fear that it would jeopardize future Nike footwear deals). On the Internet, "fan clubs" of sorts began to pop up, as though the grandfa-therly secretary were Britney Spears. And, *la pièce de résistance*, the *National Review* went so far as to feature a preening caricature of Rums-feld headlined, "The Stud: Don Rumsfeld, America's New Pinup."

SIR RUDY

"Every wall is a door."

Ralph Waldo Emerson

The hunger for a compassionate leader combined with a personal crusade to heal New York City knighted Rudy Giuliani

Prior to 9/11, Rudy Giuliani was getting attention for his messy divorce, his prostate cancer, and his aborted bid for a U.S. Senate seat. A few months later, he was named *Time* magazine's Man of the Year, and was knighted by the Queen of England.

The change in Giuliani's fortunes is attributable to the savagery of the terrorist attacks on the World Trade Center and his response to the tragedy. As with Rumsfeld and Bush, the attacks gave Guiliani moral authority. New Yorkers—not to mention most Americans—wanted Giu-liani to succeed, an external factor that should not be lost on students of crisis management. When a leader, in effect, becomes a victim, we want him to overcome the odds that have befallen him.

MAN ON THE SCENE

In times of crisis, corporate or political, we like our leaders to be on the scene of the disaster. It's not so much a desire to see our leaders injured

THE NUMBERS DON'T LIE

Dropping Popularity, but Who Cares?

The main point of this chapter is simple: that in times of crisis, strong leadership carries the day. I have argued that the decisive actions taken and clear rhetoric used by Bush, Rumsfeld, and Giuliani shaped the strategy that followed in an overwhelmingly positive way. But don't take my word for it; let's look at the numbers.

In the months leading to September 11, 2001, the three public figures examined in this chapter suffered to varying degrees the slings and arrows of outrageous polling. Their "numbers" were down. Why? Bush was still feeling the ill effects of his Election 2000 hangover in that his critics were far from reticent in pointing out that Al Gore actually had won the popular vote and more than eager to trumpet the "Bushism" du jour. Despite his significant involvement in previous administrations, Rumsfeld remained a name familiar only in Beltway circles. And as a lame duck mayor immersed in marital scandal, Giuliani detractors outnumbered Giuliani supporters.

According to data provided by David Winston of The Winston Group, Bush's approval rating during July and August 2001 hovered

as it is a need for confirmation that they don't hold themselves out as being superior to the rest of us mortals. Giuliani was at the World Trade Center shortly after the attacks and risked injury to be there.

Not only was Giuliani on the scene immediately, he was constantly recorded there from that point on. He offered round-the-clock updates on recovery efforts and conveyed a critical combination of moral outrage and confidence that the city was doing everything that it could to find casualties.

And for this reason—Giuliani's association with action—he garnered comparisons to one of the utmost respected wartime leaders of the twentieth century: Winston Churchill.

In addition to the Churchillian rhetoric woven into his public decla-

steadily in the mid-50s. Even a poll taken during September 6–9, 2001, rated him nationally at 55 percent. Giuliani during the year 2000 plateaued comparably. And Rumsfeld—to again emphasize his obscurity—did not even merit consistent tracking.

So what effect did the September 11 terrorist attacks have on the way Americans viewed these three pivotal players? Put simply, their numbers went off the charts.

In the week immediately following September 11, Bush's job approval rating jumped, depending on the poll examined, to around 80 percent. Similarly, Giuliani scored an instant 90 percent. And Rumsfeld, moving from off-stage to the spotlight, had reached a 75 percent job approval rating by mid-October.

Some may argue that this massive shift reflected not that triad's leadership qualities, but rather a massive influx of patriotism and national rallying. This is true. A similar spike occurred when George Herbert Walker Bush led our country a decade ago into the Persian Gulf to defend Kuwait. What does, however, suggest leadership qualities of a more enduring nature is that unlike Bush the Elder, Bush the Younger, Rumsfeld, and Giuliani managed to maintain their popularity beyond the initial crisis. The outcome of the Iraq and North Korea conflicts, not to mention the economy, however, will certainly test Bush and Rumsfeld's popularity.

rations of unity and strength, the comparison held true because of the plain physical situation. Giuliani in 2001, like Churchill during World War II, was leading a city in ruins. Giuliani, like Churchill, was out among the masses, inspiring his city and charting out recovery. Rightly anointed, he was "Churchill in a Yankees cap."

But as with Bush and Rumsfeld, Giuliani's success was not due only to his strength of leadership. It also depended on circumstances—the nebulous things that presented the leader with the opportunity to lead. Of course, Giuliani seized the reins with full force once called upon, but without the reins being there in the first place, it certainly is not a given that he would have left office as a hero.

Institutions in crisis are served best by leaders who embrace the limelight during crisis. Planning helps but cannot replace telegenic leaders who communicate using simple, emotionally resonant rhetoric. When that rhetoric is matched with stark and measurable results, the recipe for success is complete.

20. *The Limits of Spin*

In times of crisis, spin isn't much more than a wives' tale.

"A good name, like goodwill, is got by many actions, and lost by one."
Lord Jeffrey

The calls began coming in shortly after the 9/11 terrorist attacks and became progressively stranger with the ensuing onset of the anthrax scare and the Enron and Arthur Andersen scandals. The calls were mostly from journalists, and they involved spin. I was asked questions such as, How could we have better educated Islam in a way that could have prevented the terrorist attacks? Why did the government botch the handling of the anthrax panic? What would I advise Enron to say to get them out of their bankruptcy mess? What should Martha Stewart do to escape allegations of insider training? Prior to 9/11, the big question was, What should Congressman Gary Condit do to dodge the mess that erupted after the disappearance and (presumed at that time) murder of intern Chandra Levy with whom the married Condit was alleged to have been romantically involved?

I concluded that either my contacts in the news media had an obscenely inflated view of my talents or the culture at large has come to confuse crisis management with alchemy.

I decided it was the latter. After two decades in damage control, the thing that surprises me the most is the evangelical belief that our culture has placed in spin—the notion that communications can solve serious and fundamental problems that go far deeper than "positioning." How could any grown person really believe that our problems with radical Islam could be addressed with a slick advertising campaign? Didn't people recognize that the reason why the anthrax scare caused such panic was because we know so little about it? When a mammoth company such as Enron collapses due, allegedly, to fraud, could a guy like me whip together a slick statement on behalf of the company with the buzzwords of New Age sensitivity—caring, empowerment, et al.—and actually make the crisis go away?

Of course not, but I'm asked the questions nevertheless. Which leads to the operative question: Why the questions?

I believe that America's faith in communications alchemists is a direct result of staggering affluence and the insulation the country has enjoyed from life's sharper edges for so many decades. Prolonged comfort has led generations of Americans to assume that peace and prosperity are guaranteed norms, and that terrorism, recession, wars where people actually die, and not having tens of millions of dollars in stock options are aberrations that result from systematic incompetence, not from factors beyond one's control. The concept of "uncertainty"—that events exist that cannot be controlled—has become increasingly unfamiliar as we have become more and more accustomed to statistical models and behavioral analyses which tell us exactly when, how, and why things will come to pass. Put another way, contemporary Americans do not believe in acts of God.

This chapter examines the shortcomings of "spin" in the face of true crises—conflicts which hinge not on simple misunderstandings which education can address, but rather deep-rooted (and sometimes irreconcilable) differences that hit on the level of core values and cultural norms. In other words, this chapter sets out to demonstrate how talk is not action, and why a lack of action sometimes is not good crisis management.

BEFRIEND ISLAM?

"Propaganda does not deceive people; it merely helps them deceive themselves."

Eric Hoffer

In October 2001, advertising veteran Charlotte Beers was confirmed as undersecretary of state for public diplomacy and public affairs. Or, in Madison Avenue parlance, she was tapped by a major client—the White House—to construct and lead a new campaign to build the American brand and "sell" it to the outside world.

So will it work?

The short answer is no, and the short explanation is that "America" is an idea, not a soap.

It is infinitely more difficult to sell ideas than it is to sell products, and the simple fact is that America cannot be merchandised as a product. Instead, America is the headline for a story which explains not a simple thought which sprung up overnight, but rather a complex system of social and economic ideas and which has taken hundreds of years to mature. To do it justice would require the talent and appreciation for nuance of Thomas Jefferson, not an ad agency creative honcho.

But in creating a "propaganda machine," that is exactly what Charlotte Beers has been tasked with doing. She is under pressure to reduce the American way of life—and the war against terrorism—into a single digestible sound bite which will appeal to a multitude of audiences, in a multitude of countries, who speak a multitude of languages, and who may or may not have heard of the United States, more or less the September 11 attacks.

Formidable as they may seem, those obstacles—the obstacles of general communication—are not insurmountable. Effective communications can be tailored to build so-called global brands. Take, for example, Coca Cola. The soft drink behemoth quite nicely has managed to mold a value-neutral global environment (that is, one in which the audiences have only negligible positive or negative bias toward the brand) into a profitable playground.

Overcoming the obstacles of a value-negative environment takes significantly more effort, if they can be overcome at all. The notion of building an "American" brand is inherently flawed in that it assumes that its operating environment is, in fact, value-neutral.

POSITIVE FACTS DON'T NEUTRALIZE NEGATIVE EMOTIONS

"I can promise to be sincere, but not impartial."

Goethe

Large corporate clients often ask me why they have come under attack. We create jobs, they argue, we create shareholder value, and our products make the world a better place. So why are we finding nasty letters in our mailboxes and picketers outside our annual meetings? My response is simple: If you are successful, people will want to see you fail, and if you symbolize a given value linked with that success, people who adhere to the opposite value will want to see you fail.

People want to see the United States fail, especially militant Muslims. America has become the leading global economic engine, and that carries with it resentment. In addition, America symbolizes a certain set of values, values for which some groups are willing to die to oppose.

In the value-negative environment America is operating in, what becomes the highest priority is not to "educate" or "dialogue with" your opponents and make them become your best friends, but rather to make them go away. Some people simply do not—and never will—like America. No matter how many leaflets these people see, they will not change their minds. No matter how many bulleted lists of good things America has done for the world, they will not change their minds because positive facts don't neutralize negative emotions.

Spin is appropriate in some situations, but our conflict with militant Islam is not one of them. And for those who remain unconvinced, think about how well Americans have received the spin and propaganda that runs counter to their beliefs (e.g., the notion that the suicide bombers were "martyrs" and that 9/11 casualties were somehow deserving of their fate) and originated in the hills near Tora Bora.

What, then, should Charlotte Beers do? The short answer is to examine how military propaganda—which *is* what we're talking about here—has worked throughout history. Successful propaganda is anchored in two objectives: Rally your friends and frighten your enemies.

America and its allies must be presented with emotionally resonant messages and images of Western moral superiority and strategic effectiveness. Sound arrogant? Fine. Our target audience should be those who are already inclined to support us. Most human beings have Darwinian impulses toward survival and, therefore, our outreach efforts must hammer home the message that the United States is on the winning side of the current struggle between one civilization that is rocketing into the future and another which is hell-bent on bombing humanity into the past. Success should be measured by a lack of tangible obstructions to America's war on terror, not on how wildly the world expresses love for our country.

As for America's enemies, the best spin isn't spin at all, but astonishing military superiority. Power talks, "dialogue" walks. Islamic extremists will disrespect us by precisely the amount that we "seek resolution" and other rhetorical passports of new age sensitivity. We are up against fanatics, not a game show where a bland but deliberate host declares a winner, and all contestants return home with a door prize.

To be sure, this approach will not deter all of America's enemies, but this brings us back to the thesis of this chapter—that first-rate strategies will not exempt us from acts of God and madmen, and that perfect strategies must not become the enemy of decent ones.

REMAIN CALM? HANDICAPPING ANTHRAX CRISIS MANAGEMENT

"The enemy is anybody who's going to get you killed, no matter which side he's on."

Joseph Heller, *Catch-22*

There was a flawed assumption in much of the coverage of how the anthrax scare was handled, namely that the main goal of crisis communications is to calm everyone down. I believe that sometimes there is a reason to panic. In the case of anthrax, we were confronting a lethal chemical that we knew very little about, which was almost certainly delivered by a homicidal terrorist, foreign or domestic. While the discomfort that is caused by panic is certainly painful, it is not necessarily irrational, nor does it mean that someone botched the communication. In the scheme of things, I would argue that a little panic actually provides incentive to track down the perpetrator and take tangible steps to prevent additional horrors.

While certain aspects of the crisis might have been handled better, it shouldn't be lost on anyone that the biggest challenge was that no one knew very much about anthrax. It's hard to communicate effectively about something that we know so little about. Therein lies what became the biggest problem: The habitual tendency for government flacks to imply that everything was under control when it wasn't.

Perhaps the most extraordinary mistake was made by U.S. Postmaster General John E. Potter. Amid swirling speculation over the safety of the Brentwood facility—which was the distribution hub for mail delivered to the U.S. House and Senate—Potter elected to hold a news conference at the facility itself, assuring the media and the public that it was safe. Within days, however, new stories broke that two employees who worked at Brentwood were dead, with anthrax as a "highly probable" cause, and that two others had tested positive. Reporters who toured the facility—in addition to Brentwood employees—suddenly began Cipro treatment and rather than having a calming effect, the press conference further fueled public concern.

So much for the "all's well" message.

But in Potter's defense, he was acting under guidance from the Centers for Disease Control. As the agency responsible for handling anthrax-related events, the CDC initially gave the assessment that it is "highly unlikely to virtually impossible" for infection or death to result from cross-contamination, in which anthrax spores from one contaminated letter jump to another. But in the wake of the Brentwood deaths, the CDC changed its tune and released "tips" on handling mail for the obviously worried public.

In addition, the White House initially announced that it was working under the "operating suspicion" that the domestic cases of anthrax were related to al-Qaeda and the September 11 terrorist attacks. What the White House did not announce, however, was the foundation for the "suspicion," nor did they offer any compelling proof. And at the time of this writing, the White House still has not produced a plausible suspect and remains overwhelmingly unsure as to who actually was behind the attacks.

All parties involved were operating within the difficult parameters of the unknown. Nobody—the public, the media, our government officials—had ever confronted this sort of event and as a result, a template plan to manage the crisis did not exist. But I also said that certain aspects of the crisis could have been handled better, and that remains true.

The following checklist may seem simple but, as I have so often seen in over a decade of crisis management, simplicity in a time of uncertainty is golden:

1. Define What Is Known—All audiences want information and, to the extent possible, a reasonable effort must be made to give it to them. You must say what you do know, but you must do so in a clear and nonspeculative way. Pretend that the listening group is Sgt. Joe Friday—it only wants the facts.

2. Define What Is Not Known—Equally important is explaining to audiences what is not known. Do not give them the opportunity to assume that something is "safe" only to have it later emerge that it is not safe. People prefer uncertainty rooted in honesty over reassurance rooted in nothing.

3. Provide a Steady Stream of Information—The overriding factor when managing a crisis is the trust bank the communicator must build with the audience. And the easiest way to do that is to provide a steady stream of reliable information. When you learn something, keep your audience in the loop.

THE CONDIT AFFAIR

> "Every Halloween, the trees are filled with underwear. Every spring, the
> toilets explode."
>
> Dean Wormer in *Animal House*

Gary Condit may not be guilty of murder, but he is guilty of being
unlucky, unsympathetic, and uniquely incapable of even the most basic
elements of damage control.

In early May of 2001, news reports broke around Washington, D.C., that
an intern from the Bureau of Prisons, Chandra Levy, was missing. Circumstances surrounding her disappearance were described by Detective Sgt.
Ronald Wyatt as "unusual," but that was that. The police were continuing
their search and canvassing for information that might produce leads.

Enter Gary Condit.

Initially, Condit's involvement was limited to that of Chandra's
home-district representative and "good friend." He contributed $10,000
to the fund established to reward information leading to Chandra's
recovery but largely remained out of sight.

But then, as rumors surfaced that Chandra had a "mysterious boyfriend in politics," the Fourth Estate smelled scandal and the Beltway
once again became the Beltway. With great speed the media moved their
story outward from reporting on a missing person to delving into a possible romantic link between Levy and Condit. Accusations of clandestine
trysts and foul play followed shortly thereafter, catalyzing a maelstrom of
media attention which, in a shark attack–dominated stagnant news cycle,
sucked everything into its screaming vortex.

LEGAL VS. PR APPROACHES

When he came under attack, Condit stayed mum—sometimes. Other
times, his office answered questions from the media, including ones characterizing the congressman's relationship with Chandra Levy as that of a
friend and a concerned party.

The trouble with this striptease approach is that it promised the news media that the more they camped outside of Condit's home and office, the greater their chances were of getting an answer out of him. It worked. Condit smiled at the cameras—wholly inappropriate given the backdrop of the disappearance and alleged murder of a young woman—and kept quiet until his office or publicist released a statement.

As a rule, lawyers want their clients to stay quiet and communicators want them to talk. Both are correct. Lawyers want their clients to keep quiet because anything they say could be thrown back at them in court. Communicators want their clients to talk in order to appear more human and likable. It was clear, by virtue of Condit's having hired power lawyer Abbe Lowell, not to mention the implication that he was involved in Levy's demise, that the Condit camp feared he would end up in court. If Condit had not been a public figure, the best move for him would have been to remain silent. Totally silent.

However, Condit had another objective: He wanted to remain in office. To remain in office he'd have to explain himself, convey empathy, and stay in touch with his voters. In order to do this he'd have to answer fundamental questions. Did you kill Chandra Levy? What was your relationship with her? To do this he would have to violate the basic tenets of a legal defense and talk, a nearly impossible tightrope to walk.

For a time, Condit attempted to walk this tightrope by hiring a spokesperson—apart from his congressional office—to handle media inquiries. This spokeswoman, a reputable pro named Marina Ein, was put in an impossible situation. By announcing to the world that an external spin doctor had been retained, every word Ein uttered fell under ripsaw scrutiny. And by declaring the fact that District police didn't name Condit as a suspect a "home run," Ein played into their hands. After all, the logic went, a true "home run" would have been finding Levy alive and well.

Soon the story was not that a young woman was missing, but about whose handlers were better! Some pundits had the audacity to suggest that the reason why the Levys were beating Condit in the handling wars was because they had retained better advisors, as opposed to a more visceral truth. The Levys—rightly—had a sympathetic message: Where's our daughter? Condit didn't: Wasn't me. The infamous Connie Chung interview in August 2001 is the quintessential example.

Condit came off looking bad with Chung because, the logic went, he was ill-prepared. Nonsense! Condit had the luxury of essentially hand-picking his inquisitor and, one would hope, had by that point undergone hours upon hours of media training to hone his message and practice his delivery. Nevertheless, when Chung stayed focused on Condit's other purported extramarital activity, the congressman played the deer in the headlights.

So was it the handlers' fault? Did they not adequately prepare their client? Of course not. What happened was simply that Condit could not make Chandra materialize from the Green Room as though this were an episode of *Candid Camera* taken to a ludicrous extreme. He also had a stiff and cold demeanor, which made viewers dislike him more intensely. Slick media training cannot change terrible circumstances, not can it change someone's core personality.

The Levys had a missing daughter and undeniably had the moral upper hand in the battle against Condit. In his situation he could have retained the Wizard of Oz and still looked awful.

INOPERABLE

I did a lot of media commentary during the Condit affair, and my posi-tion—not popular in the PR community, incidentally—was that his crisis was, for the most part, inoperable for six reasons:

1. The married Condit appeared to be, at the very least, guilty of being romantically involved with a young intern—not to mention other women—in the post-Lewinsky era. Regardless of how one feels about this morally, it's hard to sympathize with a man in power who is this reckless, especially given Lewinsky's wake.
2. The crime that was implied—the murder of a young woman—is so serious that the culture was unwilling to give Condit the benefit of the doubt, as they did when President Clinton became involved with Monica Lewinsky. Whereas Washington-area police were combing through local landfills searching for Levy's body, during

the Lewinsky scandal everyone knew that Monica was alive and affluent with her mother in the Watergate condominium.

3. The Levy family had the resources and sophistication to keep Chandra's story in the news. Sadly, most families of missing people don't have the wherewithal to hire Washington big-name attorneys and public relations firms. That the Levys were able to prosecute a concerted campaign, which included lawyers, PR people, media interviews, rewards, and leaflets with their daughter's photo, helped keep the story in the news.

4. There was no competing news. Sometimes how long a crisis stays in the news depends upon what crises it's competing with. In the summer of 2001, all was well with America, and we had the luxury of a sideshow like the Condit-Levy affair. That there was no resolution to the crime—or even proof that there was a crime—fueled endless conspiracy theories, which served as a catalyst in the Condit story's viral nature. As callous as it seems to speculate, had Levy disappeared in the days immediately prior to the September 11 terrorist attacks, the matter may very well have ended up being just another missing persons case.

5. There was no foil or alternative villain or explanation for Levy's disappearance. There was no Kenneth Starr to blame for meddling in the private lives of others, no crazed ex-boyfriend to arouse suspicion. While this didn't mean that Condit was guilty, it did mean that he was the sole focus.

6. Condit was a remarkably unsympathetic figure, personally. In an attack situation, personality means a lot. While Condit would have been in deep trouble no matter what, if he had been a more Clintonian figure, better able to convey vulnerability by admitting at least some of his mistakes, some might have cut him some, but not much, slack.

In short, had Condit been my client, I would have advised him not to run again. Condit lost his reelection bid and, in May 2002, a year after she disappeared, Chandra Levy's skeletal remains turned up in a Washington park. Had her body been discovered shortly after her disappearance, it would have likely shortened the half-life of the Condit story, especially if he had been discounted as a suspect by forensic evidence. Perhaps he could have even turned the controversy into a story about a witch-hunting media, but I doubt it. The whole affair was such an assault on conventional morality that it would have still been unspinnable.

THE ARTHUR ANDERSEN SALVAGE JOB

"An example from the monkey: the higher it climbs, the more you see of its behind."

Saint Bonaventure

The venerable Arthur Andersen accounting firm found itself in a "perfect storm" of horrible crisis management conditions. When Andersen's client Enron collapsed, creating the largest bankruptcy in American history, the mainstream and business media swiftly decided that accounting shenanigans played a significant role in the crisis. Another Andersen client, telecom upstart Global Crossing, imploded soon after. Bookkeeping malfeasance was alleged in this case, too, and scrutiny descended on the accounting industry, an endeavor known heretofore for certifying the veracity of the Academy Awards, not to mention its capacity to bore people into a coma. Soon, corporate giants as worshiped as General Electric were forced to answer questions about the legitimacy of their finances, something that would have been unthinkable in earlier times. Accountants had even made their way into the popular culture with President Bush declaring that, "We just received a message from Saddam Hussein. The good news is that he's willing to have his nuclear, biological, and chemical weapons counted. The bad news is, he wants Arthur Andersen to do it."

Complicating matters was the public's poor understanding of accounting. After all, the industry's key selling point was trust in a field where the rest of us felt ill-qualified to render judgment. When the financial statement in a company's annual report stated that the enterprise sold a thousand widgets, shareholders simply assumed that somebody trustworthy had added up all the numbers. To harbor any other thought was to concede that we had absolutely no understanding or control of our investments, and that unscrupulous executives could run wild.

The collapse of Enron and other huge companies confirmed our worst nightmares, namely that our collective ignorance of accounting had indeed led to world-class swindles, an anxiety that was not helped by a recession and the swift degeneration of the technology sector. In uncertain times there needs to be a witch, a clear-cut sponsor of our misery. On the corporate side, that villain was Enron and the politically connected executives who ran the company. On the accounting side, Arthur Andersen became that villain, especially when it was revealed that the company's Houston office had shredded many of its Enron files. By the time congressional hearings were held on Enron, Andersen, and Global Crossing, the public and the news media, understandably, hadn't the slightest interest in learning about the complexities of these cases. Witches were witches.

Arthur Andersen was indicted for shredding its Enron files in March. The shredding of sensitive materials, of course, is routine. However, shredding becomes a criminal act when it is done in response to a legal inquiry, as opposed to being done for proprietary reasons.

Suddenly, it was about damage control, saving what was savable. Andersen took several steps, which, while by no means cure-alls, were responsible experiments in damage control.

FIRING THE PERCEIVED PERPETRATOR

One of the first moves Andersen made was firing the Houston-based leader of the Enron account, David Duncan.

To be sure, Duncan's attorneys argued that Duncan was being made a scapegoat for broader problems. This was no doubt true, however, the consequences of not firing Duncan would have been immediate and devastating. It's a sure bet that the company would have been widely perceived as being unresponsive, unrepentant, and, worse, actively enlisting Duncan to cover up its misdeeds. Andersen chose the best of its bad options.

On March 25, 2002, the *New York Times* reported that Andersen was apparently cozying up to Duncan so that he would not portray the company to the Justice Department as having engaged in an active conspiracy to destroy evidence. The ostensible objective was now to communicate a unified message—that any shredding that occurred had been done as a matter of course in order to protect both Enron and Andersen from competitive snooping, as opposed to a criminal inquiry.

The article begged the question, Should Andersen have kept Duncan on staff rather than fire him? My answer is no; Andersen should have fired him because the consequences of keeping Duncan on the inside were far worse. But whether Andersen arguably erred was when the company later tried to rekindle its relationship with Duncan in order to minimize his impact on the case.

For one thing, Andersen should have plotted its strategy around the assumption that once terminated, Duncan likely would want to protect his reputation. And that such protective measures, logically, would involve tarnishing Andersen's reputation. Given the initial cold shoulder and the later—almost afterthought—attempt at reconciliation, it would seem that Andersen did not think through this element of its program. As a result, Duncan, who pleaded guilty to an obstruction of justice charge in May 2002, became one of the prosecution's lead witnesses, and Andersen's problems compounded.

THE ADVERTISEMENTS

In the days following the company's implication in the Enron collapse, Andersen bought full-page advertisements in the major national newspapers: the *New York Times*, *Wall Street Journal*, and *Washington Post*.

The advertisements, which featured an open letter from then-CEO Joseph Berardino, made a strong appeal to the public and as a proverbial "first step" did two important things right:

1. They came from above—If a company is in trouble, the public not only expects but demands that initial and important news come

from senior management. While somewhat superficial, this demonstrates that the company is taking the matter seriously to such an extent that top executives have made crisis management their job. For that reason, it is good that Berardino, as opposed to a lower-ranking lieutenant, signed the ads.

2. Catalogue actions—People like to know what's going on, and the open letter adequately catalogued what the company has done and what it plans to do.

But unfortunately, Andersen's woes did not end with the advertisements. Additional gaffes and information was made public that pointed to a larger problem than one rogue employee, which made the stance outlined indefensible and the actions promised undeliverable. Remember: the American public often is willing to give exemption from its wrath, but only if it sees tangible results—and fast.

THE EMPLOYEE RALLIES

In a combination of spontaneous outrage and orchestrated mobilization, Arthur Andersen held rallies in key cities across the country, namely Washington, D.C., and its home-base in Chicago, in order to protest the Justice Department's indictment. At these rallies many employees wore T-shirts inscribed with the powerful message "I am Arthur Andersen." Their point: It is unfair to punish 28,000 employees in the United States with an indictment that was predicated on the possible actions of a few.

Certainly not all of its employees had been indicted, but Andersen characterized the indictment as a "death sentence" for any accounting firm. University of Chicago law professor Randall Picker concurred, stating in May, just before the federal trial began, "The indictment itself was akin to a death sentence for Andersen because clients fled." And that flee could translate into thousands of lost jobs.

At the time of these rallies, I was routinely contacted by the news media with inquiries about whether or not I thought the rallies would "save" Andersen or "improve Andersen's image." My answer: Of course not, but in grave circumstances, damage control techniques such as the rallies are designed to impact the crisis at the margins, the same way that pain-killing medications may not cure a gravely ill patient, but keep him comfortable, a legitimate objective. Rather, I believed that the rallies were designed to accomplish three aims.

1. Salvage employee morale—Understandably, Andersen employees were distressed by the allegations that their firm was the Antichrist. They had, after all, considered themselves to be good people engaged in an honest profession and were greatly unprepared for the public criticism which erupted. The rallies, therefore, were a way for the collective Andersen psyche to undergo a much-needed purge in which the uninvolved could say to the world: certain people made bad decisions, but we did not.

2. Attempt to have a chilling effect on prosecutions—The Justice Department, like all government agencies, is a political animal. While not directly elected, Justice Department officials have to answer to those who are elected and can become serious liabilities to administrations, as Attorneys General Janet Reno had become to President Clinton and Edwin Meese had been to President Reagan. In the wake of the Enron and Andersen debacles, not only did the public demand that a witch be punished, but many media reports suggested that the corruption may go all the way to the president and vice president of the United States. The Justice Department's decision to indict Andersen was harsh but understandable given the political climate. Given this, Andersen workers had only one viable argument, which was that the government's actions harshly punished thousands of innocent people. Andersen's strategy was to introduce risk to the government by putting a human face on its position.

3. Protect its remaining asset: Andersen's people—As a profession driven by relationships and reputation, accounting relies heavily—if not exclusively—on its human capital.

One of the best damage control strategies for a troubled company is to sell out to a suitor in order to recoup at least some financial reward, not to mention share its burdens with a stronger partner. Despite protests to the contrary, the minute Andersen's troubles began, it was on the block. Big accounting firms have two assets, their reputations and their personnel, both of which work to attract and keep clients.

With its indictment, Andersen's reputation was destroyed, as evidenced by the stampede of clients to the exits. Much of Andersen's staff, however, remained. In better times the company could have been sold at a premium. Not anymore. All Andersen had left was the hope that decent, hardworking people would stay so that the company could retain some of its clients and be someone marketable on the selling block.

At this writing, Arthur Andersen is in talks with the Justice Department about reaching a settlement. The very fact that these discussions are taking place, I would characterize as a testament to the effectiveness of Andersen's damage control strategy. Contrary to conventional wisdom, given the conditions surrounding its adversity, a buoyant recovery was never an option. This was a salvage job from the beginning. If Andersen reaches a reasonable settlement with the Justice Department, or if a jury vindicates the company on some of the charges it faces, this consultant will declare its damage control program a success.

I would like to see damage control studied like a social science rather than a movie script, which is the current state of the art. This means embracing a doctrine of salvaging what's salvageable—the way a trauma surgeon would—rather than implying that well-executed maneuvers can always deliver victory.

There is something to be learned, however, about crisis management from the dramatic arts. As any Hollywood producer knows, in a drama, the audience needs someone to like and someone to dislike. In crisis situations, these irrational emotions play a viral role in the spreading of hostilities against institutions and individuals. Long before Martha Stewart was accused of insider trading, the news media—with the full backing of the public—enjoyed attacking her. Was such hostility all due to resentment of a woman's success? Not really. After all, Oprah Winfrey, who was arguably more successful than Stewart, was never attacked so brutally.

Stewart's savaging has had much to do with her air of queenly superiority and perfection, which may have helped her sell magazines and household items, but it provoked the wrath of a democratic public that is deeply insecure about its own caste. The cuddly Winfrey, on the other hand, with her well-chronicled hard childhood, her struggles with weight, and romantic setbacks, tacitly conveys, "If I can make it, so can you."

21. *An Outlook for Damage Control*

September 11, the collapse of Enron, and true diversity in the news media have changed the climate for crisis management.

"We're going to nail your ass! Nail your ass!"
Hillary Rodham Clinton, during her Capitol Hill internship,
to the CEO of Minute Maid

CRISIS MANAGEMENT MEANS ALWAYS HAVING TO SAY YOU'RE SORRY

Following the dual wounds of Vietnam and Watergate, American businesses began to embrace the rhetoric of their fiercest critics, even when those critics were wrong. Complicating matters were the high-profile corporate debacles of Love Canal, the attempt to corner the silver market by the Hunt Brothers, and the insider trading scandals of the late 1980s. Crisis management became rooted in apologies and the belief that if we are simply nice to our critics, they will go away. The past thirty years have taught many businesses the opposite lesson, namely that New Age rhetoric—"engaging in dialogue," "sharing ideas," "exchanging views," and "tolerance"—has not only not defused attacks, but in many cases emboldened their adversaries.

September 11 served as a symbolic turning point. While not a business crisis per se, one thing that many corporate leaders learned from the global fallout was that the world is not a happy place peppered with simple, easily resolved misunderstandings. There are people out there who hate us and are willing to undertake despicably violent actions to demonstrate their beliefs. To be sure, no sane person should compare the murderous acts of terrorists with civilized opposition to business practices, but the unavoidable truth remains: A business crisis is an opportunity for one's attackers—trial lawyers, labor unions, activist groups—to characterize all corporate criticism as fair-minded discourse and all corporate defenses as corruption.

ENRON GOES DOWN

"The most accomplished confidence man since Charles Ponzi."
                                       Sen. Peter Fitzgerald (R-Ill.)
                                   on Enron's former CEO, Kenneth Lay

If September 11 taught corporate leaders that symbolic towers of strength can fall under certain conditions, the collapse of energy giant Enron showed that businesses that do bad things can be destroyed in a climate of intense scrutiny.

Previously hailed as a Wall Street darling, and having operated on the cutting edge of the emerging energy trading market, Enron's fall ostensibly has ushered in a new era of corporate distrust. Initially it appeared to be a routine case of earnings restatements and corporate impropriety. But when details began to emerge which pointed to greater, grander levels of manipulation, the Enron debacle cast a grave shadow over previously passive public interest in corporations.

The public and the media, for the most part, prefer recognizable scandals to which they can simply add the suffix -*gate* according to the Watergate template. Think, for example, of Whitewater-gate and Monica-gate. But with Enron came a new sort of scandal. Whitewater involved mere real estate impropriety and Bill Clinton's relationship with Monica

Lewinsky was, as far as impropriety goes, rather run of the mill in Beltway circles and the public sphere.

But Enron necessitated the use of terms like "off-balance sheet debt" and "energy trading markets" which the public didn't understand. This was not sex; this was something called "Raptor." As a result, the traditional template for corporate atonement no longer applied. Enron could not use sound bites to explain its complex financial dealings, make people understand why they were okay. Messages became muddled and, in the end, the only effective thing Enron could do was point the finger at Andersen. The problem there, of course, is that accounting is perhaps the one field more poorly understood than energy trading. People historically had put trust in the Big Five to watch their backs, and now that was in question as well.

Since September 11, some of the same clients who used to advocate appeasing their attackers even when they were on the side of right have become more willing to defend themselves aggressively because the stakes have become higher. Americans' tolerance for those who cloak their desire to destroy our institutions in moral pronouncements has weakened. The fall of Enron and Arthur Andersen, having shaken corporate leaders to their core, has also motivated them to defend themselves if and when they believe survival is at stake.

THE MEDIA BACKLASH FINALLY BEARS FRUIT

> "A paper like the *Post* is a two-ton truck, and we run over a lot of people without knowing it, and then we just roll on without even the most casual glance in the rear-view mirror."
>
> Meg Greenfield

Throughout the 1980s and 1990s, there was a great deal of carping in the business community about left-wing media bias. In my field, a left-leaning political tilt (which has more than a little truth to it) concerned me less than how the mainstream media cover issues that impact business, specifically, how allegations against businesses are characterized for the general public. Throughout my career, I have always held full-time business reporters in high esteem, but believed that "consumer," general assignment, and television network reporters tend to side with business critics, supporting a "fallacy of evil men," that is, corporate captains who sit up nights thinking of ways to hurt the little guy.

It's time to be fair: The backlash against media elites finally yielded a dividend in the form of many new media outlets, especially on cable television and the Internet, which provided the public with novel views, namely that not all business crises are created equal and that not all corporate critics are pillars of virtue. From Fox's Bill O'Reilly's probing of Jesse Jackson, a notorious corporate stalker, to the emergence of media-critical Web sites such as ratherbiased.com (a critique of CBS's Dan Rather) and consumerdistorts.com (a critique of *Consumer Reports*), these outlets have multiplied and to a certain degree edged out of obscurity and into the mainstream.

There are a number of ways to explain this recent proliferation– to the potential benefit of businesses—but I have two pet theories.

First, as competition became more brutal, news reporting lost its profit-exempt status, and top media executives recognized that there was money to be made in providing an alternative to the antibusiness ethic that had dominated the three major networks and leading print media since the 1960s. What consumers who held centrist or right-of-center views could not find in the media, they began to find on talk radio in the early 1990s, and on cable television as the millennium approached. For those who just wanted news updates without the polemics, news Web sites, TV "crawls," and just-the-facts outlets such as CNN's *Headline News* provided answers.

Declining popularity of the network newscasts also served to reallocate the power within newsrooms. Television news has historically been talent-driven, meaning that evening news anchors Dan Rather, Peter Jennings, and Tom Brokaw determined the slant of the news. If the networks had been paying those huge salaries, management rationalized, they had better be given the power to do as they pleased. To the extent that the three anchors cared about business stories at all, it was universally understood by corporate operatives like me that they tended to view corporations with distrust at best and active contempt at worst. Complicating matters was the talents' inexperience with day-to-day business affairs and the tendency to travel in social circles with people who tended to share their worldviews. They reported, in other words, through the only lens they knew, but that lens was inherently out of focus.

If the anchors tended to harbor demonizing thoughts about business, those around them often did not. After all, they operated in the trenches of corporate life themselves. News executives, while not especially pro-industry, did not see themselves and the nonmedia executives with whom they associated as being particularly sinister, and many became concerned with the gotcha mentality that came to permeate television news in the late 1980s and 1990s.

Not only did alternative media emerge, but media criticism grew into a mini-industry. At first, a select group including smartertimes.com and the *Drudge Report*, to name a few, gained momentum and developed readership simply because of what they were following and criticizing (smartertimes.com tracks inaccuracies in the *New York Times* and initially the *Drudge Report* took shots at Bill Clinton).

But as with all evolutionary trajectories, the watchers soon became the watched as more and more specialized purveyors of original content (like salon.com) and so-called Blogs (or Web Logs) sprouted up to simply assimilate and disseminate items speaking from a particular viewpoint and/or on a particular topic. For every strong opinion in the mainstream media, you now can find at least five contrarians on the Internet, as well as at least five countercontrarians for each of those—and, yes, people do read many of these. Technology has empowered the individual to become more selective in what he or she reads. It also has allowed once obscure or unheard points of view come center stage and add variety to the front pages of old.

The second reason why I believe media have sprung up that have the potential to cover businesses more favorably has been the recognition that businesses under attack have been hitting back in the wake of harsh, and sometimes incorrect, coverage. Media chiefs have come to recognize the dangers of having young, inexperienced reporters on jihads covering corporations who will hit back if they get things wrong. A producer's worst nightmare, after all, is being called into the office of the network's legal counsel and hearing that they got it wrong.

The rise of conservative and other alternative media has impacted business coverage of old line media as well. While it's hard to document, I have found that some of the same media outlets (e.g., the original three networks) that would have instinctively assailed a vulnerable company years ago now think twice before taking such a hackneyed stance for fear of being ridiculed in alternative media, which operatives like me will unflinchingly exploit.

While the objects of scrutiny inevitably deny that criticism has any impact, my anecdotal experience has been that it has had a chilling effect on attack journalism.

HOW RINGLING BROS. AND BARNUM & BAILEY CIRCUS FOUGHT BACK AGAINST THE ANIMAL RIGHTS JUGGERNAUT

The "Greatest Show on Earth" did not stand for a smear campaign and the news media did not side with the activists.

Attack Summary: Ringling Bros. Circus/Mark Oliver Gebel— Before	
Victim:	Asia, the elephant
Villain:	Mark Oliver Gebel, Ringling Bros. Barnum & Bailey Circus
Vindicator:	Humane Society of Santa Clara Valley
Void:	Animal rights agenda
Vehicle:	Criminal charges filed against Gebel
Value:	Protecting animals

On August 25, 2001, the Humane Society of Santa Clara Valley (HSSCV) cited animal circus trainer Mark Oliver Gebel for animal abuse under an odd California law that gives animal rights activists law enforcement authority. HSSCV's Christine Franco, a deputized "humane officer," accused Gebel of stabbing a performing elephant, Asia, with a metal training device called an "ankus." Gebel, who devoted his life to animal training (his father was the legendary animal trainer Gunther Gebel Williams), didn't do it and was acquitted in a December 21, 2001, trial in San Jose, California.

Since Gebel was acquitted in court, one might ask, what's the big deal? In a nutshell, the problem is that hundreds of media reports prior to and after the trial repeated the disturbing accounts of the alleged "stabbing." When one's stock in trade is a love for animals, the media spectacle of a lovable giant bleeding after being struck by a profiteering trainer is one that doesn't evaporate after "the facts" are shared.

The news media were quick to traffic in the allegations against Gebel in the weeks leading up to the trial, but many—to their credit—were also willing to reexamine the case after his acquittal. This reexamination would not have happened, however, had the circus's owner, Kenneth Feld, not engaged in an audacious program to force a new round of news coverage.*

KEEPING A CONTROVERSIAL STORY IN THE NEWS

Conventional wisdom would have it that it's best to stay out of the press in the wake of controversy, especially after a high-profile vindication. In many cases, it doesn't pay to remind the public about unpopular charges. But for Kenneth Feld, the attack on Gebel represented a seminal event that struck at the soul of the circus and could not be ignored. The accusation against Gebel marked that rare turning point in business where commercial obligations collide with moral ones. After Gebel's acquittal, Feld bought full-page advertisements in the *New York Times*, the *Los Angeles Times*, the *Washington Post*, and *Daily Variety* and other influential publications to protest the animal rights movement's deployment of the legal system to attack the circus and its star trainer. Feld supplemented the ads with numerous television and print interviews, including appearances on NBC's *Today Show* and Fox's *Hannity & Colmes*.

---

*I have worked with Ringling Bros. in the past and am not an impartial observer in this conflict.

"I decided that to remain silent while fine men and women and a beloved American institution were slandered would be unconscionable," Feld said. "I wanted to hold these special interest groups accountable for their destructive actions especially since they have been universally assumed to be ethical and credible for decades."

In his advertisements and media appearances, the soft-spoken Feld did not hold back. Gebel was like a son to him, he explained, having been raised in the circus by his father, the legendary Gunther Gebel-Williams, who had died of cancer six months before. Animal rights activists, expectedly, had shown up at Gunther's funeral. A press release issued by the People for the Ethical Treatment of Animals (PeTA) stated, "Gebel-Williams created a hell for animals in Ringling Bros. and Barnum & Bailey Circus. Odds are that he's in the real one now."

Feld's response was anchored equally in fact and emotion. Unless the alleged witness possessed X-ray power to see through elephants, she couldn't have seen the incident—Mark was on the opposite side of the four-ton pachyderm. The videotapes that activists were peddling to the news media of animal abuse had been, in fact, recorded many years earlier at non-Ringling circuses. The very same media that eagerly reported the accusation against Gebel were willing to hear the other side of the story, especially since one side had been relentlessly hoodwinking them with disinformation. Liberal or conservative, vegan or steak-lover, reporters are people and people don't like being lied to, and this was reflected in the media's often blistering questioning of the activists, a new phenomenon.

Feld also argued that it defied logic that someone who had virtually been raised in the circus would get some perverse joy out of hurting animals. Finally, Feld argued, that the oft-fabled "wild" where elephants belonged did not, in fact, exist. In the much romanticized "wild," elephants are being slaughtered by poachers for their ivory. Ringling, which does not take elephants from the wild, has established one of the most successful breeding programs for Asian elephants in the world. Fifteen baby elephants have been born in the past nine years.

To be sure, Feld's defense of the circus will not make the institution's critics disappear, the fantasy of most corporations under siege. Damage control is a game played at the margins; rarely do singular actions reverse

chronic problems. Rather, by fighting back, the circus introduced something to its critics that they had never known before: risk. For decades, the
news media lapped up what the activists spewed because they knew how
to package attacks. There was a victim (animals), a villain (the circus),
and a vindicator (activist groups). It wasn't until the movement, like any
force that goes virtually unchallenged, became arrogant and smeared an
innocent and beloved figure like Mark Oliver Gebel that the circus had
the weapons to "flip" the narrative and reveal a movement fully capable
of treachery.

Counterattack Summary: Ringling Bros. Circus/
Mark Oliver Gebel—After

Victim:	Mark Oliver Gebel
Villain:	Humane Society
Vindicator:	Justice system
Void:	Framing an innocent man
Vehicle:	Advertising and media outreach by Ringling Bros.
Value:	Protecting animals

Text of letter:*

Vienna, VA—January 7, 2002—The following open letter is from Kenneth Feld, Chairman and Producer of Ringling Bros. and Barnum &
Bailey®, in an appeal to the animal rights organizations that continue to
waste their members' valuable financial contributions and the organizations' human resources attacking responsible animal care providers,
instead of spending them on the care of animals.

* * * * *

Contents of the open letter issued today:

---

*http://www.ringling.com/lava/release.asp?rtype=nr&docid=0000004874

An Open Letter to Animal Rights Groups

After sitting through a trial in San Jose, California, that should never have come to court, and witnessing a senseless waste of taxpayer's money, I am writing with the hope of appealing to your heart, your conscience, and your common sense.

Your organizations publicly claim thousands of members and tens of millions of dollars raised on behalf of animals. Yet The Associated Press* reported that in 1999, PeTA confiscated 2,103 pets and killed 1,325 of them. Did PeTA appeal to its members for homes? How much, if any, of its more than $15 million in resources did PeTA spend on their care? How much money raised by PeTA and like-minded groups was spent on creating politically motivated lawsuits, violent and sexually titillating ads, publicity stunts, and support of politically extreme groups such as the Animal Liberation Front† (listed as a terrorist organization by the F.B.I.), as well as traveling people around the country to harass those with whom they disagree?

I am appealing to you to use the millions you raise from your well-intentioned members to positively affect the lives of animals who are starving, ill, overpopulating, and dying in habitats that can no longer support them. Instead, your resources are being spent attacking Ringling Bros. and Barnum & Bailey® and other responsible organizations such as licensed zoos and aquariums who care for, raise, live, work, and play with their endangered animal partners under carefully regulated laws enforced by the United States Department of Agriculture. Your millions of dollars could be so much better spent in the care of animals in real distress, rather than manipulating well-meaning hearts and minds into believing that there is a "wild" which, in reality, no longer exists.

People need to know the truth. It's disingenuous at best to suggest that endangered animals should be put back in the wild, and very destructive to the cause of conservation at worst. They are dying out there. A wild environment is far from peaceful for endangered species. For example, Asian elephants have dwindled to a worldwide population of less than 50,000 because of poaching and competition with humans for resources and food. Experts believe they may disappear entirely if conservation and breeding efforts are not more successful. This is why

---

*July 30, 2000, *Washington Post* (Associated Press)
†September 29, 1997, *Newsweek* ("Breaking the Cages")

Ringling Bros. has established the Center for Elephant Conservation, one of the most successful breeding programs for Asian elephants in the world. We are proud to say we have had 12 babies in the last 9 years, with 3 more on the way in 2002. We spend our resources directly working with worldwide partners to breed, study, and care for these highly endangered animals.

Isn't it time to paint the full picture in your fundraising drives? Ringling Bros. and Barnum & Bailey does not take animals out of the wild, and we have not done so for over 26 years, following the introduction of the CITES treaty in 1975. The truth is no one is more concerned with the well-being of animals than Ringling Bros. We have a lifelong emotional and financial commitment to our Asian elephant partners. Animals who are born in the care of humans, grow up with humans, and live with humans are comfortable working with humans. Our animal partners are healthy, well cared for, and content, and we know that because we have individual relationships with each and every one of them.

We urge you to develop relationships with individual animals as we do, and to spend your dollars and efforts caring for them as individuals. Use your money and resources where they are needed most, and stop targeting responsible animal care providers for political reasons.

Sincerely,

Kenneth Feld
Chairman and Producer
Ringling Bros. and Barnum & Bailey

CONCLUSION

"Everything is in the hands of its enemies."

Assumption of Murphy's Law

Much of what becomes a crisis depends upon what it's competing with. In the months prior to September 11, Americans were preoccupied with killer sharks and Gary Condit. Now, we're duly concerned about suicide bombers and boardroom sleight-of-hand.

If September 11 provoked Americans to circle the wagons to protect their institutions, the Enron and Arthur Andersen debacles, rightly, gave us pause. Attacks on businesses, legitimate or not, will continue in part because the vehicles of communication have multiplied and individuals have more leverage to lash out at oppressors, real and imagined. The greatest threat to businesses is the mindset which much of the world shares: specifically, the belief that success and immorality are one and the same. We can expect to see the vilification of success and the exaltation of weakness continue because it's a great story line. Many businesses will respond to hostilities with cuddlier-than-thou PR programs to convince the public that captains of industry toss and turn in their beds at night as they dream up ways to "nurture solutions." Well, they don't, and the public knows it.

I'm a big fan of drawing attention to real achievements, and often team with conventional advertising agencies and PR firms to this end. If a company has done something good, why not publicize it? I see nothing wrong with that. What I object to, however, is hollow "image building" campaigns designed to neutralize biases that are visceral and intense.

There is an enormous and vital difference between a classroom and a mugging. In a classroom, the consensual objective is to exchange ideas and, through dialectic, work toward synthesis. Everybody is both teacher and student; everybody is there to learn. It is in this realm that so-called happy PR operates—a value-neutral environment.

In a mugging, however, the mugger wants the victim's wallet, and that's that. There is little room for "education" or "dialogue." In the midst of a fight, you cannot explain that it is your wallet and that you should not have to give it up. Attack targets must eliminate the notion that a "communications breakdown" has occurred. The mugger almost certainly has heard and understood your appeal; he simply doesn't agree and doesn't care. This is a value-negative environment and, unfortunately for business, it's the rule, not the exception.

As was true when this book was first published, the core lesson is that business leaders must stop whining about what's fair, cease pie-in-the-sky flirtations with utopian strategies, and explore the imperfect options at our disposal to fight winnable wars. It's time to get some backbone, make a stand, and take your wallet back.

Clinton and Sexgate:
Three Damage Control Fallacies

**Clinton's political skills and his
good luck—not "spin"—saved him.**

"It would have been painful, grotesque, but a scandal was after all sort
of a service to the community."

Saul Bellow, *Herzog*

A WHITE HOUSE APPRENTICESHIP
IN PUBLIC RELATIONS WIZARDRY

My White House bosses were depressed. The nation was in a deep recession and the president's motorcade had just been pelted with rocks in Florida. As a young aide in the fall of 1982, I remember watching their pained faces as they debated what to do about President Reagan's terrible image. Having little to contribute at this stage of my career, all I remember doing was watching; watching my mentors struggle with the consistently awful news.

President Reagan and his wife, Nancy, could do no right. The country was furious that Mrs. Reagan got new china for the White House. They didn't care for the First Couple's hoity-toity friends, either. Placards reading

"Reaganomics Sucks" were commonplace. How would "we" (I saw myself, however self-delusional, as part of the team) get out of this mess?

A few months, a stock market rally, and an economic turnaround later, Reagan was riding high. My depressed bosses were no longer depressed. In fact, they were being hailed widely as image control geniuses. The smart ones rolled their eyes at the nonsensical attribution. Others honed a skill of smiling archly, ushering in the age of the over-hyped spin doctor.

At the time, the miraculous turnaround meant nothing to me. Sixteen years later, however, what I saw helped me make sense of the public opinion puzzle that was being called "Sexgate."

Within the first few weeks of the Bill Clinton–Monica Lewinsky scandal, the news media and the public fell into a stale triad of conventional wisdom about the case that very few challenged. This conventional wisdom held that "spin" was responsible for the president's miraculous survival. Wizards of spin shouted from the sidelines that the president should have "come clean" and admitted to his affair with White House intern Lewinsky. Pundits echoed each other's assessments that the public was sick and tired of the scandal, which was supposedly contributing to Clinton's survival.

The central problem with challenging these notions was that most folks benefited from them financially, politically, psychically, or just because they were easy concepts to grasp. Notions of brilliant spin, confession, and public disinterest had little, if anything, to do with President Clinton's survival.

FALLACY #1: WHITE HOUSE "SPIN" WAS RESPONSIBLE FOR CLINTON'S HIGH APPROVAL RATINGS IN THE WAKE OF SCANDAL

Spin didn't save Bill Clinton. It doesn't work. Spin is dead because everybody knows what it is. The whole idea behind spin was to convey sincerity. Today, the media openly cover spin itself, so the public is on guard and tunes out. This doesn't stop pundits, reporters, and the public alike from believing in spin: alchemy, stealth, and public relations tricks to fool the public against its will. "Spin doctor" first appeared in the dictionary in 1984 and its very definition implies subterfuge: "A representative . . . who favorably interprets words or actions."

The media attribute outcomes to spin because the concept is a catch-all that allows reporters to appear to have gotten to the bottom of a complex case without doing any work:

"How did Clinton survive?"

"Spin."

"Ahhh."

The mythical power of spin is further aggravated by codependent flacks and reporters who narcissistically attribute the outcome of current events to their own skills. Accordingly, things that go well are attributed to "brilliant staging." Events that go poorly were "mismanaged"—by someone else, of course.

The legend of spin offers everybody a benefit. The spin doctor becomes known as a genius, which inflates his career marketability; the media run with an inside scoop showing how they exposed the impenetrable world of political spin; and the public has its suspicions confirmed about trickery and wicked masterminds in Washington without having to accept any of the blame for how things turned out.

If spin didn't protect Bill Clinton, what did? Clinton's success has been attributable to his personal gifts and incredible luck. His personal gifts include charm, a genius for lying and getting away with it, his ability to mobilize allies, and a capacity for generating empathy among people who should know better, or who are persuaded by Clinton not to attack him.

After Clinton confessed to an "improper relationship" with Lewinsky, his wife and daughter held his hand on the White House south lawn. The very same feminists who devoured Supreme Court Justice Clarence Thomas and Senator Robert Packwood either stood by Clinton or said little or nothing about his behavior. Rather than testify against Clinton, his one-time business partner Susan McDougal chose to go to prison for contempt. None of these exigencies were engineered by spin doctors or consultants. They resulted from Clinton's own skills and political appeal.

Clinton has also been very lucky. I've never seen anything like it in business or politics. Examples of Clinton's luck have included a booming economy; the convenient death of his former business partner and Whitewater witness James McDougal; and the serendipitous bombing of the U.S.

embassies in Tanzania and Kenya shortly before his grand jury testimony in the Lewinsky affair. Clinton responded to the terrorist bombings by retaliating against the perpetrators with cruise missiles, which knocked the Lewinsky matter from "above-the-fold" media coverage status to second page news.

FALLACY #2: CLINTON SHOULD HAVE COME CLEAN RIGHT AWAY

Rule #1 of introductory public relations dictates that if you are accused of doing a bad thing, and you actually did it, you should confess. This is a charming and wishful little chestnut, but it has little use when survival is at stake.

When under attack, any person or institution instinctively reaches for proven resources to survive. Bill Clinton's chief resources have been his charm and his proven ability to lie and get away with it.

Contrary to the hackneyed sound bite that "Clinton thinks he can get away with lying," Clinton *has* gotten away with lying his entire life. Most of us who think we can get away with lying publicly would be considered delusional in addition to being dishonest. When Clinton has thought he could get away with lying, however, he was making a calculated risk based on a track record of getting away with it. That's how life works for certain people. Life is a different adventure for the gifted, who can fool all of the people who want to be fooled all of the time. In other words, Clinton *is* special.

In the wake of the Lewinsky revelation, Clinton's polls were quite high. Women, the population most likely to be offended by Clinton's behavior, defended him aggressively. Feminist organizations were silent. The president's Congressional support was strong, the stock market was roaring, the economy was growing, and America's international standing was solid. Virtually nothing on the political landscape begged for a change in strategy. In fact, an early confession may have unnecessarily spiked the president's support, which was critical to the White House's successful campaign to demonize Independent Counsel Kenneth Starr.

The "come clean" strategy was anchored in the belief that morality mattered in the Lewinsky affair. In the early days of the scandal, armchair damage control counselors dove before news cameras to ascribe their own morals to Clinton. *"Repent!"* they admonished. Unconsciously, they were also applying to Clinton's predicament their own sense of what *they* would be able to get away with in a bind.

My colleagues call my position on Clinton's escape from crisis my "crime pays" theory. Do I believe that lying is a viable strategic alternative? they ask. I don't. I am just bringing to light the harsh truth that the rules aren't the same for everybody. I don't counsel my clients to lie because it's morally wrong and because they would get caught. This doesn't mean, however, that others don't lie and get away with it. In fact, my experience has been that the most effective attackers—and survivors of attack—are utterly audacious, unrepentant, and absent of any limiting self-awareness or conscience. Clinton is the quintessential attack survivor because he has the survival attributes of a quintessential attacker.

People who pursue the presidency care about one thing: being president. Once they become president, they care about staying president. If they're moral, it's charming but optional.

To have written off Clinton as just a liar grossly underestimates the man. Clinton is a *gifted* liar with a track record of making lying work. Said Comedian Bill Maher in *Playboy*, "The people want to be lied to. They want to be lied to by the smoothest guy."

Maybe, but don't ever try it.

The Legal Issue

In addition to my "crime pays" theory of Clinton's survival, there is an even more important reason Clinton couldn't easily "fess up": A confession would have complicated and perhaps destroyed his legal case.

Communicators and lawyers are often in conflict. Lawyers want their client to be silent because anything they say could incriminate them in court. Communicators like myself like clients to confess because openness is the biggest factor in being trusted. What was lost on most of the pundits—and the public—was that the independent counsel's investigation was a *legal* inquiry, not an informal inquisition.

Despite the embarrassment of Clinton's later reversal, it did not hurt his impeachment case; he won. Even if the reversal does hurt his future

legal problems, that damage must be weighed against the political benefits that it accrued. Powerful members of Congress were sending signals
shortly before Clinton's reversal that a confession might avert impeachment. They had been sending no such signals earlier. As with most negotiations, legal and political, time had to play out before concessions were
made. In the short term, Clinton had to keep quiet regardless of how frus-
trating it was to many. In the long term, his handling of events yielded the
best possible results given his predicament.

FALLACY #3: THE PUBLIC WAS SICK OF THE LEWINSKY CRISIS

The Clinton White House (and an assortment of pundits) floated the line
that the American public had grown tired of the Lewinsky scandal. The
thinking was that if they could get the public to repeat the "we're sick of
it" mantra loudly enough, Clinton's attackers would back off.

Nobody backed off. The attacks continued and the public remained
transfixed by the scandal regardless of what they said in man-on-the-street
interviews. Every day I watched from my office window as a swarm of
news cameras waited outside of Monica Lewinsky's lawyers' offices on
Connecticut Avenue in Washington. One of my young colleagues remarked, "They're not waiting out there because no one's interested."

No they were not. When the public is truly sick of something, they
tune out; they do not make Independent Counsel Starr's report a best-
selling book. There is nothing that the media—and shrewd pollsters—can
detect faster than apathy. (It's possible for people to *say* that they disapprove of coverage and still watch, is it not?) Barbara Walters's March 3,
1999, interview with Lewinsky was the most-watched news program ever
aired by a network (ABC). Said pollster Frank Luntz, "It is socially unacceptable for people to tell pollsters they are intrigued by matters of sex."

The public felt obligated to say it was sick of the Lewinsky matter in
the same spirit that very few people admitted to voting for Richard Nixon
and very few radio listeners concede that they listen to shock jock
Howard Stern: Feigning disinterest in Lewinsky was proper etiquette.

As with the O. J. Simpson case before it, the Lewinsky scandal made reality more amusing than anything Hollywood could produce. It was just the latest consumer product to keep Americans entertained. The Simpson case brought consumers sexy buzzwords ("bloody glove," "plaintive wail") and high-minded debates (spousal abuse). Lewinsky, too, delivered buzzwords ("stained dress," "presidential kneepads") and noble crusades (the character issue) to justify prurient interest.

The scandal sparked the news media and consumers to strike up a tacit bargain: The media would provide an endless supply of soft-core porn disguised as public controversy and, in return, consumers would tune in for "Breaking News" about oral sex and cigars used as sex toys.

Despite the public's commitment to the entertainment aspects of the scandal, Americans were concurrently worried about what it was doing to the nation's moral fabric. The public was genuinely concerned about distractions from more important issues. Americans were titillated by the amusement value of the scandal but were repelled by its policy implications. This, more than pure disinterest, probably accounted for all of the "I'm sick of it" statements.

WHAT CLINTON'S OPERATIVES DID RIGHT

While Clinton's survival has been due primarily to his charm and his luck, his staff—to which I add the First Lady, Hillary Rodham Clinton—played a valuable supporting role. They did five things in particular that were very smart.

Good Move #1: Characterize the Independent Counsel's Investigation as Being about Sex

The White House characterized Independent Counsel Starr's investigation as being about sex when it was about obstruction of justice. To investigate the obstruction of justice charge, however, Starr needed to determine whether or not Clinton was being truthful about his relationship with Lewinsky. In a court of law, lies—even about seemingly trivial matters—constitute perjury.

The public has an abysmal understanding of how the law works. The

Clinton White House understood this. Americans, however, do understand sex and abhor the specter of law enforcement nosing around in people's sex lives. The White House chose to make sex the issue, not because it really was the issue, but because it was what resonated. It more than resonated. It drove people crazy.

Yes, the independent counsel ended up nailing Clinton on the seemingly trivial issue of sex. Yes, it is mindboggling—and pathetic—that the leader of the free world could fall because of oral sex. However, the government ended up nailing the murderous Al Capone for tax evasion and convicts numerous criminals for things like wire fraud (using the telephone do dirty business) and mail fraud (sending bad stuff through the mail). I have a client who went to prison because he didn't call the Environmental Protection Agency within the designated amount of time (I think it was thirty minutes) from when a chemical spill occurred. Why did he fail to comply? He was frantically trying to prevent the chemicals from flowing into a nearby schoolyard.

Was his punishment unfair? I think so. But the law and fairness are different concepts.

Good Move #2: Mobilize the First Lady

Many people believed from the beginning that the Lewinsky matter was a marital issue, not a political or legal one. Americans reasoned that if Hillary was okay with her husband's behavior, they were, too.

The substance of the First Lady's defense of her husband was irrelevant. She didn't win points for her husband by characterizing the independent counsel's investigation as being motivated by a "vast right wing conspiracy" or her freakish reference to prejudice against people from Arkansas. She shored up public support for her husband just by displaying personal, spousal support for him.

Good Move #3: Pre-Leaking the President's Reversal on Having Sex with Lewinsky

By leaking President Clinton's reversal on his vehement "I did not have sex with that woman" position, his aides took the sting out of the president's stunning contradiction. By the time Clinton spoke to the American public forty-eight hours after the leaks, he was not really breaking any news. His surrogates had done it for him. There is a reason leaders have press secretaries and hatchet men: It works.

The *source* of the news matters. People remember the specifics of getting big news, good or bad. The public does not separate the message from the messenger any more than they separate a leader from the economic conditions he presides over. Had Clinton been the one to originally confess to the public, he would have soldered himself to the bad news—the sex, the lying, the un-presidential nature of the whole mess.

Good Move #4: Blowing Up Afghanistan and Sudan

Three days after he admitted to an "improper relationship" with Monica Lewinsky, President Clinton ordered the military to fire seventy-five cruise missiles at suspected terrorist sites in Afghanistan and Sudan. Was Clinton "wagging the dog"—distracting attention from his woes by exploiting another event? Maybe, but even his critics concede he was justified. Fate sent Bill Clinton another valentine.

The missile strikes knocked the Lewinsky story into remission. I watched the camera crews that had been staking out Lewinsky's lawyers' offices next to mine vanish within moments of the announcement of the air strikes. Missiles talk, spin walks. Furthermore, the only thing the American public likes more than a sex scandal is to watch the long arm of the U.S. military hammer terrorists into the grasp of Allah.

Good Move #5: Press Secretary McCurry Kept Plausible Denial

By most accounts, White House Press Secretary Mike McCurry kept away from discussions about the details of President Clinton's relationship with Lewinsky. This was smart because the worst McCurry could be accused of is spreading Clinton's lies, not his own.

Unfortunately, the nuance of "not knowing" is important in crisis communications. The media find deliberate lying unforgivable but will

tolerate having been misled if they believe the intermediary did not know
the truth. In McCurry's case, the news media trusted him because he had
a history of being trustworthy and empathized with the awkward position
he was in.

McCurry had ample justification for not knowing the facts: Discussions about the Lewinsky matter were privileged and McCurry was not a
member of the legal team. He should not have been.* Had he been a part
of the legal team, McCurry would have been in a terrible position as the
president's spokesman, having to constantly say "no comment" on the
grounds that his statements were privileged. Even though he would have
been justified in keeping mum, his silence would have enraged the media
and the public, who often confuse silence with guilt.

"Damage Control" vs. "Damage Disappearance"

Clinton has been terribly hurt by the Lewinsky crisis despite his effective
crisis management. Nevertheless, he was hurt more by the original sin
than by his "handling" of it. Once the Lewinsky matter broke, there was
no "smart bomb" that could have made the entire crisis go away. Pundits
characterized confession as this smart bomb, which reveals maddening
naivete about how soupy real controversies are.

Damage control is an earthy endeavor where an attack target must
take actions that are doable given the circumstances. In the fog of crisis,
targets must reach out for the best solutions, not the perfect ones they see
in the movies. Clinton's actions, and those of his wife and his staff, controlled the damage well. While many of these tactics were morally repugnant, they were the best weapons available. The Clinton camp's inability
to make Monica Lewinsky disappear was a failure of Clinton's behavior,
not the crisis management process. Wrote *National Journal* editor
Michael Kelly, "What guaranteed the eventual disclosure of the president's sex with the intern was the president's sex with the intern."

---

*In many of my firm's cases, we are part of a legal team and our work is protected
by attorney-client privilege even though we are not attorneys.

Glossary of Terms

Allegation Forum. Setting, such as Internet "chat rooms" or afternoon talk shows, where an attacker can level charges with little to no resistance.

Attack. Intense, often unwarranted, public scrutiny aimed at hurting a *target*.

Attacker. One who seeks to damage a *target*.

Barnum Effect. Belief in a symptom or allegation by virtue of its having been suggested.

Character Crisis. Attack where the inherent trustworthiness, quality, or competence of a *target* is questioned. (Contrast with *Sniper-Fire Crisis*.)

Connie Confessional. Attempt by a savvy journalist to get a naïve individual to go "off-the-record," fully knowing that whatever is confessed will be made public, to the confessor's embarrassment.

Coronation. Second stage of *schadenfreude* where the greatness of the *target* is widely publicized.

Culture of Attack. Society that demands *attacks* and/or is increasingly comfortable with them.

Debate. Opportunity to humiliate a *target* in a forum that inherently favors the *attacker*.

Discovery. First stage of *schadenfreude* where a *target* is initially identified as a savior or panacea.

Display behavior. Human behaviors such as facial expressions and body language of a *target* that impact likability.

Dissuasion. Aggressive stance by a *target* that introduces personal risk to *attackers*.

Dr. No. A visual filming technique that makes a *target* look bad, even if he is engaged in a benign act (e.g., walking to his car wearing sunglasses).

Einstein. An ostensibly scientific independent test used to validate a particular agenda.

Elvis. One who attacks in order to gain recognition.

Flaming. Internet-launched smear campaign.

Flaw Detection. Third stage of *schadenfreude* where a *target*'s weakness is first noticed.

Godzilla Meets Bambi. Technique of enumerating alleged misdeeds committed by a strong party against a weaker party.

Goodwill. Perceived trustworthiness and likability of a *target*.

Guerrilla. *Attacker* adept at using modern communications to injure a *target*.

Handler. Omniscient genius thought to be in control of all elements of public perception, usually on behalf of a political or corporate interest. Also called "Spin doctor."

"Holy Shit!" Story. News story that will shock the public and boost the career of the reporter who uncovers it.

Humiliation. Fourth and final stage of *schadenfreude* where the *target* is embarrassed and positioned as having betrayed the public trust.

Icky Feeling Hypothesis. Data collection method consisting of an *attacker*'s personal belief that an allegation is true.

Liberal Bias. Perceived political motivation of the news media, however incorrect.

Marie Antoinette. Inciting resentment against a *target* by making reference to the target's wealth.

Marketplace Assault. Attack on a business *target* by a competitor that is packaged as a legitimate issue of public concern.

Media. Vague cabal of journalists and communications vehicles that the public blames for destructive cultural trends rather than accepting responsibility for its own contribution to these trends.

Nailing prerogative. Unrestrained option exercised by some reporters to use the power of their institutions to attack a *target* they do not like.

Placido Domingo. Technique used by *attackers* to shout down an adversary in a *debate*.

Plausibility. Quality of an allegation appearing to be true. Defined downward at the millennium to mean "could conceivably be true since the marketplace wants it to be."

Prime Time Subpoena. TV magazine program technique of handing a document to a befuddled *target* and requesting that it be reviewed while the camera is rolling.

Ratings Bias. True motivation of the news media.

Resonance. Staying power of an allegation due to marketplace demand.

Right-to-Know. Excuse or "beard" used by *attackers* to justify vicious scrutiny. The subtext is that a concern for public welfare justifies the attack.

Schadenfreude. Enjoying the misery of others, usually someone (or something) more successful. Derives from German *schaden* (damage) and *freude* (joy).

Scoreboard. High-profile ranking of people, products and institutions that inevitably provoke *attacks*.

Silkwood Analogy. Reference made by *attackers* upon receiving criticism to the death of anti-nuclear activist Karen Silkwood, presumably at the hands of corporate interests. The reference is an attempt at self-martyrdom.

Sniper-Fire Crisis. attack that is perceived to be caused by an outside force—not the *target* (contrast with *Character Crisis*).

Spectral Evidence. Highly subjective "test" used during Salem witch trials to identify a witch. In layman's terms, *spectral evidence* means that the public doesn't like the *targets* and wants to convict them independent of the truth.

Spin. Trickery, slick characterizations, and clever word turns that are widely—and wrongly—believed to be effective in fooling the public.

Sweaty Al. Use by an *attacker* of the worst (least attractive) video clip or sound-bite of a *target*.

Target. Object—or potential object—of *attack*.

Value. The social principle under which an *attack* is justified.

Vehicle. The medium in which the *attack* is delivered.

Victim. One who genuinely suffers or who claims to suffer.

Victim's Network. Coalition of self-described *victims* who attack a specific *target* that they blame for their misfortunes.

Villain. The *target* believed to have inflicted harm on the *victim*.

Vindicator. External redeemer who is believed to right the wrong.

Void. An unfilled need for an *attack* that the public demands be met.

Yenta Quotient. Jump or migration of bad information from the Internet (or other unreliable source) to the mainstream media.

Bibliography

BOOKS

Barrett, Stephen, and Ronald E. Gots. *Chemical Sensitivity: The Truth about Environmental Illness*. Amherst, N.Y.: Prometheus Books, 1998.

Barrett, Stephen, William Jarvis, et al., eds. *Consumer Health: A Guide to Intelligent Decisions*. 6th ed. New York: Brown & Benchmark Publishers, 1996.

Bastian, Misty L. " 'Bloodhounds Who Have No Friends': Witchcraft and Locality in the Nigerian Popular Press." In *Modernity and Its Malcontents: Ritual and Power in Post-Colonial Africa*. Edited by Jean and John Comaroff. Chicago: University of Chicago Press, 1993.

Bonovolanta, Jules. *The Good Guys*. New York: Simon & Schuster, 1996.

Boorstin, Daniel J. *The Image: A Guide to Pseudo Events in America*. New York: Random House, 1961.

Boyer, Paul, and Stephen Nissenbaum. *Salem Possessed: The Social Origins of Witchcraft*. Cambridge, Mass.: Harvard University Press, 1974.

———. *The Salem Witchcraft Papers: Verbatim Transcripts of the Legal Documents of the Salem Witchcraft Outbreak of 1692*. New York: DeCapo Press, 1977.

Breggin, Peter R. *Talking Back to Prozac*. New York: St. Martin's Press, 1994.

Brunvand, Jan Harold. *Curses! Broiled Again!*. New York: W. W. Norton & Company, 1989.

———. *The Mexican Pet*. New York: W. W. Norton & Company, 1986.

Bugliosi, Vincent. *Outrage: The Five Reasons Why O. J. Simpson Got Away with Murder.* New York: W. W. Norton & Company, 1996.

Burrough, Bryan. *Vendetta: American Express and the Smearing of Edmond Safra.* New York: HarperCollins, 1992.

Cohn, Normal. *The Pursuit of the Millennium: Revolutionary Millenarians and Mystical Anarchists of the Middle Ages.* New York: Oxford University Press, 1961.

Colburn, Theo, et al. *Our Stolen Future: Are We Threatening Our Fertility, Intelligence, and Survival—A Scientific Detective Story.* New York: Penguin Books USA, 1996.

Dineen, Tina. *Manufacturing Victims.* Montreal: Robert Davies Publishing, 1996.

Fallows, James. *Breaking the News.* New York: Pantheon, 1996.

Fitzgerald, F. Scott. *The Great Gatsby.* New York: Charles Scribner & Sons, 1925.

Frank, Robert H., and Philip J. Cook. *The Winner-Take-All Society.* New York: Penguin Books, 1996.

Fumento, Michael. *Science under Siege.* New York: Quill, 1993.

Fussell, Paul. *Class: A Painfully Accurate Guide through the American Status System 1983.* New York: Ballantine Books, 1993.

Gelernter, David. *Drawing Life.* New York: Free Press, 1997.

Girard, Rene. *Violence and the Sacred.* Baltimore: Johns Hopkins University Press, 1972.

Henning, Chuck. *The Wit and Wisdom of Politics.* Golden, Colo.: Fulcrum Publishing, 1992.

Henry, William A. *In Defense of Elitism.* New York: Bantam Doubleday Dell, 1994.

Howard, Philip K. *Death of Common Sense: How Law Is Suffocating America.* New York: Random House, 1994.

Hughes, Robert. *Culture of Complaint.* New York: Warner Books, 1994.

Irvine, Reed, et al., eds. *The News Manipulators: Why You Can't Trust the News.* Smithtown, N.Y.: Book Distributors, 1993.

Kaminer, Wendy. *I'm Dysfunctional, You're Dysfunctional.* New York: Vintage Books, 1993.

Kramer, Peter D. *Listening to Prozac.* New York: Penguin Books, 1993.

Kurtz, Howard. *Hot Air: All Talk All the Time.* New York: Times Books, 1996.

Lewis, C. S. *The Screwtape Letters.* New York: Touchstone, 1961.

Lopate, Philip. "The Last Taboo." In *Dumbing Down: Essays on the Strip-Mining of American Culture.* Edited by Katherine Washburn and John Thornton. New York: W. W. Norton & Company, 1996.

Love, John F. *McDonald's: Behind the Arches.* New York: Bantam Books, 1986.

Maas, Peter. *Underboss.* New York: HarperCollins Publishers, 1997.

Miller, Dennis. *The Rants.* New York: Bantam Doubleday Dell, 1996.

Milloy, Steven. *Science without Sense.* Washington, D.C.: Cato Institute, 1995

Milloy, Steven, and Michael Gough. *Silencing Science.* Washington D.C.: Cato Institute, 1998.

Mills, Nicolaus. *The Triumph of Meanness.* New York: Houghton Mifflin, 1997.

Moynihan, Daniel Patrick. *Miles to Go: A Personal History of Social Policy.* Cambridge, Mass.: Harvard University Press, 1996.

Pipes, Daniel. *Conspiracy*. New York: Free Press, 1997.

Postman, Neil. *Amusing Ourselves to Death: Public Discourse in the Age of Show Business*. New York: Penguin Books, 1985.

Ries, Al, and Jack Trout. *Marketing Warfare*. New York: McGraw-Hill, 1986.

Roth, Philip. *American Pastoral*. New York: Houghton Mifflin, 1997.

Sabato, Larry. *Feeding Frenzy*. New York: Free Press, 1991.

Samuelson, Robert J. *The Good Life and Its Discontents: The American Dream in the Age of Entitlement*. New York: Times Books, 1995.

Schiavo, Mary, and Sabra Chartrand. *Flying Blind, Flying Safe*. New York: Avon Books, 1997.

Scott, James C. *Weapons of the Weak*. New Haven, Conn.: Yale University Press, 1987.

Seinfeld, Jerry. *SeinLanguage*. New York: Bantam Books, 1993.

Shaw, David. *The Pleasure Police*. New York: Bantam Doubleday Dell, 1996.

Shorter, Edward. *From Paralysis to Fatigue: A History of Psychosomatic Illness in the Modern Era*. New York: Free Press, 1992.

Showalter, Elaine. *Hystories: Hysterical Epidemics and Modern Media*. New York: Columbia University Press, 1997.

Slater, Robert. *Ovitz*. New York: McGraw-Hill, 1997.

Smolla, Rodney. *Suing the Press*. New York: Oxford University Press, 1986.

Summers, Anthony. *Official and Confidential: The Secret Life of J. Edgar Hoover*. New York: G. P. Putman's Sons, 1993.

Tenner, Edward. *Why Things Bite Back*. New York: Knopf, 1996.

Tolkien, J. R. R. *The Hobbit*. New York: Houghton Mifflin, 1937.

Wachtler, Sol. *After the Madness: A Judge's Own Prison Memoir*. New York: Random House, 1997.

Weaver, Paul. *News and the Culture of Lying*. New York: Free Press, 1994.

Wells, Tana. *Fear of Living*. Rickreall, Ore.: Agora Publishing, 1994.

Whelan, Elizabeth, et al. *Panic in the Pantry*. Amherst, N.Y.: Prometheus Books, 1992.

Wurtzel, Elizabeth. *Prozac Nation*. New York: Riverhead Books, 1994.

ARTICLES

Abramson, Jill, et al. "Anti-Trust Probe of Archer Daniels Puts Spotlight on Chairman Andreas' Vast Political Influence." *Wall Street Journal*, July 11, 1995.

Achenbach, Joel. "Reality Check." *Washington Post*, December 4, 1996.

" 'All Pain, No Gain' for Most Workers." *Washington Report* 36, no. 18 (September 20, 1996).

Alter, Jonathan. "A Call for Chinese Walls." *Newsweek* (August 14, 1995).

———. "Jessica's Final Flight." *Newsweek* (April 22, 1996).

———. "The Incendiary Aftershocks." *Newsweek* (March 15, 1993).

Alterman, Eric. "Stop the Presses." *Nation*, May 13, 2002.

Associated Press. "Giuliani Receives British Knighthood." *New York Times*, February 13, 2002.

Babineck, Mark. "Winfrey Blamed for Woes of Ranchers as Trial Opens." *Washington Times*, January 22, 1998.

Bailey, Jeff. "The Dump's Foe Is Indignant and Has the Money to Pay for a Fight." *Wall Street Journal*, June 6, 1996.

Baker, Russ. "Truth, Lies, and Videotape." *Columbia Journalism Review* (July/August 1993).

Balz, Dan, and Bob Woodward. "America's Chaotic Road to War." *Washington Post*, January 27, 2002.

———. "'We Will Rally the World.'" *Washington Post*, January 28, 2002.

———. "Afghan Campaign's Blueprint Emerges." *Washington Post*, January 29, 2002.

———. "A Day to Speak of Anger and Grief." *Washington Post*, January 30, 2002.

———. "At Camp David, Advise and Dissent." *Washington Post*, January 31, 2002.

———. "Combating Terrorism: 'It Starts Today.'" *Washington Post*, February 1, 2002.

———. "A Presidency Defined in One Speech." *Washington Post*, February 2, 2002.

———. "Bush Awaits History's Judgment." *Washington Post*, February 3, 2002.

"Be Bold, Says Beers." *O'Dwyer's PR Daily*, April 15, 2002.

Belkin, Lisa. "No One Could Save Baby Jessica's Rescuer." *Palm Beach Post*, August 13, 1995.

Bolte, William. "Minimally Disabled Must Move Aside." *Los Angeles Times*, July 7, 1995.

"Bombing Case Prompts Media Self-Examination." Reuters, October 28, 1996.

Bovard, James, and Archer Daniels Midland. "A Case Studying Corporate Welfare." *Cato Policy Analysis,* no. 41 (September 6, 1995).

Brenner, Marie. "American Nightmare: The Ballad of Richard Jewell." *Vanity Fair* (February 1997).

Brock, David. "His Cheatin' Heart." *American Spectator* (January 1994).

Brody, Jane E. "Health Scares That Weren't So Scary." *New York Times*, August 8, 1998.

Brophy, Beth. "Kindergartners in the Prozac Nation." *U.S. News & World Report* (November 13, 1995).

Brown, Chip. "She's a Portrait of Zealotry in Plastic Shoes." *Washington Post*, November 13, 1983.

Burleigh, Nina. "Clintonophobia!" *Time* (April 11, 1994).

Bushman, Richard L., and James Morris. "The Rise and Fall of Civility in America." *Wilson Quarterly* 20, no. 4 (autumn 1996).

Bynum, Russ. "Value Down for ValuJet." Associated Press, May 11, 1997.

Byrd, Joann. "TV News: The Pickup Trucks." *Washington Post*, March 7, 1993.

Cardoso, Bill. "Regional News." UPI, June 25, 1984.

Carlson, Peter. "The Player: Dwayne Andreas and the American System." *Washington Post Magazine* (July 14, 1996).

Carmody, John, and Howard Kurtz. "NBC Exec Ousted over Staged Crash." *Washington Post*, January 3, 1993.

Carney, Dan. "Dwayne's World." *Mother Jones* (July/August 1995).

Carter, Bill. "A Fountain of Youth for TV News Magazines." *New York Times*, October 19, 1992.

———. "Behind the New Apology from NBC." *New York Times*, February 27, 1993.

"Cause of the Crash of ValuJet 592 Challenged by VisionSafe's Werjefelt." Bloomberg Business News (August 18, 1997).

Charlton, Janet. "Kathie Lee: 'I'm Going to Have Frank's Baby.' " *Star*, July 22, 1997.

Chen, Kathy, Gregg Hitt, Laurie McGinley, and Andrea Petersen. "In Washington, Government Failed Anthrax-Scare Test." *Wall Street Journal Europe*, November 2, 2001.

Clark, William. "Witches, Floods, and Wonder Drugs." *Published Symposia*. New York: Plenum Press, 1980.

Collins, Amy Fine. "A Night to Remember." *Vanity Fair* (July 1996).

Colvin, Geoff. "What Can Stop the Economy?" *Fortune* (October 8, 1996).

Conant, Jennet. "Don't Mess with Steve Brill." *Vanity Fair* (August 1997).

Connolly, Ceci, and Ellen Nakashima. "CDC Sets 'Tips' on Handling Mail." *Washington Post*, December 6, 2001.

Cordle, Ina Paiva. "Airline Rebuilds Ranks, Routes under Intense Scrutiny by FAA." *Miami Herald*, May 4, 1997.

Crocker, Catherine. "Jackie's Auction's Total Haul: $34.5 Million." Associated Press, April 27, 1996.

Croteau, David. "Challenging the 'Liberal Media' Claim." *Extra!* 11, no. 4 (July/August 1998): 4–9.

Cummings, Jeanne, and Phil Kuntz. "Sorting Fact from Rumor in a Media Maelstrom." *Wall Street Journal*, January 29, 1998.

Cummings, Judith. "Lawyer Fails to Provide Sex Tapes in Court." *New York Times*, July 26, 1983.

DeBakey, Michael. "Hype and Hypocrisy on Animal Rights." *Wall Street Journal*, December 12, 1996.

Department of Justice, "Report to Congress on the Extent and Effects of Domestic and International Terrorism on Animal Enterprises." October 1993.

DePaulo, Lisa. "The Screwing of Frank Gifford." *Men's Journal* (December 1997/January 1998).

Diamond, Edwin. "Auto Destruct: NBC's Gartner Goes Boom." *New York*, March 15, 1993.

Diebel, Linda. "Anthrax Kills 2 More in U.S." *Toronto Star*, October 23, 2001.

Dong, Roger. "Jackie's Own." *People* (January 8, 1996).

Dowie, Douglas. " 'Sex Tape' Attorney Robert Steinberg." UPI, July 12, 1983.

"Drudge Inks Fox News Pact." Reuters, February 27, 1998.

Edmonson, George. "Rumsfeld's Popularity Sparks Curiosity—and Unusual Questions." *Cox Newspapers*, January 9, 2002.

Ehlers, Robert. "The Recycling Boondoggle." *Law and Politics* (October 1996).

Elstrom, Peter. "Now the Medium Is the Message Board." *Business Week* (July 8, 1996).

Eichenwald, Kurt. "Andreas Retires as Chief of Archer." *New York Times*, April 18, 1997.
———. "Archer Daniels Informer Admits Recent Deception." *New York Times*, January 15, 1997.
Farhi, Paul. "Marina Ein's Muddled Message." *Washington Post*, July 20, 2001.
———. "Ovitz Departs Disney after 16 Months." *Washington Post*, December 13, 1996.
Farquhar, Michael. "Tricks." *Washington Post*, October 27, 1996.
"FBI Reportedly Searches Contractor Linked to ValuJet Crash." Reuters, August 7, 1996.
Fallows, James. "Why Americans Hate the Media." *Atlantic Monthly* (February 1996).
Farrell, Greg. "Indictment Could Shred Andersen." *USA Today*, March 15, 2002.
———. "Andersen Workers Protest Indictment." *USA Today*, March 22, 2002.
"Few Lessons Learned after ValuJet Crash." Associated Press, August 18, 1997.
Fitz, Reginald, and Jim Nelson. "Kathie Lee Divorce Agony." *National Enquirer*, July 22, 1997.
Folkers, Richard. "When Our Worlds Collide." *U.S. News & World Report* (September 15, 1997).
Freedberg, Sydney, Jr. "Run Away." *New Republic* (June 16, 1997).
Friedman, Jon. "Bloomberg Profile: ADM's Andreas Feels Probe's Tremors." Bloomberg Business News (July 10, 1995).
Gardiner, Beth. "Royal 'Rags' Pull in $3.26 million at Christie's." Associated Press, June 27, 1997.
Gillian, Audrey. "U.S. Closer to Blaming Anthrax on al-Qaida." *Guardian*, October 24, 2001.
Gillin, Audrey. "Are You Lonesome Tonight?" *Washington Post*, August 16, 1997.
Glassman, James K. "Matt Drudge, E-Journalist." *Washington Post*, June 9, 1998.
Glausiusz, Josie. "The Chemistry of Obsession." *Discover* magazine (June 1996).
Gliatto, Tom. "Present Tense." *People* (June 2, 1997).
Goldberg, Carey. "Some Journalists Have Met the Enemy and It Is Them." *New York Times*, January 30, 1998.
Goldberg, Robert B. "The Cellular Phone Controversy: Real or Contrived." *EMF Health Report* 1, no. 1 (1993).
Gopnick, Adam. "Read All about It." *New Yorker*, December 12, 1994.
Green, Michelle. "Objects of Desire." *People* (April 11, 1996).
Grove, Lloyd. "The Reliable Source." *Washington Post*, October 23, 2001.
Gugliotta, Guy. "Sorting through Trash, Sort Of." *Washington Post*, April 29, 1997.
Gunnison, Robert B. "Drudge Dredges up the Dirt, First Reporter, a Pioneer in Internet Journalism." *San Francisco Chronicle*, January, 24, 1998.
Gunther, Marc. "Business Is TV's Newest Bad Guy: Villains of Prime Time." *Fortune* (July 7, 1997).
Harper, Jennifer. "Coverage Returns to Civic Journalism." *Washington Times*, November 14, 2001.
Harwood, John. "Public's Esteem for Business Falls in the Wake of the Enron Scandal." *Wall Street Journal*, April 11, 2002.

Harwood, Richard. "40 Percent of Our Lives." *Washington Post*, November 30, 1996.

———. "When Reporters Become 'Producers of Meaning,' " *Washington Post*, December 16, 1997.

———. "The Writing on the Wall of the Media." *Washington Post*, March 5, 1994.

Heinrich, Susan. "The Enron Fallout." *National Post*, January 17, 2002.

Hertzer, Martin. "Many at Fault, Panel Concludes." *Miami Herald*, May 4, 1997.

Hill, Michael. "The Al Sharpton, Tawana Brawley, Defamation Trial." Associated Press, February 10, 1998.

Hirsley, Michael, and Jan Crawford. "Bernardin Accuser Recants: Sex Abuse Charge Dropped for Lack of Evidence." *Chicago Tribune*, March 1, 1994.

Hitt, Greg, and David Rogers. "Critics of Bush on Terror See Caution Signs in Poll." *Wall Street Journal*, May 20, 2002.

Horovitz, Bruce. "The Race to Capitalize on Diana's Image." *USA Today*, September 3, 1997.

Horrigan, Alice, and Jim Motavalli. "Talking Trash." *E Magazine* (March/April 1997).

"Hounding Gary Condit." *Globe and Mail*, August 31, 2001.

Hunt, Al. "Anthrax: A Botched Investigation?" *Wall Street Journal*, May 9, 2002.

Iannone, Carol. "Rise of the Irrational." *Commonsense* (1993).

"Interview with Bill Maher." *Playboy* (August 1997).

Irvine, Reed. "It Was Advocacy, Stupid." *AIM Report* 22, no. 5 (March 1993).

Isikoff, Michael, Evan Thomas, Mark Hosenball, Karen Breslau, and Bob Jackson. "From Bad to Worse." *Newsweek*, September 3, 2001.

Jacoby, Tamar. "Sharpton Is Guilty of More Than Defamation." *Wall Street Journal*, July 16, 1998.

Jensen, Elizabeth. "Off the Air: NBC News President, Burned by Staged Fire and GM, Will Resign." *Wall Street Journal*, March 2, 1993.

———. "TV News Reverts to Pre-Sept. 11 Patterns." *Los Angeles Times*, May 23, 2002.

"John Chancellor's Obituary." *Washington Post*, July 13, 1996.

"Journalist Who Accused Boorda Is Challenged." Associated Press, May 16, 1997.

Judis, John B. "The Great Savings Scare." *New Republic* (January 27, 1997).

Kalb, Marvin. "Practicing Deception in the Pursuit of Truth." *Washington Post*, March 24, 1997.

Katz, Diane. "The Press's Ignominious Role." *Wall Street Journal*, August 20, 1997.

Kelley, Matt. "ADM Risks Backlash with Suit." *Journal of Commerce* (February 19, 1997).

Kelly, Michael. "It's about Fitness to Lead." *Washington Post*, August 26, 1998.

Kinosian, Janet. "Rudeness on the Rise." *Washington Post*, December 15, 1997.

Knecht, G. Bruce. "Rare Breed: Media Watchdog with Some Bite." *Wall Street Journal*, November 20, 1996.

Knox, Noelle, and Matt Krantz. "Andersen Workers Feel Maligned." *USA Today*, March 25, 2002.

Kolata, Gina. "Safeguards Urged for Researchers: Aim Is to Keep Vested Interests from Suppressing Discoveries." *New York Times*, April 17, 1997.

Kolbert, Elizabeth. "NBC News Chief Quits to Relieve Network's Pains." *New York Times*, March 3, 1993.

———. "Wages of Deceit: Untrue Confessions." *New York Times*, June 11, 1995.

Kolody, Tracy. "Crash Casts Pall over ValuJet's Annual Meeting on Thursday." *Ft. Lauderdale Sun-Sentinel*, May 22, 1996.

Kotz, Nick. "A Matter of Honor." *Washingtonian* (July 1998).

Kristol, William. "Taking the War Beyond Terrorism." *Washington Post*, January 31, 2002.

Kurtz, Howard. "CNN Retracts Allegations of Nerve Gas Use by U.S." *Washington Post*, July 3, 1998.

———. "Cyber-Libel and the Web Gossip-Monger." *Washington Post*, August 15, 1997.

———. "Press Takes a Step up in the Public's Opinion." *Washington Post*, November 29, 2001.

———. "Should Journalists Take Money from Corporations and Lobbying Groups?" *Washington Post Magazine* (January 21, 1996).

Labash, Matt. "Scaremonger." *Weekly Standard*, April 29, 1996.

Leo, John. "Spicing Up the (Ho-Hum) Truth." *U.S. News & World Report* (March 8, 1993).

Lewis, Craig. "Cheating Frank Gets a Second Chance." *Globe*, July 1, 1997.

Lieberman, David. "Too Much of a Good Thing?" *TV Guide* (March 6, 1993).

Lyons, David. "How Much Is a Crash Victim's Life Worth?" *Miami Herald*, May 6, 1997.

Markowitz, Arnold. "Typical Takeoff, Then Murky Death." *Miami Herald*, November 19, 1996.

Marshall, John. "Simpson Books Growing beyond Market Niche, into a Subgenre." *Seattle Post-Intelligencer*, April 18, 1996.

Martinez, Barbara. "Anthrax Victims' Fate Varied by What Hospital, Which Doctor They Saw." *Wall Street Journal*, November 27, 2001.

Masters, Kim, et al. "The Mousetrap." *Vanity Fair* (December 1996).

Masters, Roger D., and Baldwin M. Way. "Experimental Methods and Attitudes toward Leaders: Nonverbal Displays, Emotion, and Cognition." *Research in Biopolitics* 4 (1996).

———. "Political Attitudes: Interactions of Cognition and Affect." *Motivation and Emotion* 20, no. 3 (1996).

McBee, Barry. "Garbage? Recycling Is Here Because It Makes Sense." *Dallas Morning News*, August 25, 1996.

McClam, Erin. "U.S. Health Agency Comes under Attack for Not Testing Postal Workers." *Canadian Press*, October 23, 2001.

McClellan, Steve. "Magazines Prime Earners in Prime Time." *Broadcasting & Cable* (May 9, 1994).

McFadden, Robert. "New York Nightmare Kills a Dreamer." *New York Times*, January 5, 1999.

Menn, Joseph. "Archer Daniels Board Forms Corporate Governance Committee." Bloomberg Business News (October 19, 1995).

Mertzer, Martin. "ValuJet Fire Video Unnerving." *Miami Herald*, November 20, 1996.

Mifflin, Lawrie. " A Generation Gap in Viewership Is Suddenly Wider." *New York Times*, May 13, 1996.

Millman, Nancy. "ADM Chief's Clout Seen Waning as Shareholders Prepare for Battle." *Journal of Commerce* (October 18, 1995).

Milloy, Courtland. "Condit's Apathy for Levy Sends Chilling Message." *Washington Post*, August 26, 2001.

Mintz, John, and Bill McAllister. "Records Suggest Boorda Ineligible to Wear Pins; Navy Tightened Combat 'V' Rules in '68." *Washington Post*, May 21, 1996.

Mithers, Carol Lee. "Stress Sex." *Ladies' Home Journal* (September 1993).

Morgan, Dan, and George Lardner. "The Enigma of an Admiral's Death; to Many Colleagues, Neither Medal Controversy Nor Grueling Pace Explains Suicide." *Washington Post*, May 20, 1996.

"The Myth of the Liberal Media." *Business Week* (November 11, 1996).

Nelson, Robert H. "Chemicals and Witches: Standards of Evidence in Regulation." *The Freeman* (March 1995).

Neumeister, Larry. "Judge Sanctions Lawyer for Bringing Frivolous Lawsuit." Associated Press, June 7, 1996.

Neusner, Noam. "Archer Daniels Says EU Investigating Price-Fixing." Bloomberg Business News (June 11, 1997).

"Neutral in the Newsroom." *Wall Street Journal*, November 3, 2001.

Nicholson, David. "The King and Us." *Washington Post*, August 17, 1997.

Nocera, Joseph. "Fatal Litigation." *Fortune* (October 16, 1995).

"Of Sharks and Gary Condit." *Chicago Tribune*, September 6, 2001.

Orwall, Bruce. "Ovitz Isn't Finding Magic in Kingdom but Will He Flee?" *Wall Street Journal*, December 12, 1996.

O'Toole, James. "Spreading the Blame at Andersen." *New York Times*, March 26, 2002.

Overington, Caroline. "Andersen Slams Charges." *Age*, March 16, 2002.

Page, Susan, and Bill Nichols. "Overseas, Bush Viewed with Respect, Skepticism." *USA Today*, May 21, 2002.

Pauley, Heather. "U.S. Retailers Report Strong July Sales." Bloomberg Business News (August 7, 1997).

Powers, William. "The Feast of Diana." *New Republic* (September 22, 1997).

———. "Getting Kathie Lee." *New Republic* (June 9, 1997).

———. "Hear No Evil, See No Evil, Speak No Evil, Why the Establishment Media Wouldn't Dish the Dirt on Clinton in '96." *New Republic* (December 16, 1996).

———. "Scandal-Shy." *New Republic* (December 16, 1996).

Prager, Joshua Harris. "Death of a Princess, Birth of a Thousand Press Releases." *Wall Street Journal*, September 10, 1997.

"PR Costs More of a Concern for ValuJet Than Financial Costs." Cox News Service, May 14, 1996.

"Raging Bulls: Tom & Roseane." *People* (May 2, 1994).

Ramirez, Anthony. "Health Claims Cause Turmoil on the Cellular Phone Market." *New York Times*, January 30, 1993.

"Regional News." UPI, May 17, 1985.

Reingold, Edwin M. "America's Hamburger Helper." *Time* (June 29, 1992).

Rice, Marc. "Plotting Its Restart, ValuJet Faces Hurdles." Associated Press, August 30, 1996.

Rich, Frank. "Bob Hope Lives." *New York Times*, June 10, 1998.

———. "Ding, Dong, the Cultural Witch Hunt Is Dead." *New York Times*, February 24, 2002.

Richburg, Keith B. "Bush's Handling of Crisis Lifts His Stature in Europe." *Washington Post*, October 3, 2001.

Roberts, Catherine. "CEO of Retail Outlet for B&L Resigns." *Rochester Business Journal*, May 30, 1997.

Robins, Alisha. "Luncheon Lecture Unravels History of Salem Witches." *Lariat Reporter*, no. 137 (October 31, 1996).

Rose, Frank. "Whatever Happened to Michael Ovitz?" *Fortune* (July 7, 1997).

Rose, Matthew. "Lou Dobb's Defense of Andersen on CNN Show Raises Eyebrows." *Wall Street Journal*, April 3, 2002.

Rottenberg, Josh. "L.A. Confidential." *US* (March 1998).

Rowe, Jonathan. "Major Growing Pains." *U.S. News & World Report* (October 21, 1996).

Rudolph, Barbara. "Coping with Catastrophe." *Time* (February 24, 1986).

Russakoff, Dale. "Decade after Tawana Brawley Episode, Trial Looms." *Washington Post*, November 17, 1997.

———. "Sharpton Found Liable for Defamation." *Washington Post*, July 14, 1998.

Salerno, Steve. "The Interview That Didn't Happen." *Wall Street Journal*, July 29, 1996.

Santana, Arthur. "NW Woman Missing for a Week." *Washington Post*, May 11, 2001.

———. "Lack of Answers Frustrates Family of Missing Woman." *Washington Post*, May 16, 2001.

Satel, Sally. "Freud—Is He Just Another Dead, White Male?" *Psychiatric Time*s (August 1993).

Schoofs, Mark, and Gary Fields. "Anthrax Probe Was Complicated by Muddled Information, FBI Says." *Wall Street Journal*, March 25, 2002.

Schwartz, John. "Andersen's Retired Partners Fear Benefits May Slip Away." *New York Times*, April 3, 2002.

Scott, Janny. "Rules in Flux: News Organizations Face Tough Calls on Unverified Facts." *New York Times*, January 27, 1998.

Sella, Marshall. "The Red-State Network: How Fox News Conquered Bush Country—and Toppled CNN." *New York Times Magazine*, June 24, 2001.

Shafer, Jack. "The Web Made Me Do It." *New York Times*, February 15, 1998.

Shepard, Alicia C. "Going to Extremes." *American Journalism Review* (October 1996).

Sherrid, Pamela. "The General Custer of Shareholder Lawsuits?" *U.S. News & World Report* (April 21, 1997).

"A 'Sleazy' Attack." *Wall Street Journal*, Review and Outlook, February 2, 1997.

Spinner, Jackie, and Susan Schmidt. "Andersen Wants Quick Trial on Obstruction Charge." *Washington Post*, March 16, 2002.

Squeo, Ann Marie. "ADM Former Execs Indicted for Alleged Price-Fixing." Bloomberg Business News (December 3, 1996).

Starr, Alexandra. "Charlotte Beers' Toughest Sell." *Business Week*, December 17, 2001.

"Statements Made on Television Show Deemed Admitted after No Response; Pagones vs. Maddox." *New York Law Journal* (June 1, 1998).

Stengel, Richard. "Fly Till I Die." *Time* (April 22, 1996).

Stevens, Amy. "Tempest in a C Cup: What's Underneath Victoria's Secret Suit." *Wall Street Journal*, May 1, 1996.

Stockwell, Jeff. "Getting Swamped." *Premiere* (January 1997).

Stone, Andrea. " 'We've Got Work to Do' on Image with Muslims, Bush Says." *USA Today*, February 28, 2002.

Teicher, Martin H., et al. "Emergence of Intense Suicidal Preoccupations During Fluoxetine Treatment." *American Journal of Psychiatry* 147 (February 1990): 207–10.

Tierney, John. "What a Waste." *New York Times Magazine* (June 30, 1996).

Torriero, E. A., and Robert Manor. "U.S. 'Feeling Heat' on Andersen Trial." *Chicago Tribune*, May 5, 2002.

Traub, James. "No-Fun City." *New York Times Magazine*, November 4, 2001.

Trunzo, Candace. "Cheating Frank's X-Rated Video." *Globe*, May 27, 1997.

"Tylenol Extortionist Leaves Prison Today." *Roanoke Times*, October 13, 1995.

Uelman, Gerald F. "Perspective on the Media: Not All News Leaks Deserve Law's Shield." *Los Angeles Times*, December 30, 1996.

Vogelstein, Fred. "Giving Credit Where Credit Is Undue." *U.S. News & World Report* (March 31, 1997).

"ValuJet Airlines Was Allowed to Grow Too Fast." Reuters, June 15, 1996.

"ValuJet Crash, Competition Dampen Enthusiasm for Startups." Bloomberg Business News (September 16, 1997).

"ValuJet Crash Preventable with Fire Equipment NTSB Expert Says." Bloomberg Business News (August 19, 1997).

"ValuJet Expects to Fly Next Month; Cancels Leases at Three Airports." Associated Press, July 10, 1996.

"ValuJet Has Lengthy Record of Problems." Cox News Service, May 14, 1996.

"ValuJet Hearing Reveals Truths about Passenger Perception." *World Airline News* (August 22, 1997).

"ValuJet Name Retired as Airline Changes Images." UPI, September 4, 1997.

"ValuJet Shares Rise 33% on Name Change to AirTran." Bloomberg Business News (September 4, 1997).

Varadarajan, Tunku. "Serious CNN, Foxy Paula: What a Dilemma." *Wall Street Journal*, January 11, 2002.

Wallace, Mike. "The Press Needs a National Monitor." *Wall Street Journal*, December 18, 1996.

Warnecke, A. Michael, Roger D. Masters, and Guido Kempter. "The Roots of Nationalism: Nonverbal Behavior and Xenophobia." *Ethology and Sociology* 13 (1992): 267–82.

Waxman, Sharon. "Wetland of the Giants; Environmentalists Balk at Studio Site." *Washington Post*, August 6, 1996.

Wayne, Leslie. "Networks Gain Riches from News Magazines." *New York Times*, October 25, 1993.

Weiss, Michael. "The High-Octane Ethanol Lobby." *New York Times*, April 1, 1990.

"What Happened at Brentwood?" *Washington Post*, October 23, 2001.

"What's Going on Charlotte?" *O'Dwyer's PR Daily*, March 27, 2002.

Whittle, Thomas, et al. "The Story Behind Prozac." *Freedom* (November/December 1993).

Whyte, Murray. "Connie Chung Lands the Big 'Get.' " *National Post*, August 22, 2001.

Wickham, De Wayne. "Sammy the Bull—Singing for Himself." *USA Today*, July 15, 1997.

Wilkinson, Peter. "The Trash Man." *US* (February 1998).

Williams, Melissa. "Cowboys Used Informant's Residence for Wild Sex, Drug Parties, He Says." Associated Press, May 14, 1996.

"Williams Sues Dallas Police Station." UPI, February 12, 1997.

Winkler, Claudia. "True Lies." *Weekly Standard*, March 5, 2002.

"Writer Commented Boorda Might Shoot Himself Over Medals." Associated Press, New York, May 21, 1996.

Zachary, G. Paschal. "CEOs Are Stars Now, but Why? And Would Alfred Sloan Approve?" *Wall Street Journal*, September 3, 1997.

Zuckerman, Mortimer. "Internet Cranks Up the Rumor Mill." *USA Today*, November 25, 1996.

Zwecker, Bill. "O.J. Friend Bares All in *Playboy*." *Chicago Sun-Times*, August 28, 1994.

MISCELLANEOUS

"Additional ValuJet Comments in Response to the NTSB's Findings and Probable Cause Statement." *PR Newswire*, August 19, 1997.

Association of Certified Fraud Examiners. Internet, www.cfenet.com (December 18, 1996).

Boerner, Christopher, and Jennifer Chilton Kallery. "Restructuring Environmental Big Business." Center for the Study of American Business, Policy Study Number 124, January 1995.

Breen, Michael J. "A Cook, a Cardinal, Priests and the Press: An Analysis of Media Agenda Setting in Stories about Clergy Following Child Abuse Scandals." Submitted to the Mass Communication and Society Division of the Association for Education in Journalism and Mass Communication (AEJMC), Syracuse University. Internet, http://web.syr.edu/~mjbreen/cardinal.html (April 17, 1995).

"Business Behaving Badly." Special Report, *Media Research Center*, June 16, 1997.

Buzbee, Sally. "U.S. Finding Arabs Difficult to Woo." Associated Press, April 17, 2002.

Cellular Phone Use Included in Upcoming Study of Brain Tumor Risks." *National Cancer Institute*. Internet, www.oncolink.upenn.edu (February 1993).

"Cellular Telecommunications Industry Association. "Wireless Phones Used for Over 59,000 Emergency Calls Every Day." Press release, May 20, 1997.

———. "The Wireless Revolution Continues." Press release, March 3, 1997.

Center for Science in the Public Interest, Internet, http://www.cspinet.org/orgs/public_citizen/hits.html (August 19, 21, 1997).

Corn, David. "The Loyal Opposition Losing the PR Battle." TomPaine.com, November 9, 2001.

"Confessions of an Insurance Fraud Offender." *National Insurance Crime Bureau*, Internet, www.nicb.org.

Crotty, James. "FOX and the Hounds." WorkingForChange.com, February 26, 2002.

Dallas Morning News Internet Home Page, dallasnews.com (January 27, 1998).

Defillo, Lt. Marlon. "Law Enforcement Response to Urban Legends about Kidney Theft." *City of New Orleans Department of Police*, January 30, 1997.

"Easing One's Mind with Prozac." Student Publications Inc., Kansas State University, February 21, 1996.

Edelstein, Ken, *Creative Loafing Network (online newsweekly)*. Internet, web@cln.com (January 18, 1997).

Editors. "Marching Orders Redux." *New Republic Online*, January 28, 2002.

Electronics Industry Association, Statistics obtained by Eric Dezenhall via telephone, August 19, 1997.

"Endangered Cures." Foundation for Biomedical Research, June 1996.

Flanders, Laura. "Pushing the Media Right." WorkingForChange.com, November 12, 2001.

"The Founding and Beginnings of CCHW." *CCHW Center for Health, Environment and Justice Home Page*. Internet, www.essential.org//CCHW/ (August 11, 1997).

Frandsen, Jon. " 'Highly Probably' that Anthrax Killed Two D.C. Postal Workers." Gannett News Service, October 23, 2001.

Gallo, Carmine. "Eyeing the Sunglass Market." *CNNfn*. Internet, http://cnnfn.com (May 23, 1997).

Hayward, Douglas. "Diana: Net Conspiracy Theories Begin." TechWire, Internet, www.erols.com/igoddard/pbs.htm (September 2, 1997).

"Interview: Parent Seeking Help in Locating Missing Daughter Chandra Levy." ABC News: *Good Morning America*, May 14, 2001.

"Jewell's Search for Justice." *Creative Loafing Network*. Internet, web@cln.com (November 2, 1996).

"Juror Bares All." *Patriot Ledger*, Snapshots section, January 4, 1996.

Klein, Naomi. "Brand USA." AlterNet.org, March 13, 2002.

Lamer, Timothy, and Alice Lynn O'Steen. "Businessmen Behaving Badly: Prime Time's World of Commerce." *Media Research Center*, June 16, 1997.

Lechtzin, Ed, General Motors, Interview with Eric Dezenhall, November 24, 1997.

Lester, Will. "Bush's High Poll Numbers Drift Down." Associated Press, April 19, 2002.

Lieberman, Adam J., and Simona C. Kwon. "Facts versus Fears: A Review of the Greatest Unfounded Health Scares of Recent Times." *American Council on Science and Health*, 3d ed., June 1998.

Lipsett, Brian. "Witness Statement: McDonald's Corporation v. Dave Morris and Helen Stee." Internet, www.mcspotlight.org/people/witnesses/recycling/lipsett_brian.html (August 11, 1997).

Loney, Jim. "Shark Expert Seriously Injured by Shark in Bahamas." Reuters, April 12, 2002.

Love Canal Collection, University Archives, State University of New York at Buffalo. Internet, http://ublib.buffalo.edu/libraries/projects/lovecanal (February 12, 1999).

Luntz, Frank. Interview with Eric Dezenhall, August 26, 1998.

Mansfield, Seymour, et al. "Legal Restraints and Crisis Management." Mansfield & Tanick P.A. white paper, 1994.

Maxa, Rudy. Interview with Eric Dezenhall, April 30, 1997.

MediaNomics. "Flat Earth Environmental Reporting." *Media Research Center*, July 1997.

———. "Poll: Workers Happy. Media: Yawn." *Media Research Center*, June 1996.

———. "Reporters Say American Dream Stolen." *Media Research Center*, October 1996.

———. "Trying to Break the Chains." *Media Research Center*, November 1996.

Mei, Suzanne. "Who Is Autumn Jackson?" Internet, ABCNEWS.com (July 25, 1997).

"The NewsHour with Jim Lehrer." *PBS*, September 2, 1997.

The Pepsi-Cola Company. "The Pepsi Hoax: What Went Right." Published by Pepsi-Cola Public Affairs, 1993.

Photo Marketing Association, documents obtained by Eric Dezenhall via fax on August 14, 1997.

Politically Incorrect with Bill Maher, November 30, 2001.

"Poll: Muslims Doubt Arabs Mounted Sept. 11 Attacks." Reuters, February 27, 2002.

"Press 'Unfair, Inaccurate and Pushy': Fewer Favor Press Scrutiny of Political Leaders." *Pew Research Center for the People and the Press*. Internet, www.people-press.org (March 1997).

Price, Matthew. "Paging Winston Churchill." Salon.com, November 7, 2001.

"Problems Continue to Plague ValuJet." *CNNfn*. Internet, http://cnnfn.com (May 16, 1996).

Rainie, Harrison, Margaret Loftus, and Mark Madden. "The State of Greed." *US News & World Report Online*. Internet, www.usnews.com (June 17, 1996).

"Report to Congress on the Extent and Effects of Domestic and International Terrorism on Animal Enterprises." Department of Justice (October 1993).

"Report to the Nation: Occupational Fraud and Abuse." *Association of Certified Fraud Examiners*, Austin, Tex., 1996.

Solomon, Norman. "The Televised Greatness of George W. Bush." Alternet, October 18, 2001.

Statler, Jean, Wirthlin Worldwide. Interview with Eric Dezenhall, November 18, 1997.

Sutton, Jane. "Despite Frenzy, Shark Attacks Declined in 2001." Reuters, February 19, 2002.

Trull, Frankie, Foundation for Biomedical Research. Interview with Eric Dezenhall, January 23, 1998.

"The Tylenol Murders." Internet, http://www.facsnet.org/report tools/guidesprimers/tampering/perspct3.html (October 4, 1997).

U.S. Department of Defense. "Secretary Rumsfeld Interview with NBC Meet the Press." January 20, 2002.

ValuJet Annual Report to Shareholders, 1996.

"ValuJet Struggling to Overcome Woes." *CNNfn*. Internet, http://cnnfn.com (May 16, 1996).

Warren, Robert S. (Gibson, Dunn & Crutcher), and Lewis B. Kaden (Davis Polk & Wardwell). "Report of Inquiry into Crash Demonstrations Broadcast on *Dateline NBC*, November 17, 1992." March 21, 1993.

Weber, Joseph. "Andersen's Dark Day—and No White Knight." Business Week Online, March 15, 2002.

Yudkowsky, Chaim. "Byte of Success." SmartPros.com, February 2002.

Index